Utah
BOULDERING

By **Chris Grijalva**
Noah Bigwood
Dave Pegg

Front cover: Noah Bigwood on *Chaos* (V8), Big Bend, page 190. Photo Dave Pegg

© 2003 Wolverine Publishing LLC All rights reserved. This book or any part thereof may not be reproduced in any form without written permission from the publisher.

ISBN# 0-9721609-0-6

Wolverine Publishing is seeking manuscripts and ideas for guidebooks.

Wolverine Publishing
5439 County Road 243
New Castle
Colorado
81647
970-984-2815
dave@wolverinepublishing.com
wolverinepublishing.com

Printed in Korea

So that's how they do it! Ben Moon getting high on *Black Lung* (V13), Joe's Valley — with a little help from Boone Speed and Jerry Moffatt.
Photo: Ray Wood

THE WORLD'S #1 PRICE / QUALITY CLIMBING SHOES

WWW.ROCKSHOES.COM
1-877-YA-CLIMB

The black sheep of the family.

Why follow when you can lead? bufo has the highest quality climbing shoes for the lowest price. Don't be like all the other sheep out there.

See website for extensive dealer listing.

choose your weapon.

1-877-YA-CLIMB
www.rockshoes.com

---

ex·cep·tion·al
(bufo-climbing-shoes) *adj.*

1. Bufo shoes are exceptional. They combine high performance, superior quality with an ethically founded & revolutionary price.
2. Winner 2001 and 2002 Climbing Magazine Gear Guide Award for best rockshoe product.
3. Available at an enlightened Dealer near you.
4. For black sheep only. See website for more beta.

www.rockshoes.com

1-877-YA-CLIMB

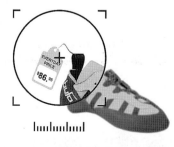

choose your weapon.

Contents

LITTLE COTTONWOOD 9
- Secret Garden 14
- Cabbage Patch 22
- 5-Mile Boulders 26
- Riverside 30
- Mr. T 36
- The Gate 38
- The Swamp 46
- The Hillside 50
- The Glen 54
- Hidden Forest 61
- Campus Boulder 65
- White Pine 66

JOE'S VALLEY 75
- Left Fork 79
  - Crack Boulder 80
  - Mine Cart 81
  - Trent's Mom 82
  - Right Sign 84
  - Riverside 88
  - Big Joe 92
- Right Fork 96
  - Boy Size 98
  - Gun Shot 102
  - Man Size 104
  - Black and Tan 108
  - Warm-Up Boulder 112
  - UMWA 114
  - Buoux 116
  - ALL 118
  - No Substance 120
  - Minute Man 122
  - Moby Dick 124
  - The Hulk 128
- Innumerables 130
- New Joe's 135

IBEX 161
- Ibex Crags 164
- Topus Mountain 176
- Stagger 178
- Other Areas 179

BIG BEND 181

OGDEN 199
- Lower Boulders 202
- Patriot Crack 210
- Upper Boulders 212

OTHER AREAS 216

Emma Medara on *Mr Trujillo's Big Day* (V2), Big Bend, page 192.
Photo: Dave Pegg

INTRODUCTION

This book was conceived in a pullout at Joe's Valley in the fall of 2001. Chris Grijalva and I were stretched out inside the camper shell of his truck, sharing a beer and basking in the afterglow of a brilliant day of climbing. I'd bouldered at Joe's before but had never had as much fun as I'd had today. The difference was that I had been climbing with Chris who knew the area well. He had given me a guided tour, taking me to a bunch of new areas and pointing out many great problems that I would otherwise have missed.

The experience sparked the idea for this book: *Utah Bouldering* — a comprehensive guide to the best areas in the state. Written by climbers who knew the areas well, it would provide the same quality of information you'd get if you asked these local experts to personally show you around. Chris did the bulk of the work, writing and researching Joe's Valley sandstone and Little Cottonwood Canyon granite — two massive areas that rank among the country's best bouldering destinations. He also documented the excellent and largely unheralded quartzite bouldering that lies a few minutes from his home in Ogden. Noah Bigwood of Moab supplied the information for Big Bend, a historic desert-sandstone area with some of the hardest problems (and grades!) in the state, and I spent a week and half in the desert researching the superb quartzite bouldering at Ibex when plans for a Salt Lake City climber to write this section fell through.

Because we wanted this book to provide the same quality of information you'd get from a human guide, we paid a lot of attention to the details. The authors mapped every single boulder in this book with graph paper and a compass. They checked all the problems, climbing the vast majority of them and attempting the rest. We tried to be explicit about starting holds and used a four-star rating system to help you identify the best problems at a glance. One thing this book can't do is shout encouragement, but we hope the production standards, tick lists, and action photographs provide at least some of the motivation you'd get from a good friend during a great day of bouldering.

If you enjoy *Utah Bouldering*, take a look at *Western Sloper*, our guidebook to the sport climbing at Rifle Mountain Park, The Fortress of Solitude (home of *Flex Luther* and *Kryptonite*), and other crags in western Colorado. You can find out more about us and the climbing on western Colorado limestone at wolverinepublishing.com.

— *Dave Pegg*

SAFETY

Bouldering is hazardous. Every time you fall, you hit the ground, risking a bruised ego, a bruised body ... or worse. I've broken two ankles bouldering and consider myself lucky. Please boulder prudently and use a crash pad and spotters, which will reduce your chances of injury.

In this guide we have used symbols to indicate problems that we think are especially risky or dangerous (see "What Does It All Mean?" on the following page). We hope these symbols are helpful. Nevertheless, they are subjective and incomplete assessments of risk. We cannot anticipate all potential hazards, which include but are not limited to bad landings, big or awkward falls, loose rock, and your ability. Remember, there are no "safe" boulder problems. Use your own judgment to assess the risks before attempting to climb any of the boulder problems in this book.

THE AUTHORS AND PUBLISHER MAKE NO REPRESENTATIONS OR WARRANTIES, EXPRESSED OR IMPLIED, OF ANY KIND REGARDING THE CONTENTS OF THIS GUIDEBOOK, AND EXPRESSLY DISCLAIM ANY REPRESENTATION OR WARRANTY REGARDING THE ACCURACY OR RELIABILITY OF INFORMATION CONTAINED HEREIN. THE USER ASSUMES ALL RISK ASSOCIATED WITH THE USE OF THIS GUIDE.

WOLVERINE THANKS

Chris Grijalva for taking on a huge amount of work and getting the job done. Noah Bigwood for doing an equally great job. Fiona, for everything. Tracy Martin of Painted Wall and Rock and Ice for her help with the cover. The staff of Rock and Ice and Climbing Magazines for their help and support. Mick Ryan for getting me started. Photographers: Wills Young, Andrew Kornylak, Jim Thornburg, Ray Wood, Cory Rich, Cameron Lawson, and everyone else who sent in shots. And last, but not least, the many climbers who have contributed to the development of the bouldering areas described in this book.

Introduction

The Love Cushion
... the best damn bouldering pad in the world!

Zealot
Climbing Products Incorporated

p.o. box 4957
clifton park, new york
12065.0859

phone: 518.383.5441
web: www.zealotclimbing.com
e-mail: info@zealotclimbing.com

photo: Josh Helke

Our pads... good to land on.

Their pads... good to stand on.

GRADES

US	Font
V0	4
V1	5
V2	5+
V3	6a
	6b
V4	6c
V5	6c+
V6	7a
V7	7a+
V8	7b
V9	7b+
V10	7c
	7c+
V11	8a
V12	8a+
V13	8b
V14	8b+

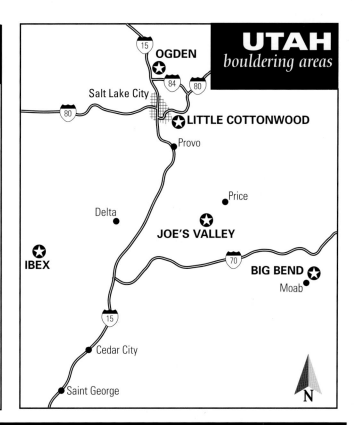

UTAH bouldering areas

What does it all mean?

The sit start and heart-flutter symbols are the copyrighted material of RockFax guidebooks. A big "thank you" to Mick Ryan of RockFax USA for permission to use these symbols in this guidebook.

Stars indicate boulder problem quality

        No stars. Don't bother.

★   Worth doing but nothing to write home about.

★★   Good problem. Recommended.

★★★   Excellent problem. Highly recommended.

★★★★   World class. An area classic.

 Sit start.

 Scary or potentially dangerous problem. **NB: The absence of this symbol does not mean the problem is "safe." It is possible to hurt yourself on any problem in this guide. Use your own judgement when deciding which problems you attempt.**

 Extremely serious problem. Don't fall! **NB: The absence of this symbol does not mean the problem is "safe." It is possible to hurt yourself on any problem in this guide. Use your own judgement when deciding which problems you attempt.**

 Eliminate problem. Read the description carefully. The big jug that you're hanging from may not be allowed.

 Trick, stunt, or just plain stupid problem. Expect bizarre moves.

 And for those of you who forget, there's the "**don't take it too seriously**" symbol.

Introduction

Little
COTTONWOOD

By Chris Grijalva

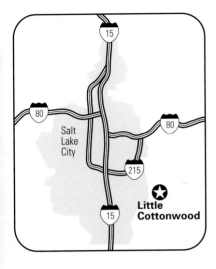
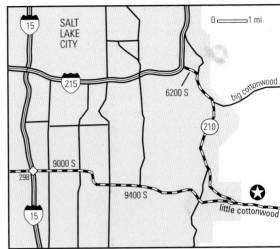

INTRODUCTION

With its soaring granite cliffs, waterfalls, 11,000-foot peaks, tall pines, and deciduous trees that add vivid swaths of color in autumn, Little Cottonwood Canyon (LCC) is one of the most beautiful places in the Wasatch Mountains. Conveniently located, in the heart of the range, yet only 15 minutes drive from downtown Salt Lake City, this deep, glacier-eroded canyon has something to offer any outdoor enthusiast. Winter brings tons of the "greatest snow on earth" and endless skiing adventures, from backcountry touring, to plunging downhill at the world-class resorts of Alta and Snowbird. It also brings ice climbs, and with them the ice climbers prepared to do battle with their frozen foes. Warmer weather delivers an even wider array of recreational activities in the canyon: mountain biking, hiking, running, and of course rock climbing. Climbers have been hiking to the granite cliffs lining both side of Little Cottonwood Canyon since the 1960s. Later, as bouldering became a popular and serious pursuit, further exploration of the canyon revealed hundreds of well-featured granite boulders of all shapes and sizes. Today, LCC is a world-class bouldering destination with something for every level of climber.

GETTING THERE

Little Cottonwood Canyon lies on the eastern edge of Salt Lake City. There are many different ways to approach the canyon, although none avoid the city traffic. The two easiest approaches are described below:

If traveling north on Interstate 15, take the 9000 South exit. Drive east on 9000 South until it joins 9400 South. Continue east on 9400 South until it joins Little Cottonwood Canyon road at the mouth of Little Cottonwood Canyon.

If traveling south on Interstate 15, take the Interstate 80 East exit. Drive east on I-80, exiting onto I-215. Follow I-215 south and take the 6200 South exit. Continue south on 6200 South until it merges with Wasatch Blvd (highway 210). Follow Wasatch Blvd south, past Big Cottonwood Canyon, until it winds into Little Cottonwood Canyon, and Little Cottonwood Canyon road.

If traveling from the east or west on Interstate 80, exit south onto I-215. From here, follow the directions above.

Little Cottonwood Canyon

SEASON

The best times to boulder in Little Cottonwood Canyon are September through November, and March through May (although the duration of the spring season depends upon when the snow melts). Summer bouldering can be tolerable, although the heat makes the already slick rock even slicker, and boulderers usually flee the canyon in high summer. In winter, the sun sinks below the high ridges to the south, and sunlight rarely visits the canyon floor. After the first winter storms, most of the boulders remain blanketed in snow until the spring thaw.

ACCESS

Located just 15 minutes from downtown Salt Lake City, with hundreds of killer problems within seconds of the car, it's not surprising that LCC is becoming a more and more popular place to climb. All of us need to do our best to minimize the negative impacts of this increased use. As always: Do not clear vegetation from the base of the boulders, walk on established trails, and pick up any trash (even if it is not yours). These obvious precautions should not have to be mentioned, but a small percentage of climbers treat the canyon as though it were a dingy basement woody. For example, in the summer of 2001 someone left a rotting and unsightly couch next to the main boulder at the Cabbage Patch area. Presumably, this person thought that sitting on the dirt while bouldering outside was far too crude for his or her tastes. Another time someone placed a large tarp over the entire south face of the Fly Boulder at the Gate Area in an attempt to shield it from snow. The tarp quickly blew off, and was left ripped and torn in an ugly heap. These sorts of practices have no place at any climbing area. If you need a place to boulder when the snow falls and a comfy place to park your butt between attempts, go to the gym.

Another issue is that some bouldering areas, like The Gate, lie on private property owned by the Church of Jesus Christ of Later Day Saints. Currently, the church allows access to The Gate, but climbers must realize that climbing on this and other private land to which they are granted access is a privilege, not a right. Act appropriately and responsibly to ensure continued good relations with all parties involved.

CAMPING

All overnight camping is prohibited, except in established campgrounds. The closest campground to the climbing is Tanner Flat. It is located approximately four miles up the canyon and sites cost $14 per night. Further up the canyon, at the end of the road, is Albion Basin Campground. Sites here cost $12 per night, but the campground is only open between July 3 and September 2. Reservations for both campgrounds involve a $9 additional fee and can be made by calling 1-877-444-6777.

SURVIVAL

Salt Lake City has everything you could possibly need. Climbing shops, climbing gyms, stores, and restaurants, are too numerous to list. Supermarkets gas stations, convenience stores, and motels are located near the canyon.

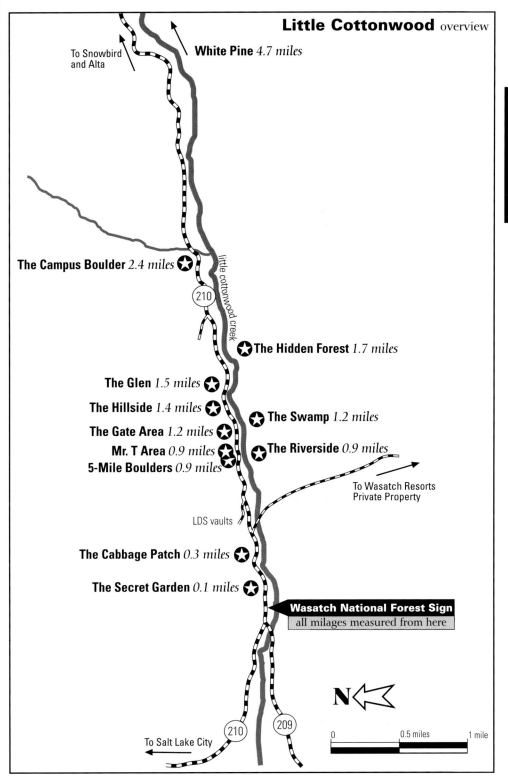

LITTLE COTTONWOOD
The Best of ...

Little Cottonwood

V0
- [ ] #33 Secret Garden ★★★ *page 18*
- [ ] #39 Secret Garden ★★★★ *page 18*
- [ ] #25 The Glen ★★★ *page 57*
- [ ] #11 White Pine ★★★ *page 68*

V1
- [ ] Haunting Mass Appeal ★★★ *page 35*
- [ ] Crystal Boulder Overhang ★★★ *page 40*
- [ ] Green Slab Center ★★★ *page 42*
- [ ] #3 The Glen ★★★ *page 54*
- [ ] #4 The Glen ★★★★ *page 54*
- [ ] #30 The Glen ★★★ *page 57*
- [ ] #7 White Pine ★★★ *page 66*
- [ ] #21 White Pine ★★★ *page 68*
- [ ] #44 White Pine ★★★ *page 72*

V2
- [ ] The Secret Garden Arete ★★★★ *page 15*
- [ ] #15 Cabbage Patch ★★★ *page 23*
- [ ] Double Dyno ★★★ *page 24*
- [ ] Big Mouth ★★★ *page 26*
- [ ] Alchemy ★★★ *page 54*
- [ ] Mud ★★★ *page 63*
- [ ] The Traverse ★★★ *page 63*
- [ ] #19 White Pine ★★★ *page 68*
- [ ] #24 White Pine ★★★ *page 69*
- [ ] #32 White Pine ★★★ *page 69*

V3
- [ ] #28 Cabbage Patch ★★★ *page 25*
- [ ] The Drip ★★★ *page 32*
- [ ] Standard Overhang ★★★ *page 38*
- [ ] EBP ★★★ *page 40*
- [ ] Don't Fall ★★★ *page 47*

- [ ] The Big Guy ★★★★ *page 48*
- [ ] You Fat Bastard ★★★ *page 57*
- [ ] #32 The Glen ★★★ *page 58*
- [ ] Sorry Charlie ★★★ *page 59*
- [ ] #35 White Pine ★★★★ *page 70*

V4
- [ ] #32 Secret Garden ★★★ *page 18*
- [ ] Carpet Roof ★★★ *page 21*
- [ ] Fat Albert Gang ★★★★ *page 23*
- [ ] Double Aretes ★★★ *page 26*
- [ ] #14 The Riverside ★★★ *page 32*
- [ ] Papa Bell's Arete ★★★ *page 32*
- [ ] #32 The Riverside ★★★ *page 35*
- [ ] Crystal Traverse ★★★★ *page 38*
- [ ] Pride ★★★★ *page 47*
- [ ] Hike ★★★ *page 47*
- [ ] Tom's Sloperfest ★★★ *page 53*
- [ ] Roadside Boulder Slab ★★★ *page 54*
- [ ] Sunday Best ★★★★ *page 57*
- [ ] The Pugilist ★★★★ *page 59*
- [ ] Charlie's Arete ★★★ *page 61*
- [ ] Dale's Arete ★★★ *page 61*
- [ ] #3 White Pine ★★★ *page 66*
- [ ] #45 White Pine ★★★ *page 72*

V5
- [ ] #22 Secret Garden ★★★ *page 16*
- [ ] Flying Carpet ★★★ *page 21*
- [ ] Fungus ★★★ *page 23*
- [ ] Salad ★★★ *page 23*
- [ ] Tom's Problem ★★★★ *page 25*
- [ ] Pump Traverse ★★★ *page 38*
- [ ] Green Slab Left Side Direct ★★★ *page 42*

Wolverine *Publishing*   www.wolverinepublishing.com

- ☐ Hong's Pinch Layback ★★★★ page 42
- ☐ #9 The Glen ★★★ page 54
- ☐ Misunderstood Dyno ★★★ page 55
- ☐ #8 Campus Boulder ★★★★ page 65
- ☐ #40 White Pine ★★★ page 71

V6
- ☐ Lance's Dihedral ★★★ page 15
- ☐ #40 Secret Garden ★★★★ page 18
- ☐ Baldy ★★★ page 27
- ☐ Heroin Face Right ★★★ page 30
- ☐ The Worms ★★★ page 30
- ☐ Garth's Other Roof ★★★ page 35
- ☐ Crystal Pinch ★★★ page 38
- ☐ #27 The Glen ★★★ page 57
- ☐ #6 Campus Boulder ★★★ page 65
- ☐ #9 Campus Boulder ★★★ page 65
- ☐ #2 White Pine ★★★ page 66

V7
- ☐ The Dean Problem ★★★ page 23
- ☐ Mr Smiley Right ★★★ page 26
- ☐ Mr Smiley Center ★★★★ page 26
- ☐ The Buzz ★★★★ page 34
- ☐ Golden ★★★ page 37
- ☐ Mr T. ★★★ page 37
- ☐ Grumpy ★★★ page 54
- ☐ #34 White Pine ★★★★ page 70

V8
- ☐ The Bear Hug Arete ★★★★ page 15
- ☐ A Bit Slopey ★★★ page 23
- ☐ Mr Smiley Left ★★★ page 26
- ☐ Butt Trumpets ★★★ page 27
- ☐ Shivers ★★★★ page 32
- ☐ Alzheimers ★★★ page 34
- ☐ Super Fly ★★★ page 38
- ☐ Huge ★★★ page 46
- ☐ The Highlife ★★★ page 52
- ☐ Fat Lady ★★★★ page 57
- ☐ Craig's V8 ★★★★ page 65

V9
- ☐ St. Nick ★★★ page 21
- ☐ The Surprise ★★★ page 35
- ☐ Ditch Witch ★★★★ page 47
- ☐ Triple Threat ★★★★ page 51
- ☐ The Egg ★★★ page 53
- ☐ Duct Tape ★★★ page 62
- ☐ Gerbils ★★★ page 62

V10
- ☐ Copperhead ★★★★ page 15
- ☐ Shingles ★★★★ page 18

V11
- ☐ Cheese Whiz ★★★ page 28
- ☐ Pro Series ★★★ page 38
- ☐ Taylor Made ★★★ page 42
- ☐ Jack Horner ★★★ page 47

V12
- ☐ Bully ★★★★ page 18

V13
- ☐ Copperhead Right ★★★ page 15
- ☐ Spinal Twist ★★★ page 42

Little Cottonwood Canyon

The Secret Garden 0.1m

The Secret Garden is the first area you reach as you drive up the canyon. It is located on the north side of the road, one tenth of a mile from the Wasatch National Forest sign. Park on the south side of the road, and walk back west (towards the entrance to the canyon). Look for a trail that enters the trees just before the "No Parking Sign".

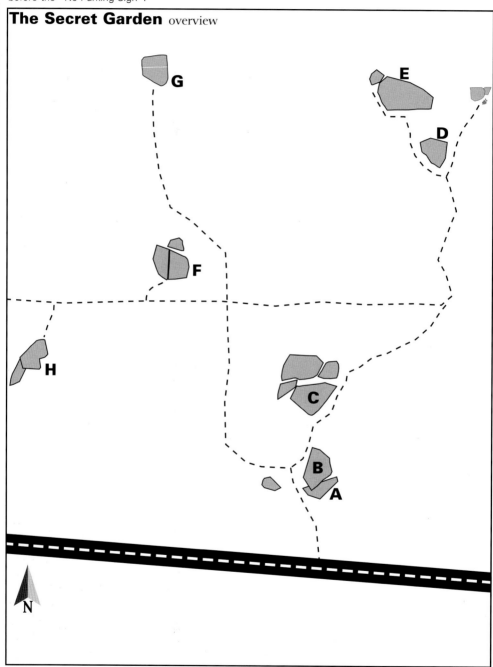

The Secret Garden overview

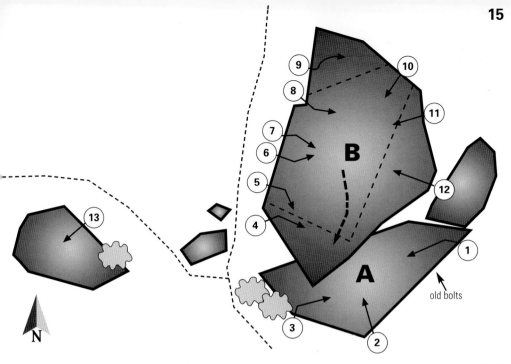

A. Shothole Boulder

The first problem you see as you walk up the trail from the road is the proud, tall Shot Hole Arete. This problem should not be missed. The boulder has two other problems, both of which are worth doing.

1. The Secret Garden Arête V2 ★★★★
Climb the right arête avoiding the boulder that leans against it. An excellent highball problem.

2. The Shot Hole Arête V8 ★★
Climb the prow using the drill scars. A little tall. Harder than it looks.

3. V2 ★★
Climb the left arête. Watch out for the tree at the start. A good warm up.

B. The Copperhead Boulder

The Copperhead Boulder is the boulder immediately behind the Shot Hole boulder. Many great problems from V1 to V13 exist, so a climber of any level is sure to be challenged. Several trees surround the rock providing shade almost all day.

4. Lance's Dihedral V6 ★★★
Start standing with both hands on the slopey ledge five feet up. Climb the dihedral topping out on the right.

5. Copperhead Right V13  ★★★
Sit start Copperhead, but grab the copperhead hold with your left hand and top out to the right. First climbed by Garth Miller. Has not yet had a second ascent.

6. Copperhead V10 ★★★★
Start standing with the left hand on a sidepull and right hand on a shallow dish. Pull right-handed to the sharp crimp then straight up.

7. Mini Arete V7 ★★
Start standing. Climb the arête and the right face

8. Twisted Dihedral V4 ★★
Climb the awkward dihedral.

9. The Bear Hug Arete V8 ★★★★
Start sitting with both hands in the underclings, climb up slapping both sides of the arête. The standing start is V6.

10. Johnny's Mantel
Start on the two slopey knobs just over the lip. Pull the heinous mantle. Not a good problem to try in hot weather.

11. Martini Face V1 ★
Start in the right-facing flake. Climb the face straight up.

12. Face V2 ★
Sit start with both hands on the lip. Pull one move to the good edges then continue up the face. The standing start is V0.

13. Shorty V2 ★
Located on a boulder left of the trail as you walk toward Copperhead. Start on the slopey crimp and the right arête. Fire to the lip and mantle. Silly and short.

Little Cottonwood Canyon

The Secret Garden ▼ 0.1m

Little Cottonwood

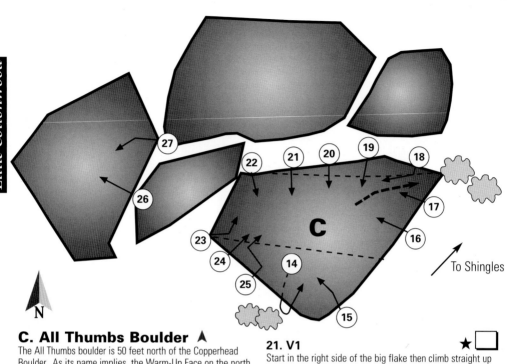

C. All Thumbs Boulder ▲
The All Thumbs boulder is 50 feet north of the Copperhead Boulder. As its name implies, the Warm-Up Face on the north side of the boulder is a great place to warm up. I've described four straight-up lines, although many eliminates on the huge drill holes that litter the face are possible.

14. All Thumbs V10 ★★ ☐
Start on the ledge under the roof, pull to the lip, and top out. A short problem that packs a big punch.

15. Arête V7 ★★ ☐
Start standing with both hands on the blunt arête.

16. Face V6 ★★ ☐
Start with both hands on the left-facing sidepull four feet off the ground. Climb the face a little to the left.

17. Face V3 ★★ ☐
Same start as Vermin Face but head right.

18. Warm-Up Arête V0 ★ ☐
Climb the arête on the left side of the Warm-Up Face.

19. V3 ★★ ☐
Start in the two drill holes. Go straight up the face avoiding the jugs to the right.

20. V1 ★ ☐
Start in the left side of the big flake and go straight up.

21. V1 ★ ☐
Start in the right side of the big flake then climb straight up

22. V5 ♥ ★★★ ☐
Start with the left hand in the right-most drilled pocket then straight up the face. Careful at the top — a fall will land you on the rock behind the boulder.

23. Careless V0 ★★ ☐
Climb the arête on the left side.

24. Slapdash V1 ★ ☐
Start with your left hand on the arête and right hand on a crimp four feet up. Climb the face and arête on the right side

25. Stevie's Traverse V5 ★★ ☐
Start on the lip just left of the trees. Traverse the lip leftwards and top out on the arête of Slapdash.

The next two problems are on the boulder just west of the Warm-Up Face.

26. Avatar V0+ ★ ☐
Climb the low-angle face using sloping dishes.

27. Avatar Right V0 ★ ☐
Start down in the space between the two boulders. Follow the rail up and left.

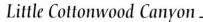

Bobby Hartage bears down on the *Bear Hug Arete* (V8), page 15.
Photo: Andrew Kornylak

The Secret Garden ▼ 0.1m

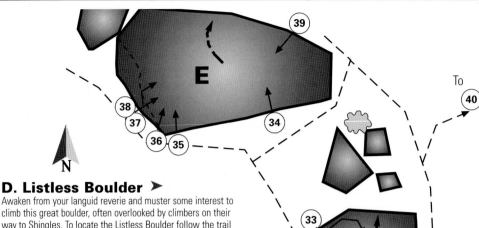

D. Listless Boulder ▶

Awaken from your languid reverie and muster some interest to climb this great boulder, often overlooked by climbers on their way to Shingles. To locate the Listless Boulder follow the trail past All Thumbs for about 200 feet, keeping your eyes open for a fork in the trail. Take the left fork for another 50 feet.

28. V0 ★ ☐
Climb the right-facing corner in the middle of the brown face.

29. V1 ★★ ☐
Climb the crack in the middle of the groove, and then continue up the slabby face above.

30. V3 ★★ ☐
Climb the blunt arête on the left side

31. V6 ★★ ☐
Start with both hands on the flake just before it disappears. Climb the face trending slightly right using small crimps and desperate slopes.

32. V4 ★★★ ☐
Start sitting with both hands in the right-facing corner. Go left handed to the left-facing flake, then straight up.

33. V0- ★★★ ☐
Follow the very easy but very fun crack up and left.

E. The Shingles Boulder ▲

The Shingles boulder is home to the highest concentration of difficult problems in the canyon, as well as two of the best: Shingles and Bully. This is the place to fail repeatedly on your lifetime project until the rage spills over and manifests itself in the form of screams and curses and childish tantrums. Don't despair. Gather yourself, rummage through the trees to find the rock shoes that you threw there during your wobbler, and walk around the back of the boulder and vent on the wonderfully pleasant problem #39, where you need not worry about failure — for if you fail your lack of consciousness and broken body will preclude any pouting about the bungled attempt. The Shingles Boulder is about 50 feet up the trail past the Listless Boulder.

34. Super G V11 ★ ☐
Start in the middle of the face. Climb up small crimps and into the underclings. A problem of very high difficulty, but not of quality.

35. Ching V12 ★★ ☐
Sit start the using the flake that is about four feet off the ground. Climb up and right.

36. Cheech V12 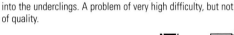 ★★ ☐
Same start as Ching, but climb up and left.

37. Shingles V10 ★★★★ ☐
Sit start using the low flake three feet off the ground and follow the left-facing flakes. The standing start is V5.

38. Bully V12 ★★★★ ☐
Do the start of Shingles. Then make a big move left and finish left. Classic. **Variation:** The stand-up start to Bully is **V7**.

39. V0 ★★★★ ☐
The tall face on the back on the Shingles Boulder. Killer. One of the best problems of the grade.

The final problem in this area is on a boulder due east of the Shingles Boulder. You can reach it by following a trail from the right side of The Listless Boulder for about 50 feet.

40. V6  ★★★★ ☐
Start sitting. Climb out the middle of the cave. Be careful you don't helicopter onto the rocks as you make the desperate lunge to the lip.

Little Cottonwood Canyon

Jerry Moffatt bullies *Bully* (V12). Photo: Ray Wood

The Secret Garden 0.1m

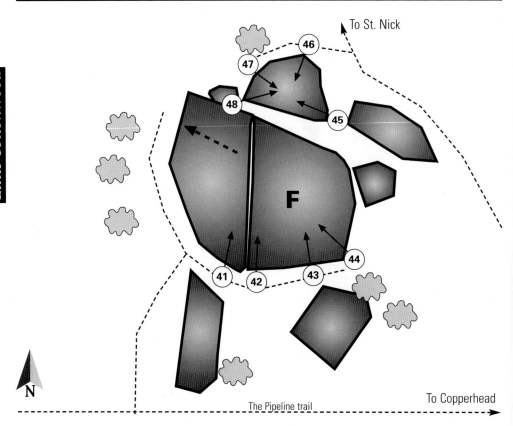

F. Boulder

To find the Boulder F, head west from Copperhead, on the trail past Shorty. Follow this trail as it turns and heads north until it intersects the Pipeline trail. Take a left on the Pipeline trail and walk for about 100 feet. Keep your eyes open for a large boulder split by a crack about ten feet off the trail on the right hand side. Most of the problems on the boulder would be excellent if the rock wasn't loose and crumbly. With traffic they may clean up and become more enjoyable — and safe.

41. V4
Climb the face just left of the crack. Loose. Dirty. Highball.

42. V3
Layback the left side of the crack. This would be a very good problem if it was cleaner.

43. Shit V4
Climb the middle of the face. Loose. Dirty. Highball.

44. Shit Right V1
The shallow groove on the right side of the boulder. Loose. Highball.

The next four problems are on the boulder behind Boulder F.

45. Ipecac V1
Start standing using good flakes at the corner. Make one or two moves to the lip and top out. The antithesis of "classic."

46. Project V?

47. Animal Dreams V4
Start with a crimp three feet off the ground go straight up using both sides of the prow.

48. Sightings V0
Start sitting. Climb the arête on the left side.

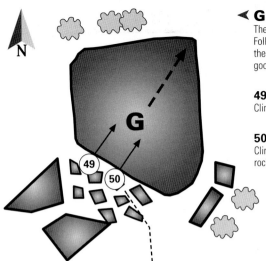

G. St. Nick Boulder

The St. Nick Boulder is about 200 feet north of Boulder F. Follow the directions to Boulder F, except when you arrive at the Pipeline trail simply cross it and head up hill. This is a good place boulder on a cold winter day as it gets sun all day.

49. Scary Tower V3 ★★
Climb the face and arete left of St. Nick.

50. St. Nick V9 ★★★
Climb the obvious seam. Hard just to get both feet on the rock. Bad landing.

Little Cottonwood

H. The Flying Carpet Boulder

This small boulder has several good problems and gets good sun exposure on cold days. To locate the Flying Carpet boulder, follow the directions to Boulder F, then continue down the Pipeline trail for about another 150 feet. The boulder is about 15 feet to the left on the south side of the trail.

51. Down Climb V1 ★
Start sitting with both hands on the triangular block, slap right hand around the corner then do the down climb. You can make the down climb easier by using the tree to the right.

52. Face V1 ★
Start two feet right of the down climb left hand on a sidepull right hand on an undercling.

53. V0 ★
Climb the slabby face using the left arête

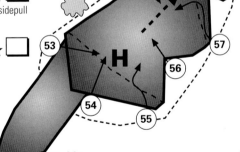

54. V1 ★
Begin with both hands on a good edge about seven feet off the ground. Climb straight up.

55. Carpet Roof V4 ★★★
Start sitting with both hands just under the roof. Follow the face and blunt arête up and a little left.

56. Groovy V0+ ★★
Climb the obvious groove.

57. Flying Carpet V5 ★★★
Start sitting with both hands on a knob three and a half feet up. Follow the sloping rail up and right. Top out just left of the down climb.

Little Cottonwood Canyon

Cabbage Patch ▼   0.3m

The Cabbage Patch is a great place for first-time visitors to get used to the rock and style of climbing in Little Cottonwood Canyon as it has many varied problems ranging from skin-friendly arêtes to razor-sharp crimps. The main boulders have a five-second approach, perfect gravel landings, and shade provided by numerous trees. They are also a good place to warm-up with many good moderate problems. To get to the Cabbage Patch, park on the south side of the road three tenths of a mile past the Wasatch National Forest sign. The boulders can be seen through the trees on the north side of the road.

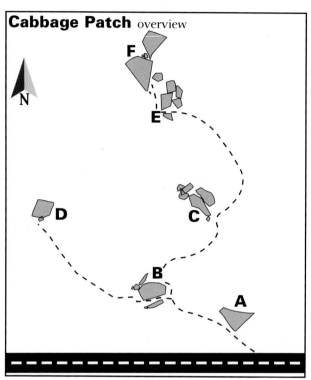

◀ A. The Brake Boulder
The small boulder nearest the road has four good moderate problems. The two arêtes are good warm-ups.

1. The Brake Arete V2
Sit start with right hand on the arête and left hand on the flat rail on the face. Climb the arête up and left.

2. Tight Shirts V3
Start in the middle of the face using underclings that are three feet off the ground. Climb straight up the face.

3. V3
Start two feet right of Tight Shirts, right hand on a knob and left hand on a small crimp. Climb up and right to join Tight Shirts avoiding the arête straight up.

4. Boter Wattle V2
For the full pump, start this problem sitting at the left end of the boulder. Follow the arête up and right.

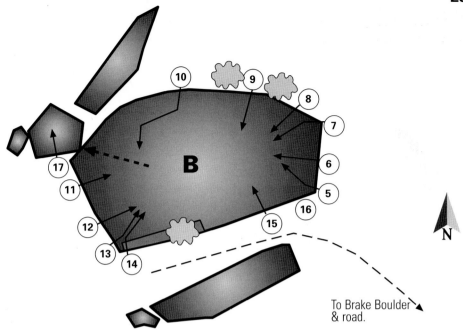

To Brake Boulder & road.

B. The Main Boulder ▲
The Main Boulder is just that: the main boulder. You'll find great problems with good landings on every face of this fine piece of rock. The boulder is 50 feet west of the Brake Boulder and about 25 feet from the road.

5. Fat Albert Gang V4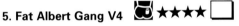
Start sitting. Climb the arête on the right side. An ultra cool little rig.

6. Fat Albert Face V8
Climb the face without using either arête. It's hard, and that's all I have to say about that.

7. Fungus V5
Start sitting with hands on little knobs on either side of the blunt arête. Climb the arête.

8. Christopher Reeve V4
Climb the face just around the corner to the right of Fungus.

9. Salad V5 ★★★
Start in between the two trees, with hands matched on the rounded flake five feet up. Climb the face. A great problem, but a little sharp.

10. A Bit Slopey V8
Start sitting using small edges, move up and right to the rail, and then follow the rail to the top making a big lunge to the lip. Avoid the drilled mono when topping out.
A **V6 variation** begins on the low part of the rail.

11. Lollypop Problem V9?
This impossible-looking line reportedly climbs the face left of the Dean Problem.

12. The Dean Problem V7
Although completely manufactured by past quarry work, this is still an enjoyable challenge. Start with both hands in the underclings four feet up. Press your feet onto the polished little dishes and fire for the first of the drilled holes, then continue up the drill holes making a big dyno to the lip, the arête to the right is off route. This used to be a fairly committing highball until a flash flood hit the area and deposited all the wonderful sand that now graces the landing.

13. Arete Left V2 ★★
Climb the arête on the left side.

14. Arete Right V1 ★★
Climb the arête on the right side.

15. V2 ★★★
Start three feet to the left of Fat Albert Gang. Climb the slabby face. A fun V2 variation that adds a little pump to this problem climbs Entrapment to the lip, then traverses to the lip and top outs on the left side of the

16. V1 ★★
Climb the slabby face using the arête with your right hand.

The next problem is on the small rock that touches the Main Boulder on its northwest corner.

17. Cronin's V3
Climb the face without using the arêtes.

Cabbage Patch

0.3m

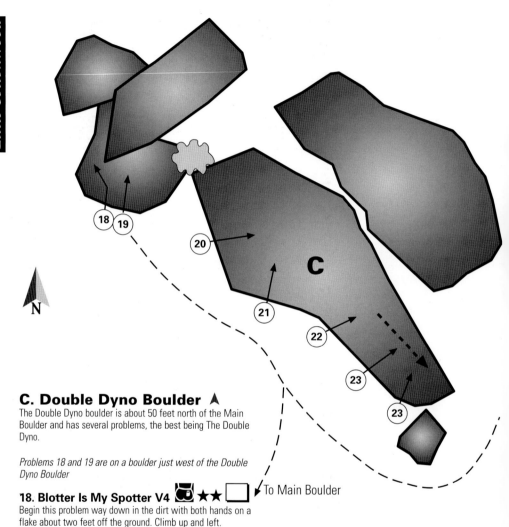

C. Double Dyno Boulder
The Double Dyno boulder is about 50 feet north of the Main Boulder and has several problems, the best being The Double Dyno.

Problems 18 and 19 are on a boulder just west of the Double Dyno Boulder

18. Blotter Is My Spotter V4 ★★
Begin this problem way down in the dirt with both hands on a flake about two feet off the ground. Climb up and left.

19. Boone's Mantel V5 ★★
Oh great! A boulder problem that consists only of a grovely mantel. Start on the lip at the middle of the boulder. Mantel.

20. V4 ★
Begin with both hands in the low part of the crack; move up to the obvious chickenhead and top out. The top out is the crux.

21. Project?
Start sitting, three feet left of the Double Dyno. Pull to the lip and make a sick-looking mantel.

22. Double Dyno V2 ★★★
Start on the big knob in the middle of the horizontal crack. Make big moves to big holds straight up. A very cool little problem.

23. Circus Freak V2 ★★
Start in the horizontal crack three feet right of the Double Dyno. Climb into the left-angling crack and top out.

24. Dim Wit V0
Climb the jugs on the right side of the boulder.

D. Tom's Boulder ▶

To reach Tom's Boulder follow a trail west from the Main Boulder, going a little uphill, for about 100 feet.

25. Lance's Mantel V4 ★ ☐
Rumored to be left of Tom's Problem.

26. Tom's Problem V5  ★★★★ ☐
We all have problems; some are worth sharing. Begin this classic standing at the right side of the face with your hands on a jug at the bottom of the rail. Climb the rail up and left to the arête. Follow the arête and top out as soon as you can on the left face. A beautiful, tall, and scary problem.

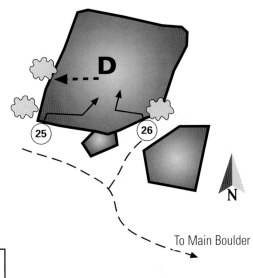

E-F. Boulders ▲ ▶

To reach these boulders follow a trail on the right side of the Double Dyno Boulder northwest up the hill for about 100 feet. I Kill Children is on the west side of Boulder E. Boulder F is 20 feet northwest of Boulder E.

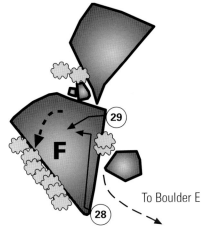

27. I Kill Children V3 ★ ☐
Begin standing with hands matched on an edge six feet up. Climb the face.

The next two problems are on Boulder F.

28. V3 ★★★ ☐
A fantastic, thrilling, and pumpy highball. The rock is a little crumbly, but with more traffic it should clean up. Start standing at the left edge of the boulder. Over the lip and just behind a small black chicken head is a drilled hole. Use this hole to get started and follow the arête up and right to the summit. If you get pumped and scared, cowardly top out at any time, but, remember — no send unless you traverse all the way to the summit.

29. V3 ★★ ☐
Another interesting and spicy little adventure that unfortunately suffers from crumbly rock. Climb the right arête to the summit. Highball, bad landing, scary.

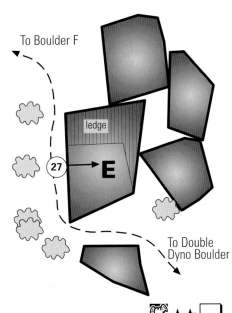

Little Cottonwood Canyon

5-Mile Boulders 0.9m

Excellent rock, an almost nonexistent approach, and loads of good climbing make the 5-Mile Boulders another classic Little Cottonwood bouldering venue. The bulk of the climbing is concentrated on the Split Boulder and its neighbor, the Butt Trumpet Boulder; however, several more climbs can be found on boulders a few yards to the north and to the east. Like many areas in Little Cottonwood Canyon, the 5-Mile Boulders are surrounded by a thick canopy of trees that provide shade during the warmer months. In fall and winter, the leaves drop and the 5-Mile Boulders can be pleasantly sunny.

To locate the 5-Mile Boulders drive up the canyon 0.9 miles, and park in a pullout on the south side of the road (this is the same parking as for the Riverside Area). The boulders are a short distance up the hill on the north side of the road, and can be seen through the trees.

A. The Split Boulder

This large and impressive boulder is the main attraction at the 5-Mile Area. It has excellent climbs of all grades, most of which have perfect flat landings. The Split Boulder is the first boulder you come to as walk up from the parking pullout. It is easily identified by the large crack that splits the boulder in two.

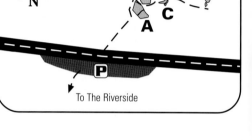

1. V0 ★
Climb the face just left of the tree.

2. Craig's Sit Down V6 ★
Sit start in a sidepull and an undercling two feet off the ground. Climb up the face via pinches, and finish on the arête to the left.

3. Sharpie V1 ★
Climb the arête.

4. V5 ★★
Start on slopers. Mantle onto the shelf, then continue up the slab.

5. V6 ★
Begin four feet left of #4 with both hands on slopers at the lip. Mantle and climb the slab.

6. Mantel Traverse V6 ★★
Begin three feet left of #5. Traverse the lip right and finish on #4.

7. The Knob V3 ★★
Climb the face right of the crack without using the crack.

8. Big Mouth V2 ★★★
Layback the offwidth crack while using face holds on the right. An excellent warm-up and good fun.

The next six problem use specific holds. See the inset topo on the opposite page.

9. Mr. Smiley Right V7 ★★★
A-B-C-D-E

10. Stand Up Right V5 ★★★
B-C-D-E

11. Mr. Smiley V7 Center ★★★★
A-B-F-D-E

12. Center Stand up V6 ★★★★
B-F-D-E

13. Mr. Smiley Left V8 ★★★
A-B-F-G

14. Stand up Left V7 ★★★
B-F-G

15. Two Giant Steps V9 ★★
H-F-G

16. Double Arêtes V4 ★★★
Climb the double arêtes. A great technical problem.

17. Webb's Slab V8 ★★
Climb the slab and arête.

18. Lance's Slab V5 ★★
Climb the slab four feet left of the arête.

19. V2 ★
Climb the arête and face just right of the down climb. Bad landing.

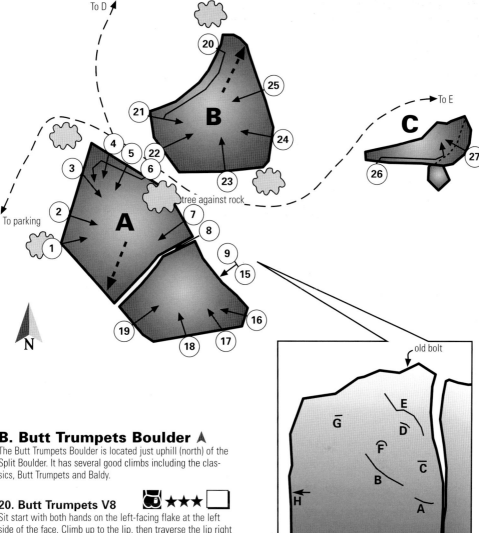

B. Butt Trumpets Boulder

The Butt Trumpets Boulder is located just uphill (north) of the Split Boulder. It has several good climbs including the classics, Butt Trumpets and Baldy.

20. Butt Trumpets V8 ★★★
Sit start with both hands on the left-facing flake at the left side of the face. Climb up to the lip, then traverse the lip right and mantel the same as for #21.

21. Baldy V6 ★★★
Sit start on good edges at the base of the arête. Climb up the arête to a hard mantel.

22. V0 ★
Climb the face to the right of #21.

23. V2 ★★
Climb the slabby face between the trees.

24. Caress V8 ★★
Sit start in the small cave; make hard moves onto the face.

25. Green Face V3 ★★
Climb the face right of # 24.

C. Razor Burn Boulder

This small boulder is located 10 yards up-canyon (east) of the Butt Trumpets Boulder. Although it does not offer much climbing, the Razor Burn problem makes a great warm up.

26. Razor Burn V3 ★★
Begin on the lip at left side of the south face. Traverse the lip right. Bad landing.

27. CB's Pit V5 ★
Sit start on the lone edge four feet up. Make one hard move up and right to an edge then the lip.

Little Cottonwood Canyon

5-Mile Boulders 0.9m

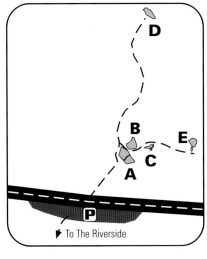

D. Cheese Whiz Boulder ▶

This boulder is located uphill (north), about 50 yards past the Butt Trumpets Boulder. One of the hardest problems in LCC is found on its overhanging south face.

28. Cheese Whiz V11 ★★★ ☐
Sit start on a good left-facing flake. Climb straight out the roof.

29. Other Roof V5 ★★ ☐
Sit start with both hands on the bottom of the sloping right-facing flake. Climb the flake up and left and out to the same finish as #28.

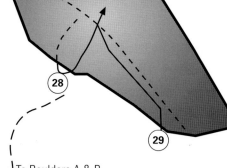

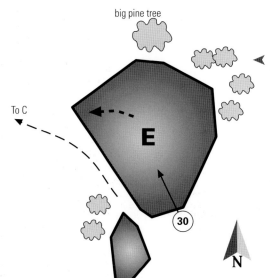

◀ E. Boulder

This boulder is 30 yards up canyon (east) of the Razor Burn Boulder. One good, hard problem ascends the blunt prow on its southeast face.

30. Rock On V8 ★★ ☐
Start standing with your right hand on small knobs five feet up and left hand on a left-facing sloper seven feet up. Make delicate moves up the prow on more slopers.

Little Cottonwood Canyon

Chris Grijalva not smiling (but having fun) on *Mr. Smiley* (V7), previous page.
Photo: Dave Pegg

The Riverside ▼   0.9m

The Riverside area is in the bottom of the canyon in dense forest and on hot days often benefits from cool breeze coming off the river. You'll find many good problems and several classic problems on the boulders spread out among the trees. They vary in style, from safe and sane to problems you would never want to fall from the top of, like Shivers and The Surprise. No matter what level you are climbing at, mentally or physically, The Riverside is a great place to climb. To access the Riverside, park on the south side of the road nine tenths of a mile from the Wasatch National Forest sign.

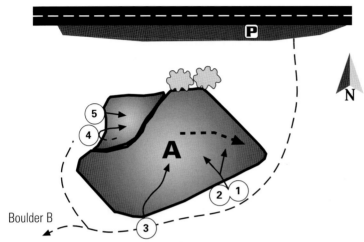

A. The Heroin Boulder ▲
The Heroin Boulder is right next to the south side of the road. Look for a trail heading downhill from the down-canyon end of the parking area, just to the left of a large boulder.

1. The Heroin Face Right V6 ★★★ ☐
Start matched on the low crimp that is four feet off the ground. Move up and left to a gaston crimp in the middle of the face, then finish to the right.

2. The Heroin Face Left V7 ★★ ☐
Same start as that of Heroin face right, but from the gaston, go straight up to the top of the boulder.

3. The Worms V6 ★★★ ☐
Begin this classic with both hands in the V-shaped scoop six and a half feet off the ground, on the left side of the face. Follow the rounded lip up and right to the summit. A variation sit start at the left edge off the face adds a few more pumpy moves.

4. V4   ★ ☐
Start sitting with both hands in the crack under the small roof. Pull the roof, then straight up the face.

5. V3   ★ ☐
Start standing in the drilled hole.

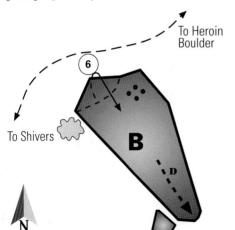

◀ B. Boulder
This Boulder is a few feet south of the Heroin Boulder. One problem is described, although several very easy climbs can be done on its low-angle faces.

6. V2   ★ ☐
Start sitting. Climb the overhung face by slapping up both sides of the arête.

WolverinePublishing   www.wolverinepublishing.com

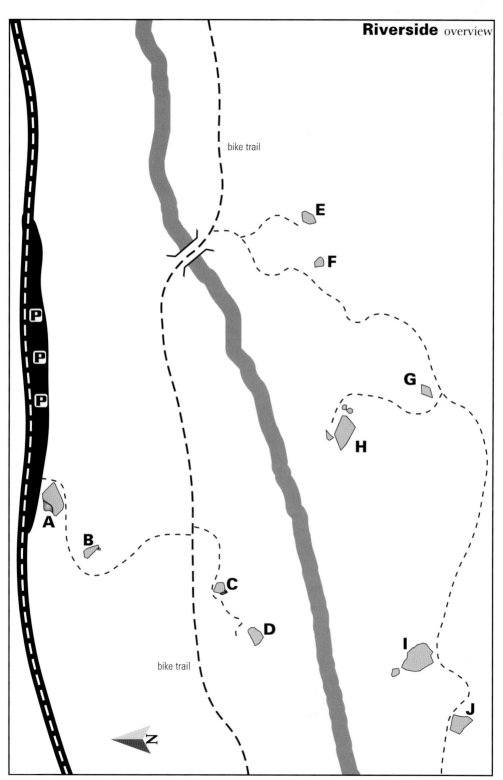

The Riverside

0.9m

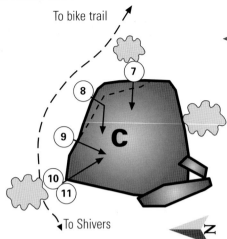

C. Papa Bells Boulder
Located on the south side of the bike trail near the river. To find this boulder, continue down the trail (south) past the Heroin Boulder for about 150 feet until you reach the bike trail. Follow the trail that crosses the bike trail and continues south and then west for about another 50 feet.

7. V3
Start in the middle of the face directly behind a tree. Right hand on a right-facing sidepull, left hand on a slopey crimp. Make one move to the jug rail.

8. V4
Start sitting three feet to the right of #7 using two right-facing side pulls, move to an edge on the face, then climb up and right.

9. Short Crack V1
Climb the crack.

10. Papa Bell's Arete V4
Walk up the arête to the summit — without using hands. The hardest part is at the top.

11. Jingle Bells V0
Climb the arête, on either side, using hands.

D. Shivers Boulder
A big, tall boulder 25 feet beyond the Papa Bells Boulder.

12. Shivers V8 ★★★★
One of the best and most intimidating problems in Little Cottonwood. Begin sitting with your right hand on a large right facing sidepull and left hand on a smaller left-facing sidepull. Climb up and left. Finish with a desperate, terrifying mantel.

13. Bronson V9 ★★
Start as for Shivers, but move right on the face and finish up #14.

14. V4 ★★★
Begin four feet right of Shivers on two opposing sidepulls. Climb up and left to the arête.

15. V5 ★★
Begin the same as #14, but climb straight up.

16. V3 ★
Start matched on edges five feet up, just right of the mossy face. Climb into the shallow groove.

17. Mike's Slab V4 ★★
Clean the rubber on your shoes before you get on this one. Slaby and thin. Climb the low-angle face three feet right of #16.

18. The Drip V3 ★★★
Start at the right end of the face with your hands matched on "the drip." Climb the blunt arête.

19. Dale's Problem V6 ★
Start with both hands in the sloping scoop directly behind the large tree. Climb straight up.

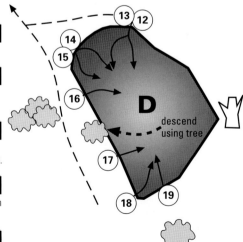

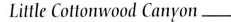

Jerry Moffatt on the fingery *All Thumbs* (V10), page 16.
Photo: Ray Wood

The Riverside

0.9m

E. The Buzz Boulder ➤
This isolated boulder has two problems, one of which is among the best V7s in the canyon. To locate The Buzz, follow the trail south from the parking area, past the Heroin Boulder, until you reach the bike trail. Follow the bike trail east for a few hundred feet, cross the bridge, and look for a trail on the right about 20 feet past the bridge. Take this trail up the hill for 30 feet towards the largest boulder with an obvious sharp arête. This arête is The Buzz.

20. The Buzz V7 ★★★★
Begin this amazing problem with your right hand using an edge six feet up, and your left hand around the corner in a flat undercling. Climb the arête. A V9 variation starts low with your hands matched on a small crimp on the right side of the arête.

21. Busy Bee V4 ★
Start sitting and climb the face five feet right of The Buzz.

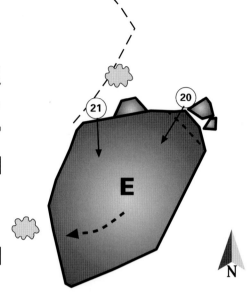

◄ F. Brutus Boulder
Brutus is 50 feet west of the Buzz.

22. Brutus V8 ★★
Start standing with your left hand on a sidepull and right hand on a crimp just below the black spot. Climb straight up.

G. Alzheimers Boulder ➤
To locate this boulder, continue west on the trail past Brutus for several hundred feet. The trail goes slightly up hill after you pass Brutus, taking you away from the river. Alzheimers is next to the trail.

23. Alzheimers V8 ★★★
This great little problem packs a lot of punch into a small amount of climbing. Start standing with your left hand on a crimp seven feet up and your right hand on a small side pull four and a half feet up. Climb straight up, clawing your way around the small bulge.

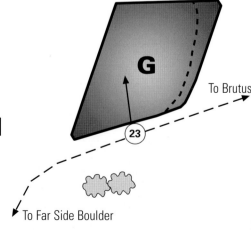

Wolverine Publishing   www.wolverinepublishing.com

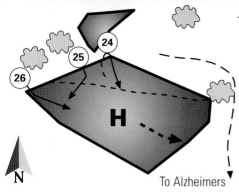

◄ H. Boulder
A lone boulder hidden in the trees 100 feet north of Alzheimers. To locate this boulder, find a trail on the west side of Alzheimers and follow it north for about a 100 feet.

24. Garth's Other Roof V6 ★★★
Start sitting with your left hand on a sidepull under the roof and your right hand on the edge of the lip. Climb the arête up and left.

25. V2 ★★
Start standing at the bottom of the rail, hand traverse the rail, and top out at the right end of the boulder.

26. Mr. Hanky V1
Climb the arete. Topout is the crux.

I. The Far Side Boulder ➤
The Far Side boulder is home to several good moderate problems, and has one of the longest approaches in the canyon (about 10 minutes from the parking area). It is common to have this area to yourself when other boulders are crowded. To find the Far Side Boulder continue for about 400 feet west down the trail from Alzheimers.

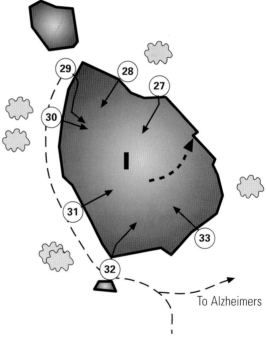

27. V0 ★
Start standing using a flake six feet up on the left side of the face. Climb the arête and face. A **V1 variation** avoids the arête and just climbs the face.

28. V0- ★
Climb the right side of the face.

29. V2 ★
Start sitting at the very bottom of the rail, traverse the rail up and right to the top.

30. V4 ★
Start six feet in from the left side of the boulder; locate two crimps in a shallow crack five feet up. Follow edges up and right.

31. Haunting Mass Appeal V1 ★★★
Start standing using jugs five feet up. Climb the face.

32. V4 ★★★
Start sitting with your right hand on a right-facing sidepull four and a half feet up; follow the arête to the "V" groove. Excellent.

33. The Back Side V6
Climb the shallow groove. Barf!

To The Far Side Boulder

◄ J. The Surprise Boulder
Located fifty feet west of the Far Side Boulder.

34. The Surprise V9 ★★★
Start sitting at the right side of the rail; follow the rail left to the arête, and follow it to the surprise — a hellish, sloping, terrifying, mantle top out. *Boo!*

Little Cottonwood Canyon

Mr T Area

0.9m

Although this small area offers only a handful of problems, most of the climbing is tall and of high quality, making it well worth a visit. The Mr. T. area lies between the Five-Mile Boulders and The Gate, and can be found by driving up the canyon 0.9 miles. Park in a pullout on the south side of the road (same parking as the Five-Mile boulders) and walk a few yards up canyon. On the north side of the road is a boulder with a red dot on its east face.

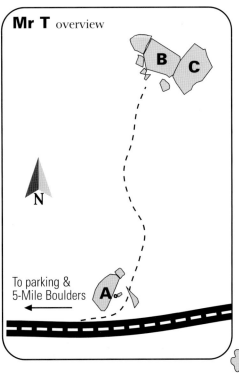

A. Red Dot Boulder
The best thing you can say about this limited boulder is that it offers a good landmark for locating the Mr. T Boulder.

1. Red Dot V0
Start on the ledge in the middle of the face. Climb straight up and mantel.

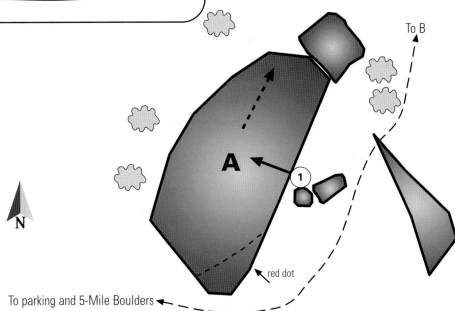

B. Mr. T. Boulder ▼

This superb golden boulder hosts three classic problems on its impeccable south face. A couple of competent spotters and crash pads are useful as the problems are tall with hard top outs, and less than ideal landings. Locate this boulder by walking 60 yards north (uphill) from the Red Dot Boulder.

2. V3
Climb the arête.

3. Golden V7
Climb the golden face between the two trees. Hard and scary turning the lip.

4. Mr. T. V7
Begin where the two thin cracks form a "T". Climb the face.

C. Boulder ▼

This large boulder is located immediately right of the Mr. T. Boulder. Two OK moderate problems climb its backside. In addition, there is a bolt on the southeast face to facilitate a top rope on what would otherwise be a very bold, and potentially deadly boulder problem.

5. V1
Climb the shallow groove.

6. V2 ★★
Begin three feet left of #5. Follow the rail up and left.

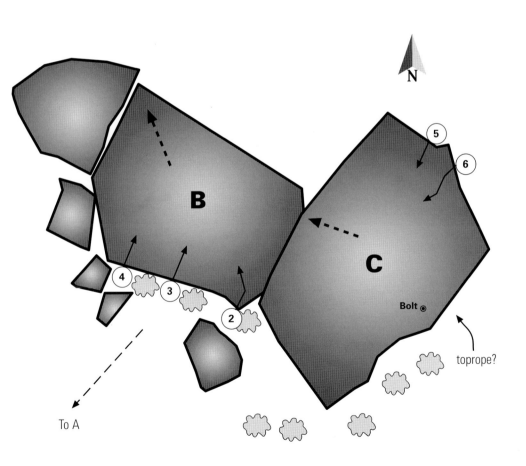

Little Cottonwood Canyon

The Gate ▼   1.2m

This popular area offers a high concentration of quality climbs on excellent rock with a variety of angles, from tall slabby faces to steep overhangs with perfect edges. With some of the hardest problems in the canyon, many hopeful suitors flock to the area in hopes of achieving fame. Hot summer days can be tolerable amidst the shade of numerous oak and maple trees; autumn and spring bring crisp temperatures and ideal conditions.

To locate the Gate boulders drive up the canyon 1.2 miles and park in the large pullout on the south side of the road. The Gate boulders are on the north side of the road. Approach via trails on either side of the fenced-in area.

Little Cottonwood

A. The Fly Boulder ➤

This is the southern-most boulder at The Gate, and is one of the finest pieces of stone in Little Cottonwood Canyon. A multitude of jugs, crimps, and pinches on its south face provide many quality eliminate problems. More good problems are found on its east and west faces.

1. V0 ★
Climb the arête on the left side

2. V0 ★
Climb the arête on the right side.

3. V0 ★
Climb jugs up the middle of the scoop.

4. V1 ★
Start on the left-facing rail at the edge of the scoop. Climb up and right onto the black face.

5. V0 ★
Start on the right side of the east face. Climb the lip up and left.

6. Pump Traverse V5 ★★★
Start on the left side of the west face. Traverse the lip right and top out on the right corner of the west face.

7. Crystal Pinch V6 ★★★
Start on the arête, move your left hand to the obvious crystal pinch then continue up to chicken-heads at the lip.

The next eight problems use specified holds. See the topo on the opposite page.

8. Standard V10 Overhang Low Start ★★★
Sit start on the footholds of the Standard Overhang, and then pull the Standard Overhang. A-B-C-D

9. Standard Overhang V3 ★★★
Begin standing with your left hand in a sidepull and right hand in an undercling. B-C-D

10. Iron Cross V5 ★★
Start in the incut edge. F-C-G-E

11. V4 ★★★
Start in the incut edge. F-C-D

12. Super Fly V8 ★★★
Start in the incut edge. F-G-E

13. Bar Fly V9 ★★★
Sit start with right hand on a small polished crimp and left in a small pocket. H-I-J-K

14. Bar Fly stand up V5 ★★★
Start matched on a crimp. I-J-K

15. Pro Series V11 ★★★
Sit start the same as Bar Fly and climb into Super Fly. H-I-F-G-E

16 Crystal Traverse V4 ★★★★
Start on edges just left of the tree. Traverse the slopey rail left and top out. L-sloper-J-sloper-sloper-E

B. Mini Boulder ➤

This small boulder is a few feet west (down canyon) of the Fly boulder. It has one very short problem on its south face.

17. Mini V1
Start sitting with two crystals at the lip. Climb straight up.

Wolverine Publishing   www.wolverinepublishing.com

The Gate overview

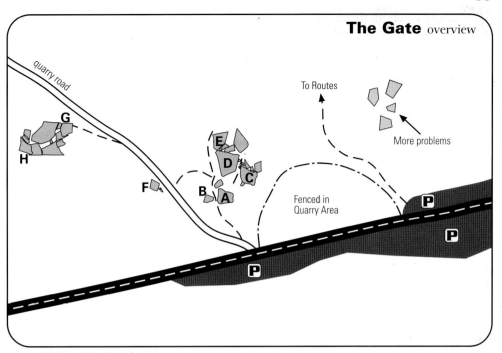

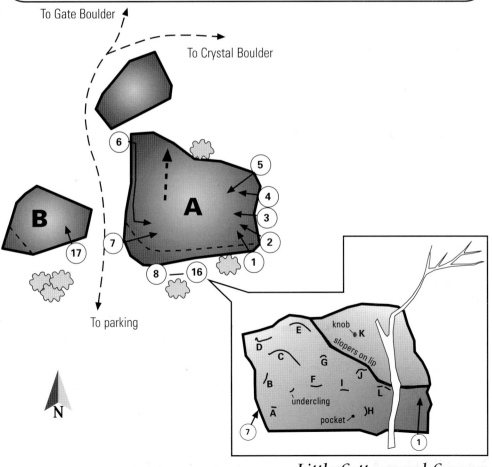

Little Cottonwood Canyon

The Gate ▼   1.2m

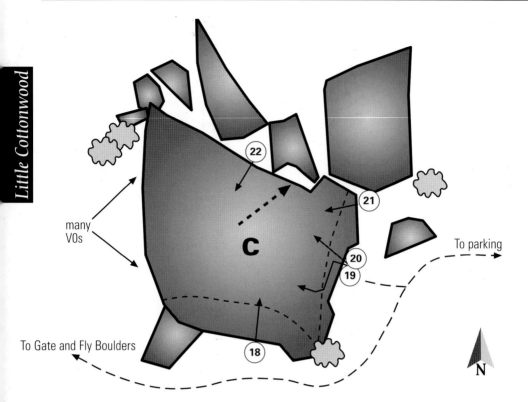

C. Crystal Boulder

The Crystal boulder is an excellent place to warm up. Although not described here, the west face of the Crystal boulder can be climbed just about anywhere at V0. This boulder is 20 yards northeast (up canyon and uphill) from The Fly boulder.

18. Arm Breaker V4
Sit start on the right-facing rounded flake on the overhanging face. Climb to the lip and mantle. Bad landing.

19. Ramp Left V4
Sit start on the left-facing slopey rail, make a big move left into the groove and follow it to the top.

20. E.B.P. V3
This is an excellent problem but with a bad landing. Begin the same as #19, but climb straight up. It is easiest to top out by moving left. It can also be done by continuing straight up to the summit, over the worst possible landing.

20a. Variation V7
Climb the face between the groove on problem #19 and problem #20.

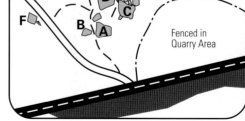

21. Overhang V1
Sit start in the small cave at the right end of the face. Follow good holds up the corner. At the big black chickenhead move right onto a ledge on the right face. This direct finish is V2 over a very bad landing.

22. Crystals V3
Begin in the middle of the north face in between the rocks at the base. Climb crystals up the low angle face.

Little Cottonwood Canyon

Tim O'Neil pumping out on
The Pump Traverse (V5),
previous page.
Photo: Jim Thornburg

The Gate ▽

1.2m

D. The Gate Boulder ▶

This large verdant boulder, located 15 yards north (uphill) of the Fly Boulder, has many excellent moderate problems. The climbs on the west face make superb highballs. If you feel uncomfortable that far above the deck, bolts at the lip facilitate toproping.

23. V3 ★★
Start matched on an edge six feet up and just to the right of a tree. Move into a right-angling crack, and top out.

24. V2 ★
Start in the good incut flake just to the left of the rock at the base of the boulder. Climb up and right.

25. V3 ★★
Same start as #26, but climb up and left.

26. V3 ★
Start in the right-facing flake five feet right of #27. Climb up and right to a slopey mantel top out.

27. V3 ★★
Sit start in a flake three feet off the ground just right of the slab. Follow good edges up and right to the same top out as #26. Avoid using the slab at the bottom.

28. Road Rash V2  ★★
That's what you get if you fall off this climb! Start standing on the slab of rock. Climb the crack into the V notch.

29. V0 ★
Begin at the right edge of the west face. Climb the arête and face.

30. Green Slab Right V0 ★★
This problem climbs the face between #29 and #31, just left of the first tree.

31. Green Slab Center V1 ★★★
Climb the face just right of a group of three trees, one alive and two dead.

32. Green Slab Left V3 ★★
Climb the face just left of a group of three trees, one alive and two dead.

33. Left Side V3 ★★
Start three feet to the right of #34. Climb the face above a very bad landing.

34. Left Side Direct V5 ★★★
Start on two small crimps, make a hard move up and right, to a good hold and continue up the face.

35. Left of Left V4 ★★
This problem starts on the left-facing rail in the small cave formed by the two boulders. Climb the left facing rail to the right onto the arête then finish the same as #34.

D. The Flake Boulder ▶

This excellent boulder touches the Gate Boulder on its north side and forms a small cave. Two of the hardest problems in LCC climb out of this cave. The west face offers one of the best V5s in the canyon, in addition to several easy problems on big holds.

36. Chimney V2 ★
Start in the back of the cave and climb out this chimney formed where the two boulders touch.

37. Taylor Made V11 ★★★
Sit start on a sloper in the back right corner of the cave. Climb out the cave and traverse left into #39.

38. Spinal Twist V13 ★★★
Start sitting. Climb the incipient black seam out of the cave and into #39.

39. Hong's Pinch Layback V5 ★★★★
One of the best V5s in the canyon. Start standing with left hand on a high crimp eight feet up and right hand on the vertical right facing flake. Continue up the flake to the top.

39a. Variation V7 ★★★
Start #39 on low holds; make one hard drive-by move to reach the left-hand starting hold for #39.

40. V1 ★★
Climb the obvious flakes to the top of the boulder. Super polished from the passage of thousands of climbers.

41. V0 ★
Start on flat edges five feet up. Climb jugs up and right.

42. V1 ★★
Same start as #41, but follow crimps straight up the face.

43. V0 ★
Same start as #41, but climb up and left.

43

Little Cottonwood

Little Cottonwood Canyon

The Gate

1.2m

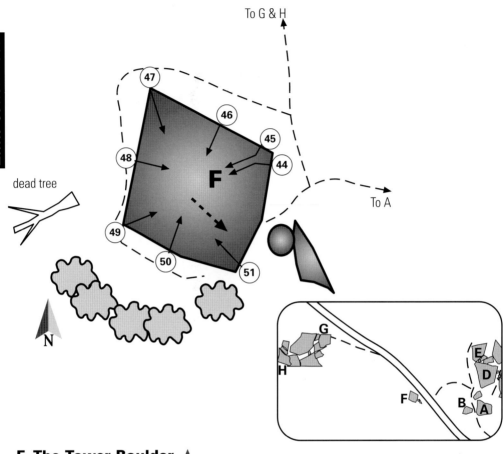

F. The Tower Boulder

This small boulder has a high concentration of climbs. It lies beside the old quarry road about 35 yards west of the main Gate boulders. With only a few small trees on its west side, the Tower Boulder is in the sun for most of the day.

44. V1 ★
Climb the arête and face on the left side.

45. V1 ★
Climb the arête on the right side.

46. V3 ★★
Climb the low angle face without using either of the arêtes.

47. V3 ★
Sit start. Climb the arête.

48. V3 ★
Start in crimps just left of the fallen log. Climb the face.

49. Easy Tower V4 ★★
Climb the arête and face.

50. The Tower V7 ★★
Start sitting in a slopey horizontal crack. Climb the face without using either of the arêtes.

51. Down Climb V0
Climb up or down the left side of the southeast face.

WolverinePublishing   www.wolverinepublishing.com

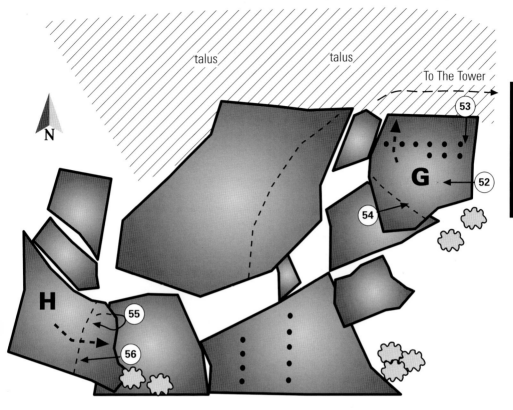

G. Boulder

The G and H boulders are located next to the old quarry road 60 yards northwest (uphill and a little down canyon) of the Tower Boulder. The G boulder has vertical blasting marks on its north face and many drill holes on its top. It sits in a group of large boulders. Although the rock is little bit crumbly, many undescribed problems have been done in this area.

52. V0
Start on the left side of the east face. Climb the face and arête.

53. V0
Start at the left side of the north face. Climb the vertical blasting scars.

54. Mind Games V4 ★★
A bit dirty, but still quite good. Start on a jug under the roof and five feet up. Climb crimps to the lip and mantle. A fall from the mantel could be serious.

H. Boulder

The H boulder can be found by walking 50 feet west from problem #54 on the G boulder. Two short and dirty problems climb out a small overhang on its east face.

55. Choose V3 ★
Sit start on good edges under the roof. Climb out the overhang up and left.

56. Waste Land V2
Sit start on a good edge beneath the lip. Make one move to the lip and mantel.

Little Cottonwood Canyon

The Swamp ▼

1.2m

The Swamp lies along the river edge in the cool canyon bottom. It has an adventurous feel with many tall, committing problems. It also has some good short problems if getting way off the deck is not your thing.

To locate the Swamp, drive up the canyon 1.2 miles, and park on the south side of the road (the same parking as the Gate boulders). Locate a large iron pipe a few yards off the south side of the road, and use it to cross the river. After crossing the river, continue south to the bike trail. The boulders are located next to the bike trail, east and west of the river crossing, and around the old house. You can also reach The Swamp by walking east (up canyon) from The Riverside area.

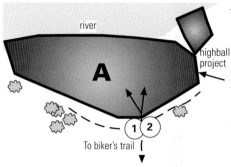

◀ A. The Tiny Boulder

The Tiny Boulder is huge. Unfortunately, it's mostly devoid of climbable features, and there is a lot of rock for just two climbs. Happily, both climbs are good. This boulder is 150 yards west (down canyon) of the old house, and 25 feet north (toward the river) of the bike trail.

1. Tiny V11 ★★
Start in the three obvious drilled holes. Climb micro holds up and left.

2. Huge V8 ★★★
Start in the same drilled holes as #1, but climb straight up past a pair of old rusty bolts.

B. Boulder
NO TOPO

This boulder is about 60 yards west (down canyon) of the old house, right off the north side of the bike trail. In addition to one bolted 5.12a route, it has numerous highballs. If you feel like doing some exciting adventure climbing, check out the boulder's tall slabs.

C. The Kewl Boulder ▼

This boulder has a couple of short problems that provide a change from the highballs hereabouts. It is located in the trees, ten yards west (down canyon) of the old house.

3. Kewl V3
Climb the arête. Weird and dirty.

4. Uber Kewl V5 ★
Start standing with your left hand on a left-facing side pull seven feet up, and right hand on whatever. Make hard slaps up the face.

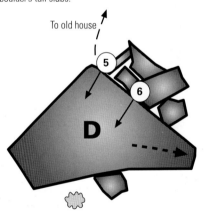

D. Boulder ▲

This boulder has two scary slab problems. It is about 15 yards from the southwest corner of the old house.

5. V2 ☠ ★★
Climb the arête and face.

6. V4 ☠ ★★
Climb the center of the slabby face, over a very bad landing.

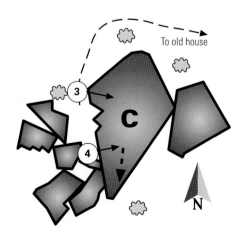

WolverinePublishing   www.wolverinepublishing.com

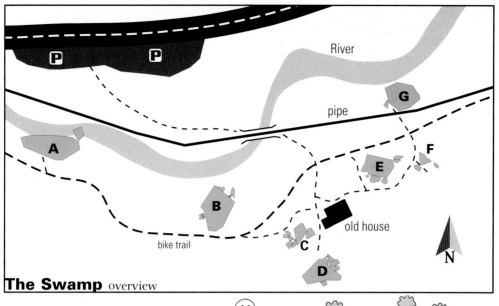

The Swamp overview

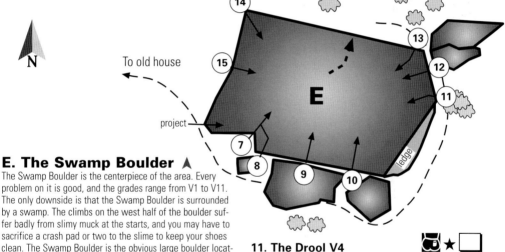

E. The Swamp Boulder

The Swamp Boulder is the centerpiece of the area. Every problem on it is good, and the grades range from V1 to V11. The only downside is that the Swamp Boulder is surrounded by a swamp. The climbs on the west half of the boulder suffer badly from slimy muck at the starts, and you may have to sacrifice a crash pad or two to the slime to keep your shoes clean. The Swamp Boulder is the obvious large boulder located about 20 yards east (up canyon) of the old house.

7. Jack Horner V11 ★★★
Climb the overhanging dihedral.

8. Ditch Witch V9 ★★★
Start on small crimps just right of the arête. Climb up the face, then move left onto the arête and top the same as #7.

9. Don't Fall V3 ★★★★
This is one of the finest V3s in the canyon. Climb the left-facing flake system up the center of the face. Can be done from a sit start.

10. Pride V4 ★★★★
This is one of the finest V4s in the canyon. Start standing at the right end of the face, and just left of a boulder at the base. Climb the face up and a little left.

11. The Drool V4 ★
Start sitting using the right-facing rail in front of the group of trees. Climb the rail up and left onto the ledge. Jump off, or continue up the tall top out.

12. Slinging Spit V8 ★★
Start on two small crimps six and a half feet up and just left of the arête. Climb more crimps up the face and join the arête.

13. B.B. Memorial Arête V5 ★★
Sit start low on the arête. Climb the arête up and left. Bad landing.

14. V1 ★
Climb the arête.

15. Hike V4 ★★★
Start with good edges six feet up. Climb straight up the scoop in the face.

The Swamp   1.2m

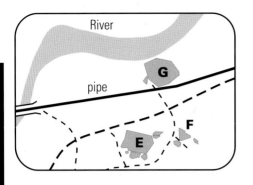

F. The Igit Boulder
This boulder has three good short problems on its west face. It is located about 15 yards east (up canyon) of the Swamp Boulder.

16. The Igit V3 ★★
Start sitting using the big ledge. Climb the face and arête.

16a. V5 ★
Start the same as #16, but dyno to the lip.

17. GED or Not To Be V6 ★
Start sitting using a crimpy edge three feet right of #16. Dyno to the top.

18. Glorified Tennis Pro V1 ★
Sit start using the rounded right facing flake. Climb the flake.

▼ G. The Big Guy Boulder
This large boulder offers few climbs although one of them is amongst the finest highballs in the canyon. It is located 25 yards north of the Igit Boulder, just north of the iron pipe, and can be reached by staying on the iron pipe after crossing the river from the parking area.

19. The Big Guy V3 ☠ ★★★★
Although this problem is completely manufactured by past roadwork or quarrying, the drill scars provide the holds for an outstanding climb. Climb the thirty-foot-tall, drill-scared arête on the west face of the boulder, at the edge of the river.

20. The Swamp Thing V3 ★★
This climb begins on the east side of the boulder in a shallow right-trending seam. Climb the seam onto the arête, then make scary exit moves onto the top of the boulder.

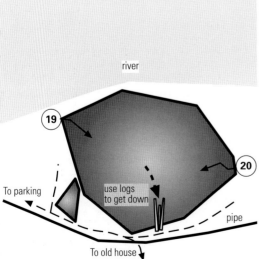

Little Cottonwood Canyon

Wills Young takes on *The Big Guy* (V3) — and he's only 5 foot 7.
Photo: Jim Thornburg

The Hillside

1.4m

Little Cottonwood

You can do a lot of walking at the Hillside as its two dozen problems are spread out on numerous boulders. The area has several good hard problems, so you can also spread the pads and work a project into submission.

To locate the Hillside, drive up the canyon 1.4 miles and park in a pullout on the south side of the road. The large and obvious Stick boulder lies right next to the north side of the road.

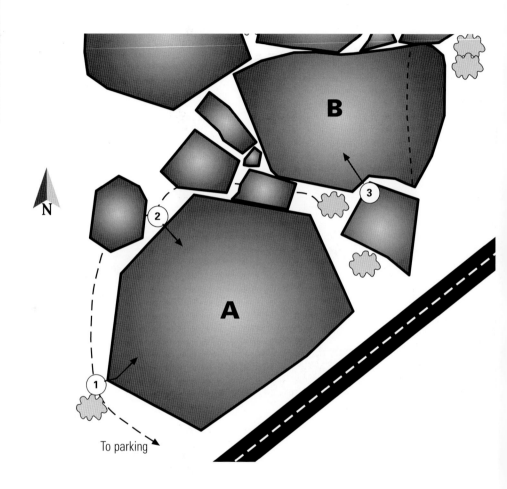

A. The Stick Boulder
Walk north from the parking area to the obvious large boulder that overhangs the road.

1. Stick Boulder Arête V4 ★★
Climb the sloping arête.

2. V5 ★
Start on a right-facing edge and undercling five feet up. Move up and right to a hard-to-see knob on the face, then finish on the slab.

B. Boulder
This large boulder is located between the Stick Boulder and the Triple Threat boulder. It has one good problem on its south face.

3. V9/10? ★★★
Begin with right hand on a positive crimp six feet up and left hand on a good edge on the arête. Climb the arête and face into the shallow seam and move left to top out. Tall with a bad landing.

Wolverine *Publishing*   www.wolverinepublishing.com

The Hillside overview

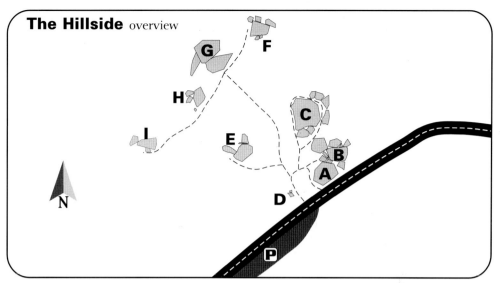

C. Triple Threat Boulder ▶

The Triple Threat boulder is the largest boulder at the Hillside. In addition to one totally classic highball, it has three bolted routes on its south and east faces. Walk north (uphill) from the parking area, or the Stick Boulder, and look for the biggest boulder around.

4. Triple Threat V9 ☠ ★★★★ ☐

This proud and intimidating line has been hailed the Midnight Lightning of LCC, although it is perhaps a bit harder, a little taller, and has a much worse landing. Start on a flat edge at the back of the overhang. Climb out the overhang until it is possible to slap the arête with your left hand. Move to good hold at the lip and finish by soloing up the tall arête and slab to the top of the boulder.

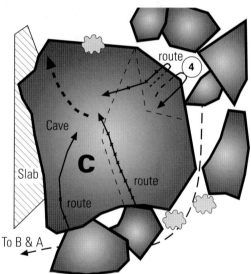

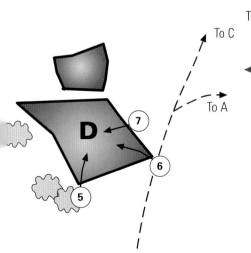

◀ D. The Obelisk Boulder

This small boulder is located in the trees, just north of the road and west (down canyon) from the Stick Boulder. It has three worthwhile V0's.

5. Obelisk Left V0 ★ ☐
Climb the left arête.

6. Obelisk Right V0 ★ ☐
Climb the right arête.

7. V0 ☐
Climb the east face.

Little Cottonwood Canyon

The Hillside

1.4m

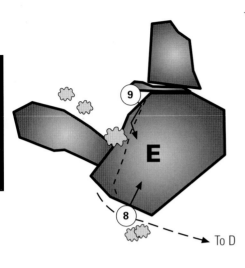

◀ E. Boulder
This is a medium-sized boulder located north (uphill) and little west (down canyon) from the D Boulder. Apparently, the entire lip from problem #8 to #9 has been climbed, but judging from the trees that lean against it blocking the traverse, it doesn't see much traffic.

8. V0
Begin on the face to the right of the overhang on good right-facing edges four feet up. Climb straight up.

9. V5
Sit start in a slopey left-facing corner. Climb up to the lip, then traverse the lip right and top out just before the tree that leans against the boulder.

F. Boulder ▶
This boulder is another fine example of Little Cottonwood Canyon granite. One very good problem climbs the arête on the south side of the boulder, and a sick-looking project has been tried using tiny dime-width edges on the impressive west face. To locate this boulder, walk the climbers' trail north (uphill) until you almost reach the Highlife Boulder, then walk east another few yards to the F boulder.

10. V7
Start with your right hand on a good edge seven feet up and your left hand on the arête. Climb the arête.

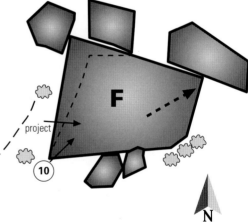

◀ G. The Highlife Boulder
If you really like desperate, slopey, greasy mantels, this is the place to be. Find this the Highlife Boulder by walking the climber's trail north (uphill) from the parking area.

11. The Highlife V8
Sit start on low crimps. Climb left to the right-facing flakes, then pull onto rounded slopey lip. Definitely not a good problem to try in hot temperatures.

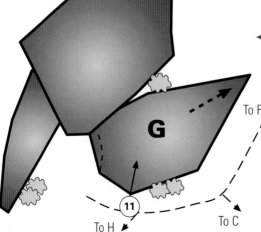

Wolverine Publishing   www.wolverinepublishing.com

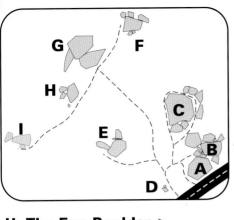

H. The Egg Boulder ▶

As the name implies, The Egg Boulder has another sick hard mantel boulder problem. It also has a pleasant V3 on its western flank. To locate The Egg, walk a few yards southwest (down canyon) from the Highlife Boulder to the obvious egg-shaped boulder.

12. The Egg V9 ★★★
Sit start under the bulge with left hand on a side pull four feet up and right hand on an edge five feet up. Make one explosive move out to the lip and mantel.

13. V3 ★★
Climb the obvious rail.

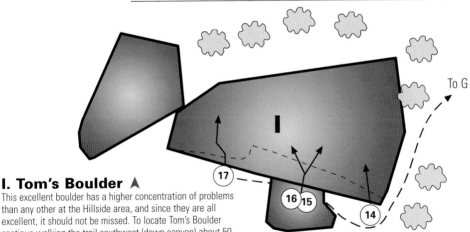

I. Tom's Boulder ▲

This excellent boulder has a higher concentration of problems than any other at the Hillside area, and since they are all excellent, it should not be missed. To locate Tom's Boulder continue walking the trail southwest (down canyon) about 50 yards past The Egg. The climbs are on the boulder's south face.

14. Tom's Arête V4 ★
Start with left hand on a knob and right hand on a pinch. Climb the arête.

15. V5 ★★
Sit start at the bottom of the right-facing flake, make a couple of moves up the flake then move right into the shallow corner. Bad landing if you fall from the top.

16. V5 ★★
Same start as #15, but stay on the flake, then moving up the face to the lip. Bad landing at the top.

17. Tom's Sloperfest V4 ★★★
Sit start with hands matched on the slopey ledge. Climb edges up and left.

Little Cottonwood Canyon

The Glen
1.5m

Similar in character to the Hillside with smaller boulders and hence shorter problems, this area is shrouded by trees in summer. After the leaves drop, its sunny location makes it an excellent winter area.
To locate the Glen, drive up the canyon 1.5 miles past the National Forest sign, and park in a pullout on the south side of the road, just past a large boulder that is right next to the road. This boulder is the Southside Boulder.

A. Southside Boulder ▶
This is only boulder at the Glen located on the south side of the road. With several great moderates it's a good place to warm up.

1. V0
Climb the face 5 feet left of the tree at the bottom of the down climb.

2. V2 ★★
Climb the left-facing edge 10 feet left of the tree.

3. V1 ★★★
Start between two rocks. Climb straight up into the water groove.

4. V1 ★★★★
Start just left of the starting rocks of #3. Climb to the tallest part of the boulder, moving slightly left.

5. V3 ★★
Start just before turning the corner with both hands on a good flake six feet off the ground. Slap to the lip and mantel.

▼ B. Roadside Boulder
The Roadside boulder is located just off the north side of the road. It has several good problems on its north and west faces.

6. Roadside V1 ★
Start with both hands at the bottom of the rail. Follow the rail up and right.

7. Waiting Room V4 ★★
Start matched on the left-facing flake. Pull to the lip and mantel.

8. Grumpy V7 ★★★
Begin with the left-facing crimp on the arête. Pull to the micro-edge with the right hand, and up to slopers. Brilliant.

9. Arete V5 ★★★
Climb the slippery arête on the left side. Pumpy.

10. Alchemy V2 ★★★
Climb the right side of the arête, and the smooth slab.

11. The Slab V4 ★★★
Climb the middle of the slab. Aretes are off.

WolverinePublishing   www.wolverinepublishing.com

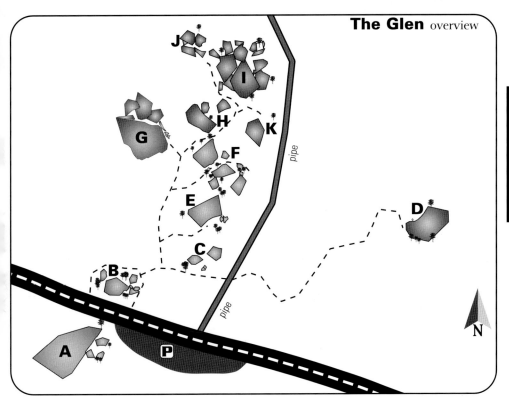

C. Misunderstood Boulder ▼
A small boulder with three problems, including the fun Misunderstood Dyno. To locate this boulder, walk up the faint trail about twenty-five yards east (up canyon) from the Roadside Boulder.

12. Borrowed Time V4 ★
Start with the left hand on a left-facing sidepull directly behind the tree; righthand on an undercling between the two black streaks. Pull to the flexing flake (that is sure to break), then to the lip right of the tree.

13. Misunderstood Dyno V5 ★★★
Left hand on the sidepull about 5 feet off the ground to the right of the black streak; right on a sidepull 4 feet off the ground. Dyno to the lip.

14. Misunderstood V1
Start standing with both hands on the arête. Climb the arête.

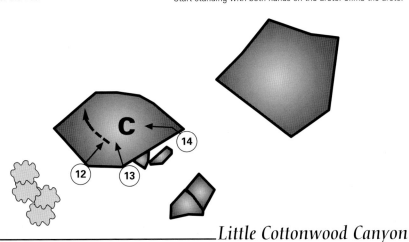

Little Cottonwood Canyon

The Glen ▼

1.5m

D. Crystal Logic Boulder ▼
A large boulder situated by itself, separate from the main Glen area. It has three OK moderates and one hard project. Locate this boulder by walking the faint trail northeast (uphill and up canyon) from the Misunderstood Boulder for about a hundred yards. Look for a large boulder amongst the trees.

15. Crystal Logic V1 ★★ ☐
A fun problem that climbs staight up the low-angle face. The flake to the right is off.

16. Flake and Bake V0+ ★ ☐
Climb the left-facing flake.

17. Project V9? ☐
Start under the lip on the blunt prow.

18. Hooloovoo V4 ★ ☐
Start standing with both hands on the lip and mantle.

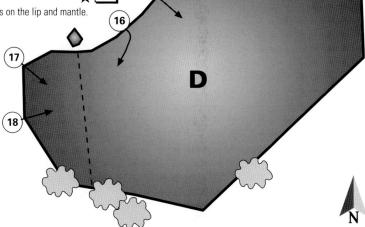

◄ E. Boulder
A large boulder with one short problem on its south face. To locate the boulder walk the faint trail north (uphill) for about 20 yards past the Roadside boulder, then walk east (up canyon) into the trees.

19. V7 ★★ ☐
Start with both hands on the rail three feet off the ground. Pull to the sharp crimper, then to the lip. Harder than it looks.

WolverinePublishing www.wolverinepublishing.com

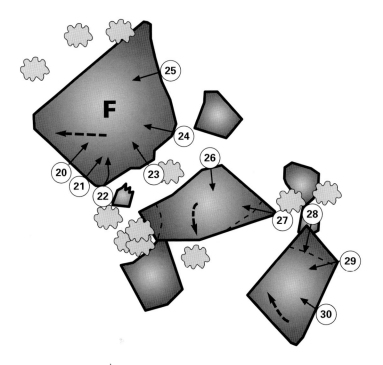

F. Fat Lady Boulders

Located at the heart of The Glen, these boulders have a high concentration of problems and some of the best climbing at the area. To reach these boulders walk the faint trail from the Roadside Boulder north (uphill) for about 40 yards, then walk east (up canyon) into the group of boulders under a canopy of trees.

20. V3 ★★
Begin standing. Right hand in the crack, left hand on the left-facing sidepull. Slap to the lip and mantle. The arête is off. Another variation begins with both hand in the crack and moves left.

21. Dun Rigil V2 ★★
Start with both hands in the crack. Climb straight up, without using the jug around the corner.

22. V1 ★★
Same start at Dun Rigil. Turn the corner to the right and topout.

23. You Fat Bastard V3 ★★★
Start standing just right of the boulder with your right hand low in the right-facing corner and your left at the bottom of a black bulge. Landing gets worse the higher you get.

24. Fat Lady V8 ★★★★
Outstanding. Start on the slopers on the right side of the blunt arête. Climb the arête using bad slopers. A cold-weather problem.

25. V0 ★★★
Great climbing up the middle of the low-angle face.

26. V1
Start on flat edges about 5 feet off the ground. The **sit start** is **V4**.

27. V6 ★★★
Begin with both hands on the very point of the prow. Move left and topout on the prow. Great.

28. Sunday Best V4 ★★★★
Begin this classic by crawling down in the dirt. Then, with both hands on the flake two and half feet off the ground, pull to the right arête.

29. V6 ★
Standing start with hands on the jug on the left arête. Dyno to the lip or pull off some slopers. Bad landing.

30. V1 ★★★
Start standing. Climb the shallow left-facing corner, staying to the right.

The Glen

1.5m

G. Tunnel of Love Boulder

This large boulder is located about 25 yards west (down canyon) of the Fat Lady Boulders. It has a couple of super scary problems on its east face, and several good moderates on its south face including the Tunnel of Love, an easy but fun water-worn groove.

31. V1 ★
Scramble up boulders at the base and climb just left of the tree. Be careful of the large loose flake. Bad landing.

32. V3 ☠ ★★★
Scramble up rocks at the base and start where the ledge forms a distinct point. Climb straight up. Bad landing.

33. V6 ★★
Start standing with both hands on the lip just before it turns the corner. Slap slopers up and to the right. Pull over.

34. V0- ★★
Around the corner from #33. Climb the groove to the summit.

35. The Trotts V3 ★★
Begin 5 feet left of #34 and just to the left of some trees. Climb micro crimps to the top.

36. V1
The shallow left-facing corner three feet left of The Trotts.

37. Screw You! Pay Me! V3 ★★
Begin in the middle of a group of trees just left of the large black groove. Climb the face and the black right-facing corner.

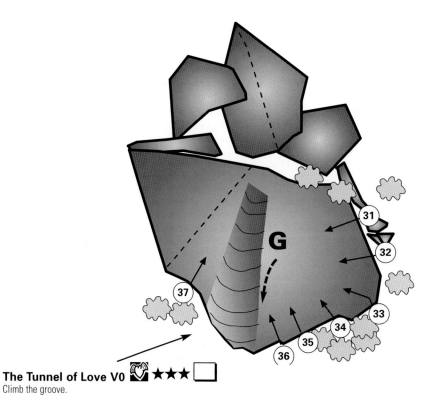

The Tunnel of Love V0 ★★★
Climb the groove.

H. No Such Place Boulders ▶

The No Such Place boulders are just a few yards north (uphill) of the Fat Lady Boulders. The two lip traverses on the first boulder are fun and good for a pump.

38. No Such Place V4 ★★
A good pumpy problem. Start with your hand on the lip of the boulder at about chest height. Traverse the lip left until your hands are on the summit. Topout.

39. V2 ★
Start matched in the good edge about six feet off the ground. Climb straight up.

40. V3
Start sitting with both hands on the lip of the boulder. Traverse the lip to the right all the way, passing a tree, and turn the corner.

41. V1 ☐
Start with hands on two opposing sidepulls. Climb straight up.

42. V1 ★
Climb the right side of the face starting with edges about six feet up.

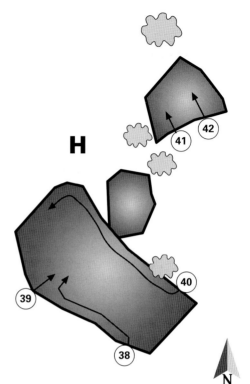

I. Pugilist Boulders

These boulders are located in the talus north (uphill) of the No Such Place Boulders. Although these boulders only have a few problems, most of them are good; the classic Pugilist should not be missed.

43. The Pugilist V4 ★★★★
Start sitting, hugging both sides of the arête. Climb the arête using both sides. Topout on the left. Excellent beautiful problem. Bad landing.

44. V2 ★★
Start sitting using good crimps in the middle of the face. Punch to the lip.

45. V1 ★
Start with both hands on the good edge 5 feet off the ground. Go right-handed to a good edge and topout.

46. V0 ★ ☐
Start on the jug in the middle of the face. Climb straight up.

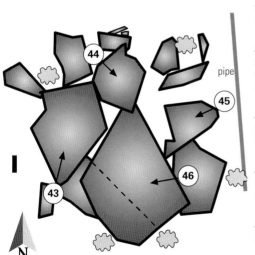

Little Cottonwood Canyon

The Glen

Little Cottonwood

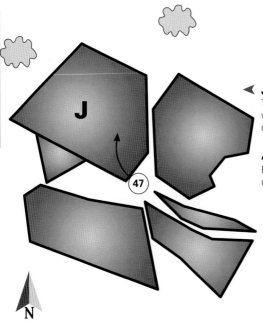

◀ **J. Boulder**
This lone boulder is located in the talus about 25 yards southwest of the Pugilist Boulder. One good problem climbs out the overhang on its south side.

47. V6
Begin with a good hold just under the lip. Slap up bad grips on the slabby face. Bad landing.

K. Boulder ▶
This boulder is fifteen yards east (up canyon) from the No Such Place Boulder and right next to the old iron pipe; it has a couple easy problems on its north side.

48. V0
Climb the left-angling rail.

49. V1
Start with the jug in the middle of the face. Climb straight up.

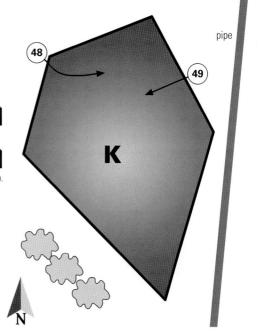

Hidden Forest ▼   1.7m

The Hidden Forest is situated at the bottom of the canyon beneath a thick canopy of trees, and is often cooler than other areas in the canyon. Considering the many nasty sloper problems and slippery mantel top outs found here, this is probably a good thing. The downside is that in late fall and winter the area gets virtually no sun, and after the first couple of storms, the Hidden Forest usually remains blanketed in snow. To reach the Hidden Forest, drive up the canyon 1.7 miles and park in large gravel parking area on the south side of the road, next to an old pump house. Walk across the bridge to the bike trail, and follow it up canyon for a couple hundred yards. When you reach a black pipe crossing the bike trail, look for a climber's trail heading south into the trees. Follow this trail a few more yards to the first boulders.

Little Cottonwood

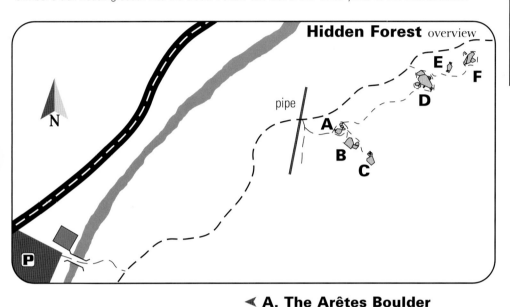

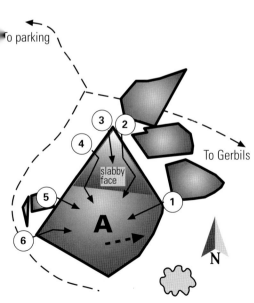

◄ A. The Arêtes Boulder
The arêtes boulder is the first boulder you come to after leaving the bike trail. It has numerous moderate problems on excellent rock with interesting features.

1. DUH V6 ★★
Start matched on the slopey ledge four and a half feet up, huck to jugs at the lip.

2. Charlie's Arête V4   ★★★
Sit start at the base of the arête. Climb the arête up and left.

3. V1   ★
Climb the slabby face between the arêtes. Bad landing.

4. Dale's Arête V4 ★★★
Start standing. Climb the arête up and right.

5. Sorry Charlie V3 ★★★
Start on the small rock at the base of the boulder. Climb small crimps straight up the face.

6. V3  ★
Sit start with your left hand on the arête and your right hand on the right-facing flake one foot off the ground. Climb the arête and face.

Little Cottonwood Canyon

Hidden Forest ▾   1.7m

B. Duct Tape Boulder ▶

This short, flat-topped boulder has two of the nastiest sloper problems in the canyon, Duct Tape and Gerbils. Each of these problems packs a V9 punch into just three moves of sloping hell. This boulder is 20 feet uphill (south) of the Arêtes Boulder.

7. Duct Tape V9   ★★★ ☐
Start on a flat edge five feet up, friction up very bad slopers. Hard for the grade.

8. Gerbils V9   ★★★ ☐
Start on the big slopey scoop five and a half feet up, slap to bad slopers just below the lip.

9. V4   ★★ ☐
Sit start in two underclings. Climb straight up.

10. V6   ★★ ☐
Climb the same as #9, but traverse left at the lip.

The next problem is on the boulder that leans against the Duct Tape boulder on its southeast side, forming a small cave.

11. Trash V5   ★ ☐
Begin on a big flat undercling, move to the crack on the left face and top out.

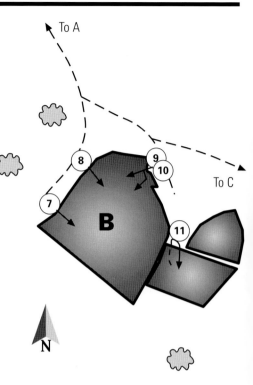

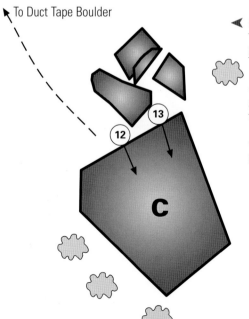

◀ C. Boulder

The north face of this small boulder has two easy but good problems. It is located 30 feet uphill (south) from the Duct Tape Boulder.

12. V0   ★★ ☐
Start in the middle of the face on left-facing sidepulls. Climb the face.

13. V0   ★★ ☐
Sit start on the left side of the face. Climb the face and arête.

Wolverine Publishing   www.wolverinepublishing.com

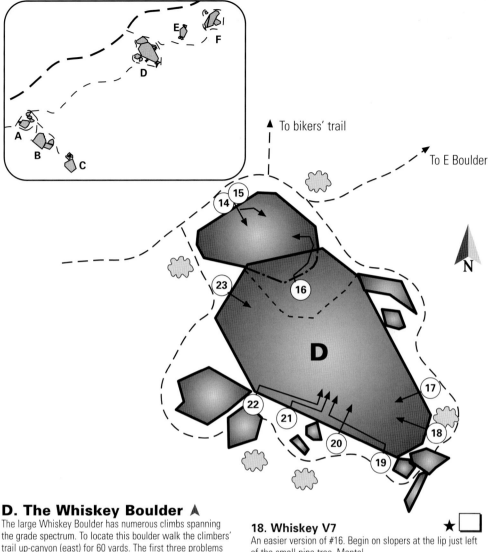

D. The Whiskey Boulder

The large Whiskey Boulder has numerous climbs spanning the grade spectrum. To locate this boulder walk the climbers' trail up-canyon (east) for 60 yards. The first three problems are found on the small boulder that is partially beneath the looming Whiskey Boulder.

14. Mud V2 ★★★
Sit start on a big blocky edge four feet up. Climb straight up.

15. Squeeze It V4
Same start as #14, but climb left onto the slab.

16. V3
Sit start in the back of the cave. Traverse the lip of the small boulder out of the cave and top out.

17. Whiskey Sour V9 ★
Stretch to reach crimps just below the lip almost eight feet up. Make whatever moves are necessary to mantel the almost featureless slab above.

18. Whiskey V7 ★
An easier version of #16. Begin on slopers at the lip just left of the small pine tree. Mantel.

19. V1 ★
Climb the slopey arête to the summit.

20. Texas V5 ★★
Start on right-facing crimpers six feet up. Climb straight up.

21. The Traverse V2 ★★★
Start in the smile-shaped rail. Traverse the rail up and right.

22. V0 ★
Climb the rounded arête to the summit.

23. V2
Not much quality here. Start with hands on the lip, and grovel over.

Little Cottonwood Canyon

Hidden Forest

1.7m

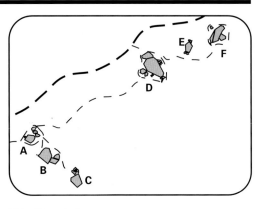

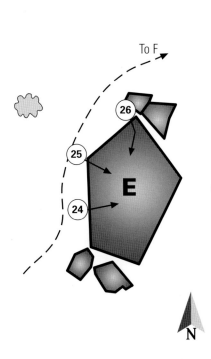

◄ **E. Boulder**
Located between the Whiskey and Slot Boulders, this small boulder has a few short lowball problems, and although less than classic, is worth a visit.

24. V4 ★
Locate some tiny crimps on the face, then friction up the slab.

25. V0
Grab the big ledge seven feet up, mantle onto it.

26. V3 ★
Climb the arête.

F. The Slot Boulder ►
This short boulder is 20 yards up-canyon (east) from the E Boulder and has several good moderate boulder problems.

26. V1 ★
Sit start. Climb the crack.

27. V1 ★★
Sit start on the flat rail three feet up. Climb obvious holds over the bulge.

28. V0 ★★
Climb the crack.

29. V1 ★★
Start on a big slopey ledge four feet up. Climb straight up.

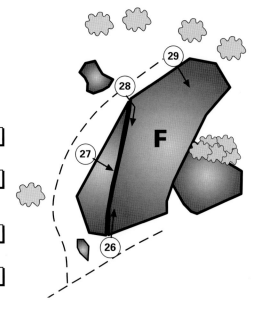

Wolverine Publishing   www.wolverinepublishing.com

Campus Boulder ▼ 2.4m

65

The Campus Boulder is situated in a beautiful location, surrounded by trees and next to a small bubbling stream. Tack on a ten-second approach and over a dozen great boulder problems and you have a splendid alternative to the more popular areas in the canyon. To reach the Campus Boulder drive up the canyon 2.4 miles past the National Forest sign and park in a pullout on the south side of the road. You can see the boulder through the trees on the north side of the road.

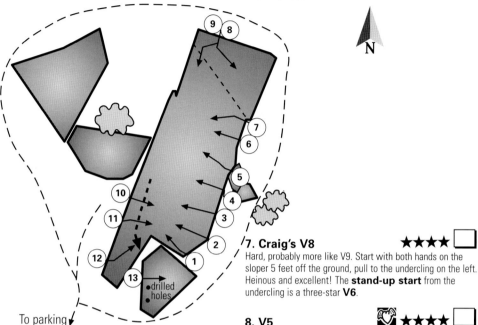

Little Cottonwood

To parking ↙

The Campus Boulder ▲

1. Campus Crack V0- ★ ☐
Start standing and layback the right side of the crack.

2. V0+ ★★ ☐
Climb the left-facing flake two feet right of the crack. Boulder to the left is off.

3. Campus Slab V3 ★★ ☐
Climb the slabby face four feet right of Nimbus Cloud. Hard start.

4. V1 ★★ ☐
Start with your left hand on a left-facing sidepull and your right on a small crimp. Short people may have a hard time reaching the first holds.

5. V3 ★★ ☐
Start standing on the rock that protrudes from underneath the boulder. Climb straight into the shallow scoop.

6. V6 ★★★ ☐
Start standing with both hands in the crack beneath the small roof. Climb the face using tiny crimps and polished footholds. Thin!

7. Craig's V8 ★★★★ ☐
Hard, probably more like V9. Start with both hands on the sloper 5 feet off the ground, pull to the undercling on the left. Heinous and excellent! The **stand-up start** from the undercling is a three-star **V6**.

8. V5 ★★★★ ☐
Start on the two-handed edge in the middle of the face, about 6 feet above the ground. Climb to the left. Fantastic, a must do.

9. V6 ★★★ ☐
Start in the same place as Campus Boy. Climb right to the arête, then up.

10. Johnny's Campus V7 Problem ★ ☐
Start on two slopers just under the lip and about 7 feet off the ground, campus to the lip. This problem is short and stupid — or maybe it just feels that way because I can't do it.

11. V5 ★ ☐
Start with both hands in the crack, place feet on the rock, move to the lip.

12. V1 ☐
There are several ways to start this problem. The most obvious is to start standing on the two-handed edge. Move to the lip.

13. V0+ ★★ ☐
This is actually a pretty good problem. Begin by squeezing between the two boulders. Right hand on the vertical drill mark, left on the arête. Climb straight up.

Little Cottonwood Canyon

White Pine

4.7m

Affording spectacular views of the peaks to the north and south, White Pine is one of the most beautiful areas in Little Cottonwood Canyon. Situated at an elevation of 7600 feet, it can be a good choice during the warmer months although some of the boulders do not receive much shade. To locate White Pine, drive up the canyon 4.7 miles past the National Forest sign, and park in a large pullout on the north side of the road. This parking pullout is located in an avalanche zone, and for safety reasons, parking is prohibited here between November 1 and May 15.

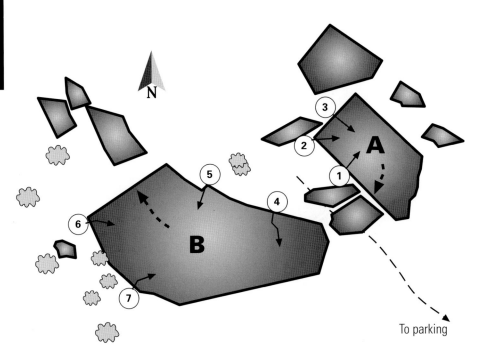

A. Boulder ➤

The first two boulders are located north of the parking area. To reach them follow a climber's trail that starts a few yards up canyon (east) from the avalanche sign. Follow the trail 50 yards north to two obvious boulders. There are more boulders further up the hill, but the rock on them is crumbly and the landings are horrible.

The A. Boulder is the eastern of the two boulders and is easily identified by its killer west-facing arête.

1. V2 ★
Sit start on edges four feet up. Dyno to the lip.

2. V6 ★★★
Sit start in an undercling two and a half feet up. Climb the arête.

3. V4 ★★★
Sit start in a good left-facing sidepull two and a half feet up. Follow the flaring crack to the top.

B. Boulder ▲

The B boulder is just a few feet to the west of the A boulder, and has several decent moderates, including a very good V1 on its southwest face.

4. V0 ★
Start on the big flat ledge five feet up. Follow crimps up and left.

5. V0 ★
Start on a big flat edge six and a half feet up. Climb into the groove.

6. V0
Climb the arête.

7. V1 ★★★
Sit start just downhill from a small aspen tree. Climb the protruding knobs up and right, and then onto the slab.

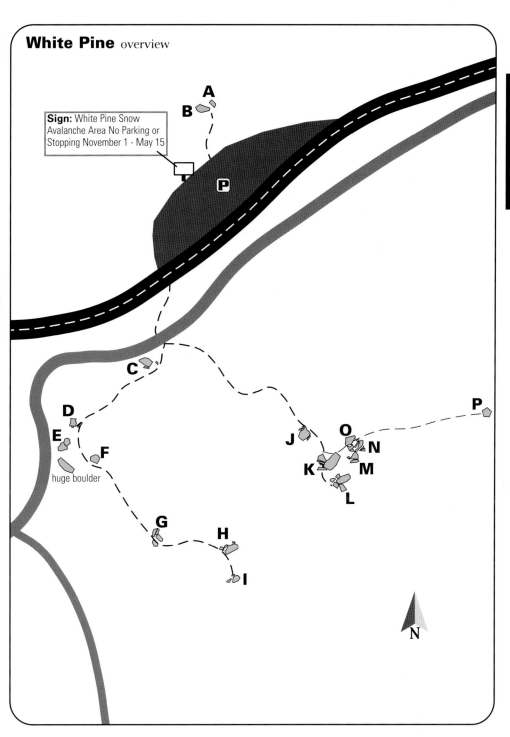

White Pine

4.7m

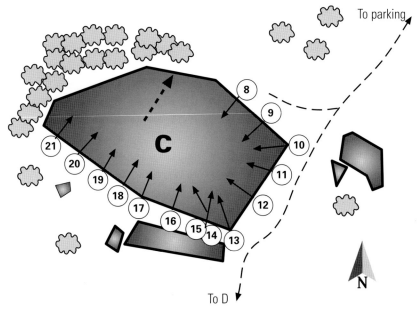

C. Boulder

This excellent boulder is situated next to the bubbling stream at the bottom of the canyon. It is the first boulder you come to after leaving the parking area, and has over a dozen high quality moderate climbs, with mostly perfect landings. To locate the boulder walk across the road (south) from the parking area, and scramble down the hill to a stream crossing; after crossing the stream, walk a few more yards down canyon (west) to the obvious boulder.

8. V1 ★
Start in a jug five feet up.

9. V1 ★★
Begin three and half feet right of the arête. Sit start in crimps just over the lip.

10. V0 ★★
Climb the arête.

11. V0 ★★★
Super fun up killer rock. Climb the juggy face.

12. V1 ★★
Sit start in the lowest holds. Climb the black streak into the V notch.

13. V0
Climb the arête.

14. V1 ★★
Start on the flat edge five feet up. Climb the face. Bad landing.

15. V2 ★★
Same start as #14, but move left to the right facing edges, then the lip.

16. V1 ★★
Sit start on a flat edge four feet up. Climb the face moving a little to the right.

17. V0 ★
Sit start where the face forms a blunt prow. Climb the prow.

18. V2 ★★
Sit start in two underclings. Climb the face using more underclings.

19. V2 ★★★
Sit start in the left facing side pull. Impeccable rock.

20. V4 ★★
Sit start with left hand in an undercling and right hand in slopey dishes, climb straight up the face. Start holds for #19 and #21 are off.

21. V1 ★★★
Sit start in right-facing sidepulls.

D. Boulder ▶

The D Boulder is another fine chunk of granite. Although a little short, it has a good concentration of quality climbs. To locate this boulder, walk down canyon (southwest) through the talus for about a hundred yards from the C Boulder.

22. V0
Begin in a triangular-shaped hole. Follow right-facing crimps up and right.

23. V3
Sit start in big holds at the edge of the roof. Make a big move right to a crimp then up the face.

24. V2
Short but super fun. Sit start in jugs at the corner of the boulder. Follow crimps straight up.

25. V4
Sit start with hands in the obvious slots. Climb straight up.

26. V0
Start on the right-facing flake. Climb the face.

27. V1
Start in the left-slanting crack. Climb the face.

28. V2
Start on a sidepull in the golden rock. Climb the face.

29. V7?
Start in the lone hold under the roof. Kick the right foot up high, make a difficult move to the lip, and then follow crimps to the top.

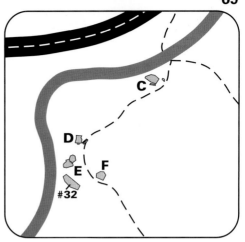

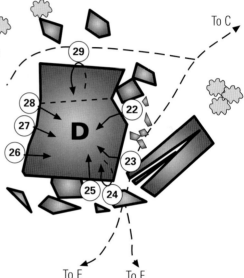

◀ E. Boulder

This boulder is 30 yards down hill (southwest) from the B boulder. The climbs are on the vertical south face.

30. V1
Start on low crimps. Climb the middle of the face.

31. V0
Start on the right-facing flake. Climb the flake to the corner.

Problem #32 is on the southwest face of the huge boulder located a few yards downhill (southwest) from the E boulder. No topo.

32. V2
This classic problem starts on a flat ledge towards the right end of the face. Climb the face to a hard top out.

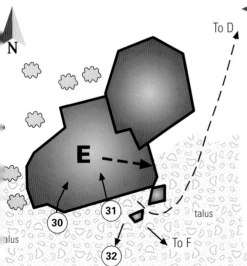

Little Cottonwood Canyon

White Pine

4.7m

F. Boulder
NO TOPO

This boulder is located in the talus forty yards uphill (south) of the D Boulder. One good steep problem climbs its overhanging southeast face.

33. V3 ★★

Sit start in a right-facing sidepull. Climb out the small cave on positive crimps. Bad landing.

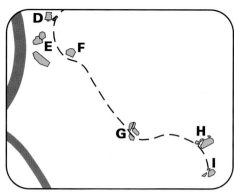

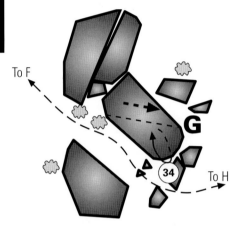

G. Boulder

This boulder is about one 120 yards up the talus slope (southeast) from the F Boulder. Look for a medium-sized boulder with a killer roof that faces south. One of the best boulder problems in Little Cottonwood climbs out this roof.

34. V7 ★★★★

Start with two good opposing sidepulls in the back of the roof and five feet off the ground. Climb out the roof onto the face. Move left on the face to top out. Amazing!

H. Boulder

This boulder is another eighty yards up the talus (southeast) of the G Boulder. Two fantastic boulder problems climb its impeccable northwest face (facing the road). Like many other boulders hereabouts, it has extremely bad landings.

35. V3 ★★★★

Sit start on a left-facing flake three feet off the ground. Climb the bulge. Fantastic. Bad landing.

36. V7 ★★★

Begin in the middle of the face on a crimp five feet up. Make a big cross with the right hand to a small crimp, and then make hard moves left to vertical fins.

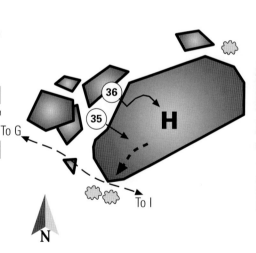

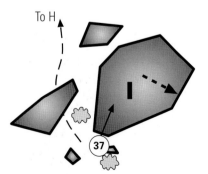

I. Boulder

This boulder has one good problem on its south-facing arête. Find it by walking up the talus (south) for about 25 yards from the H Boulder.

37. V4 ★★

Start low in the crack. Make a move or two up this, then go to the arête. Lack of footholds makes this climb harder than it looks.

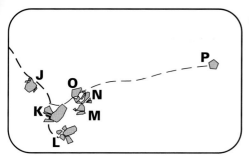

J. Boulder ▶

The J boulder, along with the remaining boulders at White Pine, is located in the middle of the large talus field, and it may be difficult to locate a single boulder among many thousands of others. The H boulder lies in a group of trees in the middle of the talus field and is just downhill (north) of a large dead tree. To find this boulder, walk southeast from the stream crossing up the talus into a group of trees.

38. V0
Start standing. Climb the right-facing flake system.

39. V5
Begin in a horizontal crack six feet up. Continue up and right following shallow seams to a solitary crimp on the otherwise blank face, move right again and finish on # 38.

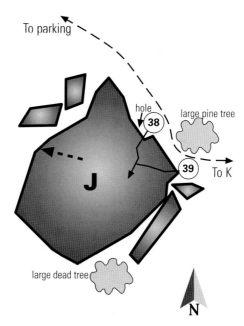

K. Boulder

As you thrash uphill (southeast) through the talus field, you'll see a group of boulders that are markedly larger than the thousands of smaller boulders surrounding them. The K through O boulders are found in this group, and are about 250 yards from the stream crossing. The K boulder is a massive boulder on the western edge of the group, with a huge overhang on its north face. Problem # 40 can be found by crawling through a tunnel at the right end of the overhang.

40. V5
Short and simple. Sit start with both hands on the low crimp four feet off the ground. Make a hard move to another crimp just below the lip, then mantel up.

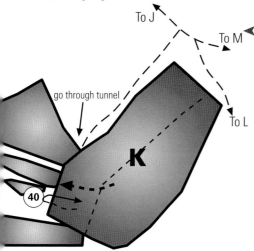

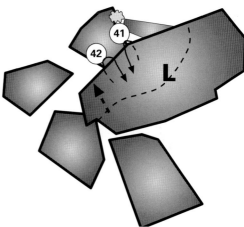

L. Boulder ▶

The L Boulder is located about 15 yards south of the K boulder. Two steep, although crumbly and dirty, problems climb out the small cave on the north side of the boulder.

41. V5
Start sitting in the cave. Climb the right-facing rail out the roof, directly over the abyss.

42. V3
Sit start on huge underclings five feet right of #41. Climb left and finish on #41.

Little Cottonwood Canyon

White Pine ▼   4.7m

Little Cottonwood

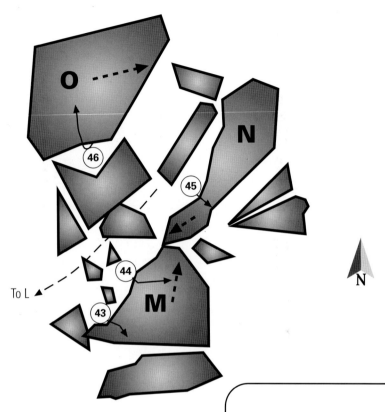

M. Boulder ⚠
The M Boulder is perhaps the easiest to identify in the K through O group. It has a very impressive tall face with an obvious crack slashing up and left. The M boulder is located a few yards east of the K Boulder.

43. V1   ☠ ★
Climb up the corner, then escape right onto a jug flake.

44. V1   ☠ ★★★
This climb is totally classic and would be worth four stars if the rock wasn't a little crumbly. Start in jug underclings then move into the obvious crack. Follow the crack up and left. A fall from the top would be disastrous. Very bad landing.

N. Boulder ⚠
This is a long boulder that touches the M Boulder on its southwest corner.

45. V4   ★★★
Sit start using blocky pinches where the boulder forms a shallow groove. Climb straight up the groove.

O. Boulder ⚠
The O boulder is a large boulder located a few yards north of the M and N Boulders.

46. V0
Climb the huge hollow-sounding flake. Choss.

N. Boulder
NO TOPO
This boulder lies at the eastern edge of the talus field. It is a large boulder with numerous V1s and V0s and excellent landings. There is no topo to this boulder here. Climb whatever looks fun!

Little Cottonwood Canyon

JOE'S VALLEY

By Chris Grijalva

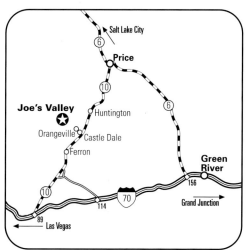

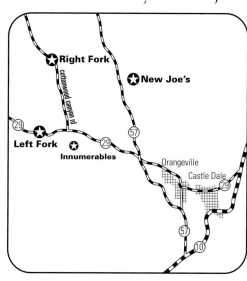

INTRODUCTION

Comprised of canyons and mesas strung out along the foothills of the Wasatch Plateau, Joe's Valley is one of the most classic, beautiful, and varied bouldering areas in the country. Discovered relatively recently, in the early 1990s, it has quickly become a major destination, attracting climbers from around the world. It is not difficult to understand why: Thousands of black and tan boulders litter the hillsides, and have produced hundreds of fun and interesting problems of every imaginable style, length, and grade. The rock is sandstone of varying quality. Some of the boulders are of such high quality that they could be mistaken for limestone. Others may look great from a distance but are a crumbling mass of detritus. Nevertheless, many possibilities exist for the first ascent connoisseur, especially on the south side of the Left Fork — so grab a brush and a pad, and look around.

A note on the rock: Sandstone loses much of its strength when wet and can easily break. Allow the rock ample time to dry before throwing yourself on the boulders. It would be a shame to lose climbs to this easily avoidable fate.

GETTING THERE

Joe's Valley is located in central Utah, just west of the small town of Orangeville, which is about 30 miles south of the large town of Price.

People coming from the Salt Lake City area will travel through the town of Price via Highway 6/191. From Price drive south on Highway 10 for about thirty miles to the junction with Highway 29. Drive west for four miles on Highway 29 to the town of Orangeville.

If approaching via I-70 from the west, take Highway 10 north to its intersection with Highway 57. Turn left and follow Highway 57 until it intersects with Highway 29.

If approaching via I-70 from the east, take a small exit signed "Moore" about 45 miles west of Green River. Follow a dirt road for about 20 miles to a junction with Highway 10 and proceed as above.

The bouldering areas are spread out in three different canyons: the Right Fork, Left Fork, and New Joe's. To reach the **Left and Right Forks**, drive west out of Orangeville on Highway 29. After 7.5 miles you will come to a fork in the road. On the right is the Right Fork (a.k.a Cottonwood Canyon Road). On the left is the Left Fork, which is the continuation of Highway 29 leading towards Joe's Valley reservoir.

To reach **New Joe's**, drive west on Highway 29 from Orangeville for 3 miles to the intersection with Highway 57. Take Highway 57 north for 3.2 miles to a dirt road on the right (east). Drive this dirt road to an oil well. Park here and hike to the New Joe's areas.

SEASON

Joe's Valley is located in a high-desert environment at an elevation between 6000 and 6500 feet. The best times to visit are September-November and March-May. Summers can be excruciatingly hot with temperatures reaching the high 90s. Winter brings cold weather and superb friction on the gritty sandstone, although storms can blow in making the climbing, and life in general, miserable.

New Joe's is the warmest area for winter climbing. The Innumerables and some areas in the Right Fork receive afternoon shade and can be tolerable when other areas are too hot.

ACCESS

The bouldering at Joe's Valley lies on National Forest and BLM lands. As of present, there are few access issues. Nevertheless, Joe's Valley has recently seen an exponential increase in the number of visiting climbers and land managers have begun to notice. It is every climber's duty to behave in a way that will negate any access concerns. Pack everything out. This includes wads of tape, wrappers, and any other form of trash. Even if it is not yours, pick it up and take it home. Walk on existing trails, and avoid trampling vegetation. Limited parking is an issue at some areas, in particular at Big Joe and The Riverside, which are popular venues with small pullouts. If a parking area appears full, it is. Do not attempt to squeeze another car into the pullout. This could present a hazard to motorists driving by on Highway 29. Numerous alternative parking areas are available up or down the canyon within an easy walking distance. Please practice good judgment for the benefit of all visiting Joe's.

CAMPING

Because Joe's Valley is part of the vast Manti-La Sal National Forest, you can camp for free just about anywhere. Many of the Right Fork parking areas are popular spots. For a more solitary experience, drive up the Right Fork, past the Hulk area, into the forest where virtually unlimited camping possibilities exist. For a few dollars a night, the campground at Joe's Valley Reservoir (at the top of the Left Fork) provides more civilized accommodations, including picnic tables, fire pits, and bathrooms. **NB: Camping and fires are forbidden at the parking areas for New Joe's and the Innumerables, which also serve as oil-well platforms.** The nearest motels are in Castle Dale, located a couple of miles east of Orangeville on Highway 10.

SURVIVAL

Orangeville has one small diner and a full-service grocery store that meets basic eating, drinking, and traveling needs, including gas. Castle Dale, located a a couple of miles from Orangeville on Highway 10, has the nearest motels and a State Liquor Store — for those who may want something a little stronger than 3.2 beer. Price has many restaurants, supermarkets, a Kmart, a Wal-Mart, two movie theatres, and everything else you would expect a fairly large town in the middle of Utah to have. The nearest climbing store is Mountain Works in Provo (801-371-0223), an hours drive from Price.

The best of JOE'S VALLEY

V0
- [ ] Riverside ★★★ page 90
- [ ] Sole Food ★★★ page 99
- [ ] Thriller ★★★ page 121
- [ ] B Sides ★★★ page 155
- [ ] Tower Down Climb ★★★ page 156

V1
- [ ] To Infinity ★★★ page 90
- [ ] Peep Show ★★★ page 101
- [ ] Faceshot ★★★ page 102
- [ ] Black Days ★★★ page 105
- [ ] Scoopable ★★★ page 112
- [ ] The Cylinder ★★★ page 125
- [ ] Sunshine ★★★★ page 127
- [ ] T-Bone ★★★ page 127
- [ ] RK Arise ★★★ page 132
- [ ] Warm Me Up Scotty ★★★★ page 136
- [ ] #10 The Closet ★★★ page 146
- [ ] Thriller (New Joe's) ★★★ page 150
- [ ] Don't Leave Thirsty ★★★ page 152
- [ ] Cherry Coke ★★★ page 152
- [ ] Orange Flakes ★★★ page 156

V2
- [ ] The Angler ★★★★ page 88
- [ ] Black Gold ★★★ page 106
- [ ] Chocolate Expresso Beans ★★★ page 109
- [ ] Easy Arete ★★★ page 113
- [ ] Prendre La Fuite ★★★ page 116
- [ ] The Buoux Crack ★★★★ page 116
- [ ] #7 No Additives ★★★ page 121
- [ ] Swine Boy ★★★ page 130
- [ ] Goatee Traverse ★★★ page 138
- [ ] Desperate ★★★ page 146
- [ ] Sunshine On a Rainy Day ★★★ page 146
- [ ] #7 Nerve Damage ★★★ page 150
- [ ] #6 The Tower ★★★ page 156
- [ ] The Edge ★★★ page 158
- [ ] Smear Test ★★★ page 158

V3
- [ ] Chi ★★★ page 90
- [ ] Michelangelo ★★★ page 104
- [ ] The Tan Streak ★★★★ page 106
- [ ] The Triangle ★★★ page 106
- [ ] Blue Eyed ★★★ page 110
- [ ] Dem Bones ★★★ page 113
- [ ] Midget ★★★ page 115
- [ ] Buoux Problem ★★★★ page 116
- [ ] Speed ★★★ page 116
- [ ] Skins Game ★★★ page 125
- [ ] Home Boy Bumping ★★★ page 131
- [ ] Lowball Productions ★★★ page 133
- [ ] Get Shorty ★★★ page 136
- [ ] Super Sloper ★★★★ page 136
- [ ] Joe Cool ★★★★ page 138
- [ ] Bad Genes ★★★ page 140
- [ ] What is This? ★★★ page 156

V4
- [ ] Amtrak ★★★ page 88
- [ ] Get Funky ★★★ page 93
- [ ] A Bobcat in The Skiparoo ★★★ page 94
- [ ] Boy Size Right ★★★ page 100
- [ ] The Comedian ★★★ page 104
- [ ] Better Than Coffee ★★★★ page 112
- [ ] Sling Blade ★★★ page 113
- [ ] Cave Man ★★★ page 113
- [ ] Tradesque ★★★ page 116
- [ ] The Bowling Ball ★★★ page 117
- [ ] #9 No Additives ★★★ page 121
- [ ] Frosted Flakes ★★★★ page 128
- [ ] Creatine Roof ★★★ page 131
- [ ] The Throne ★★★ page 132
- [ ] The Throne Traverse ★★★ page 132
- [ ] Sun In My Eye ★★★ page 136
- [ ] Snake Bite ★★★ page 136
- [ ] Idiot Man ★★★ page 142
- [ ] Pimpin' Jeans ★★★★ page 146
- [ ] Fuchsia ★★★★ page 156
- [ ] Salsa Verde ★★★★ page 158
- [ ] Big Bite ★★★ page 159

Joe's Valley

The best of JOE'S VALLEY

V5
- [ ] #7 Riverside Boulders ★★★ page 89
- [ ] Kelly's Arete ★★★★ page 90
- [ ] #3 Man Size Area ★★★ page 104
- [ ] Brawny Dyno ★★★ page 108
- [ ] Fila Void ★★★ page 110
- [ ] Smoothie ★★★ page 114
- [ ] Rug Rat ★★★ page 114
- [ ] Antaeus ★★★ page 129
- [ ] The Birth of Venus ★★★ page 131
- [ ] Horsetooth Simulator ★★★ page 132
- [ ] Phoney Baloney ★★★ page 137
- [ ] Self Service ★★★★ page 140
- [ ] Roll the Dice ★★★ page 146
- [ ] Juniper ★★★ page 156

V6
- [ ] Wills A Fire ★★★★ page 85
- [ ] Scary Monsters ★★★★ page 94
- [ ] Don't Reach Around ★★★ page 108
- [ ] 3 Weeks ★★★ page 112
- [ ] Maxi Pad ★★★★ page 121
- [ ] Minute Man ★★★ page 122
- [ ] Black and Blue ★★★★ page 125
- [ ] Moby Dick ★★★★ page 127
- [ ] The Shining ★★★★ page 129
- [ ] Profound Gratitude ★★★ page 129
- [ ] All You Sinners ★★★★ page 129
- [ ] Deformation ★★★★ page 131
- [ ] Centerpiece ★★★ page 134
- [ ] Sun In My Eye Traverse ★★★ page 136
- [ ] #16 Area 51 ★★★ page 136
- [ ] Pocket Rocket ★★★★ page 142
- [ ] Contact ★★★ page 145
- [ ] Planet of The Apes ★★★★ page 148
- [ ] Nerve Damage ★★★★ page 150
- [ ] I'd Rather Be Climbing Her ★★★★ page 152
- [ ] Roll The Bones ★★★★ page 154

V7
- [ ] Big Joe ★★★ page 92
- [ ] Boy Size ★★★ page 100
- [ ] Golden Plates ★★★ page 107
- [ ] Runt ★★★ page 115
- [ ] Buoux Problem sit start ★★★ page 116
- [ ] Water Paintings ★★★ page 118
- [ ] Pocket Line ★★★ page 133
- [ ] Big Boy ★★★★ page 137
- [ ] Phoney Baloney Traverse ★★★★ page 137
- [ ] Spam ★★★ page 138
- [ ] Chips ★★★ page 148

V8
- [ ] #2 Trent's Mom Area ★★★★ page 82
- [ ] They Call Him Jordan ★★★★ page 85
- [ ] Feels Like Grit ★★★ page 88
- [ ] No Substance ★★★★ page 120
- [ ] Team Effort ★★★ page 125
- [ ] Dirty Harry ★★★ page 128
- [ ] Posterized ★★★ page 134

V9
- [ ] Smoking Joe ★★★★ page 92
- [ ] Foxy Whore ★★★ page 93
- [ ] 3 Weeks sit start ★★★ page 112
- [ ] Hooters ★★★ page 125
- [ ] The Hulk ★★★★ page 128
- [ ] Marble Cake ★★★ page 138
- [ ] Playtime is Over ★★★ page 135

V10
- [ ] Trent's Mom ★★★★ page 82
- [ ] Nerve Extension ★★★ page 92
- [ ] Finger Hut ★★★★ page 104
- [ ] Resident Evil ★★★ page 136
- [ ] Freak ★★★ page 137

V11
- [ ] #7 Right Sign Area ★★★ page 85
- [ ] No Additives ★★★★ page 120

V13
- [ ] No Additives sit start ★★★★ page 120
- [ ] Black Lung ★★★★ page 136

LEFT FORK

The Left Fork is a deep, impressive canyon. The tall sandstone cliffs that line the rim of the canyon have shed a vast number of boulders, hosting many of the finest problems in Joe's. It also has the most potential; as the river can be difficult to cross, the south side of the Left Fork has seen little development and literally thousands of boulders remain as yet untouched.

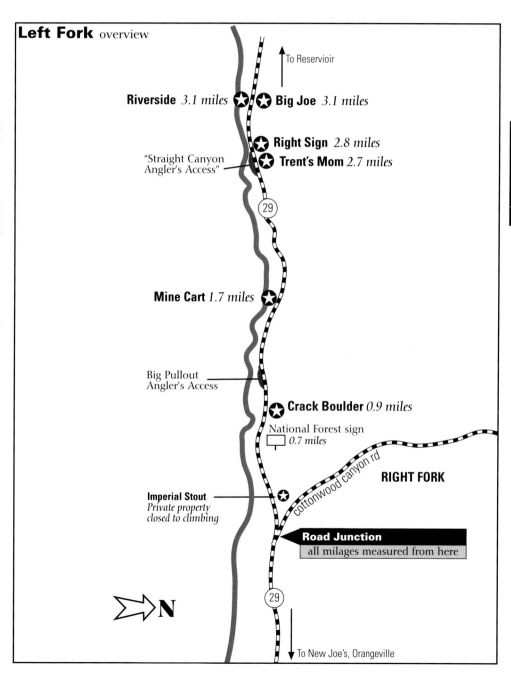

Crack Boulder ▼ left fork 0.9m

At first glance, this boulder appears to be a classic. Located right next to the road, fairly tall, well featured, and with two climbable cracks that cleave the boulder. Unfortunately, closer inspection reveals low-angle faces and inferior rock quality that leaves most of the holds perpetually sandy. Still, the Crack Boulder yields decent climbing and a distraction from other areas at Joe's. Locate this boulder by driving up the left fork .9 miles. Park in a pullout on the north side of the road; this pullout will fit two cars max. Additional parking can be found two tenths of a mile further up the left fork.

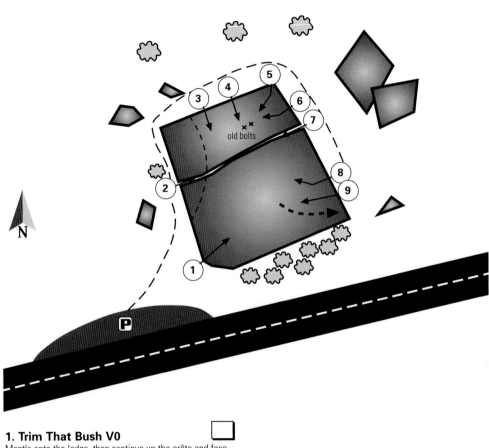

1. Trim That Bush V0
Mantle onto the ledge, then continue up the arête and face.

2. Hand Crack V3 ★★
Climb the crack. Quite good and a neat change from the crimping nasties.

3. Dirt and Grime V1 ★
Climb sandy pockets up the middle of the face.

4. Wash Out V1 ★
Climb sandy pockets up the left side of the face.

5. V1 ★
Climb the arête on the right side.

6. Beer Belly V5 ★★
Begin to the right of the crack on a slopey ledge six feet up. Climb up and right, using the arête at the top.

7. Fist Crack V3 ★
Climb the crack.

8. The Highlife V3 ★
Start on the ledge seven feet up. Climb up and right, using the crack at the top.

9. Lanky V2 ★
Same start as #8, but climb straight up.

The Mine Cart ▼ left fork 1.7m

The Mine Cart is a small, solitary boulder with a few short but worthwhile problems. It is 1.7 miles up the left fork. Park at a large pullout with a mine cart at its east end. This is a memorial to the labors of coal miners past. The problems are on the southwest and south faces of the boulder a few feet behind the mining cart.

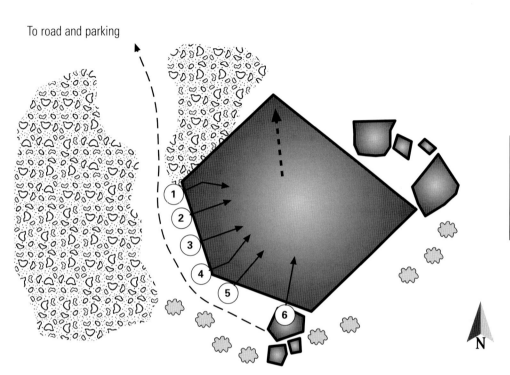

1. Rip Current V2 ★
Begin on the left side of the face and climb up using the arête with your left hand and face holds with your right.

2. Tidal Wave V3 ★
Start four feet right of Rip Current; left hand on a crimp seven feet up and right hand on shallow dishes. Make one hard move to the top and mantle.

3. The Wave V3 ★★
The line of pockets in the middle of the face.

4. The Crest V4 ★★
Begin on the right side of the face. Climb the arête up and left.

5. V0+ ★★
Start around the corner from The Crest on the south face. Climb the face.

6. V0 ★
Begin standing on the rock at the base of the boulder using a hueco and some crimps. Climb the face. Bad Landing

Joe's Valley

Trent's Mom ▼   left fork 2.7m

Trent's Mom boulder is one of the latest additions to Joe's Valley, and although it offers only three problems, they are some of the best in the valley. The boulder faces south and gets sun most of the day, making it a good choice in cold weather. To locate Trent's Mom drive up the left fork 2.7 miles and park in a pullout signed "Straight Canyon Angler's Access" on the south side of the road. Cross the road at the up-canyon end of the pullout and look for a faint trail heading up the hillside. The climbs can be seen from the parking area.

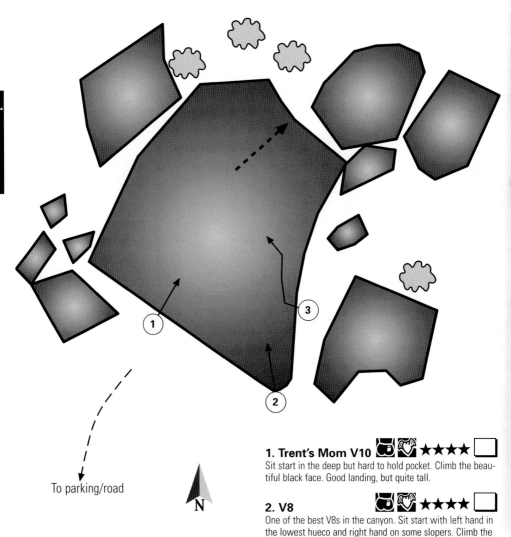

1. Trent's Mom V10 ★★★★
Sit start in the deep but hard to hold pocket. Climb the beautiful black face. Good landing, but quite tall.

2. V8 ★★★★
One of the best V8s in the canyon. Sit start with left hand in the lowest hueco and right hand on some slopers. Climb the prow. Bad landing if you fall from the top.

3. V4 ★★
Sit start on the left end of the slopey rail. Climb the rail up and right, then straight up the tall face. Very bad landing.

Cory French doing *Trent's Mom* (V10).
Photo: Dave Pegg

Right Sign Area ▼ left fork 2.8m

The Right Sign Area has a reputation for tall, scary highballs, with the commitment often increased by bad landings. The reputation is justified, although you'll also find a number of worthwhile not-so highball problems here as well. To locate the Right Sign area, drive up the Left Fork for about 2.8 miles, and park in one of several pullouts on the south side of the road. Look for a traffic sign indicating a right-hand turn in the road. Walk up the canyon towards this sign. Just before the sign, there are two huge boulders on the right (north) side of the road. A trail heads uphill between these two boulders. The first problems are on the big boulder on the left.

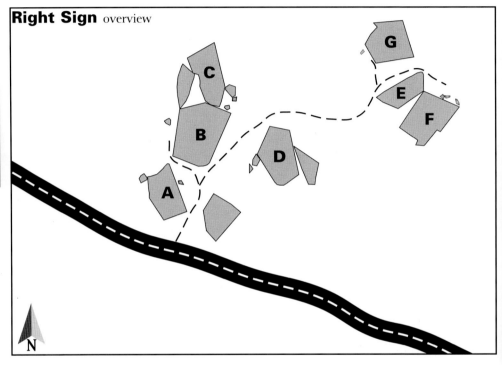

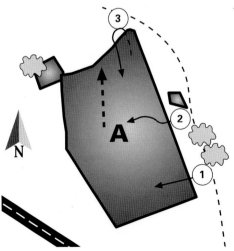

◄ A. Frosted Flakes Boulder
The large boulder on the left, as you walk up the trail from the road. I've described three problems on this boulder, but several more are possible.

1. V3 ★★
Begins on the tall black face just as you walk up the trail. Climb into the obvious right-facing flake, and then follow crimps and pockets. Move slightly right to top out. Be very careful what you pull on at the top. Highball. Bad Landing.

2. V1 ★★
An easier version of Snap, Crackle, and Pop. Begin with jugs in the tan rock in the middle of the face. Climb up and right on good holds. Highball. Bad Landing.

3. Project?
Sit start. Climb the prow.

Wolverine Publishing   www.wolverinepublishing.com

B. The Jordan Boulder ▶

The Jordan boulder is just up the hill (north) from the Frosted Flakes Boulder. The problems are on its impeccable west face.

4. Wills A Fire V6  ★★★★ ☐
Sit start using a good undercling. Follow good edges to the big pocket, move right to the crack, then back left to top out. Highball. Bad landing.

5. They Call Him Jordan V7  ★★★★ ☐
Could be the best boulder problem at Joe's! Same start as Wills a Fire, but get the big pocket with your right hand and move left to the obvious rail, then make an all-out dyno to the next rail. Highball. Photo page 97.

The next two problems are on the left side of the face, and came at the expense of the pine tree that now lays dead and rotting a few feet from the boulder.

6. Project? ☐

7. V11 ★★★ ☐
Tall black face on thin crimps.

C. Boulder ▶

The next boulder uphill from the Jordan Boulder. The climbs are located on the east face of the boulder near where the two boulders touch.

8. V6 ★★ ☐
Sit start on the left side of the face with your left hand on a sidepull around the shallow corner, and right hand on good edges. Follow good, but chossy-looking holds up and right. Top out in the black rock, avoiding the choss on the left. This problem may become easier if the finishing holds on the left are cleaned up so that they can be used.

9. V6 ★★ ☐
Begin standing on the rock at the base of the boulder with both hands on edges in the black rock. Climb straight up to the same finish as Velvet Underground.

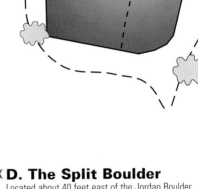

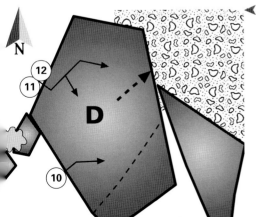

◀ D. The Split Boulder
Located about 40 feet east of the Jordan Boulder.

10. John Wayne V3 ★ ☐
Sit start in the obvious hueco. Climb up and right to an easy, but scary topout. Sandy.

11. The Split V4 ★★ ☐
Sit start in a big incut flake, move up to the left-angling crack. Follow the crack up and left.

12. V4 ★★ ☐
Same start as The Split, but from about the middle of the crack punch straight up the pocketed face.

Joe's Valley

Right Sign Area ▼ left fork 2.8m

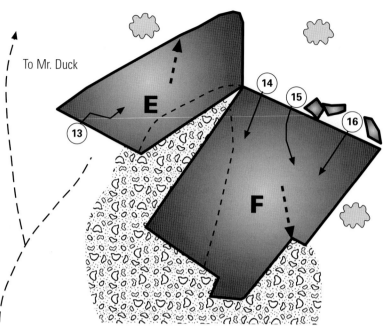

E. Why Me Boulder
You'll be thinking, "why me?" when you get to the lip of the one problem on this boulder ... No, scratch that. When you get to the lip of this boulder, you'll be thinking, "Oh shit, I'm going to die!" To reach Why Me? continue northeast up the trail, past "the Split" Boulder, for about 150 feet.

13 Why Me? ... Project? ☠ ★★★ ☐
Start standing in the obvious crack. Climb the crack up and right until it pinches closed, make a big move to edges at the lip and mantle. Don't fall!!

F. The Pistol Whip Boulder
This large boulder touches the east side of the Why Me Boulder. The north face of the boulder has three scary highballs above bad landings.

14. Pistol Whip V0   ♥ ★ ☐
Climb the crack on the right side of the face.

15. Illicit Tactics V2   ♥ ★ ☐
Start in the middle of the face follow edges up and left.

16. Drunken Stupor V1   ♥ ★ ☐
Climb the left side of the face.

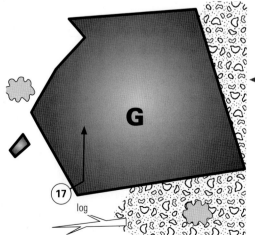

◀ G. Mr. Duck Boulder
The Mr. Duck Boulder is located just behind (north) of the "Why Me" Boulder. I've described one problem, although there's potential for many more.

17. Mr Duck V7   ★★ ☐
Sit start on the right side of the face. Climb the rounded lip up and left to the summit and mantle.

Joe's Valley

Slam dunk on *They Call Him Jordan* (V7), page 85.
Photo: Dave Pegg

The Riverside ▼ left fork 3.1m

With soft, sandy landings and wonderful boulders bordered by deep aqua-blue pools, The Riverside is popular. Climbers often come here to warm-up as the area has many good easy problems. This popularity, however, leads to parking issues. If the parking area is full, exercise your ability to walk. There are several pullouts within reasonable walking distance further up the canyon. The Riverside is on the left fork, 3.3 miles past the fork in the road. The normal parking area is in a pullout on the south side of the road under a large Ponderosa pine tree. The boulders are down the hill next to the river.

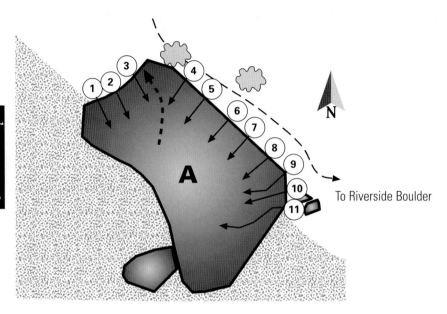

A. K-Town Boulder
The K-town Boulder is the first boulder that you come to when you walk down the hill from the parking area.

1. V0-
Climb the right side of the face on big holds.

2. V0 ★
Start sitting. Climb up the middle of the face.

3. V0
Sit start on the left side of the face, with both hands in a horizontal crack. Climb straight up.

4. V0 ★★
Start in the big hueco. Climb straight up.

5. V1 ★★
Begin four feet to the left of K-Mart with a good pocket and edges.

6. V1 ★
Start matched on an edge six and a half feet up.

7. K-Town Right V2 ★
Begin just to the right of the K-Town graffiti. Climb straight up sharp crimps.

8. K-Town V3 ★★
Climb the improbable looking slab through the middle of the K-Town graffiti. Good footholds make this easier than it looks. Photo page 90.

9. Feels Like Grit V8 ★★★
Begin to the left of the K-Town graffiti, using the arête and some face holds. Climb the rounded and desperate arête up and right, praying that your feet don't blow off the stingy footholds. A great little problem.

10. Amtrak V4 ★★★
Climb the face just left of the arête to an intimidating finish that may leave you angling for holds.

11. The Angler V2 ★★★★
Climb the amazing rail up and left. Hard to start and highball at the top. When the river is high, the majority of this problem is over the water. Is this a good thing?? Photo page 149.

Riverside overview

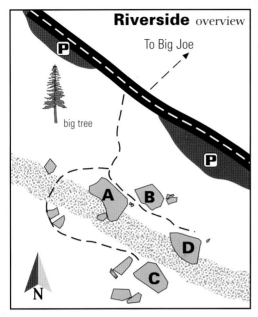

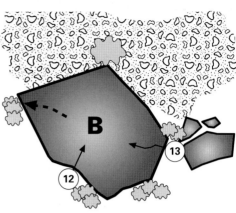

C. Far Side Boulders ▼

These boulders are located directly across the river from the Riverside Boulder, and provide three quality problems. When the water level is low the river can be easily forged a few feet upstream from the K-Town Boulder via several rocks and logs bridging a narrow portion of the river.

14. V5   ★★★ ☐
Sit start in a good right-facing flake almost in the river. Climb to the lip, and then traverse the lip to the apex of the boulder.

15. V2   ★ ☐
Start standing in the jug undercling beneath the apex of the boulder. Climb straight up.

16. V3   ★★ ☐
Sit start with both hands on the obvious and cool fin. Climb out the overhang. It's easiest to move onto the right face to top out, but can be done straight up as well.

B. The Acid Boulder ▲

The Acid Boulder is about 15 feet northeast of the K-Town Boulder. Two short, decent problems are described. Perhaps a couple more have been done, but since climbing them would damage vegetation they have not been described.

12. The Whistler V2   ★★ ☐
Start sitting with both hands on the obvious slopey knob in the groove. Climb up to the lip and mantle.

13. Lords of Acid V3   ★★ ☐
Sit start in jugs two and half feet off the ground on the right side of the boulder. Climb up and left using the shallow crack with your right hand.

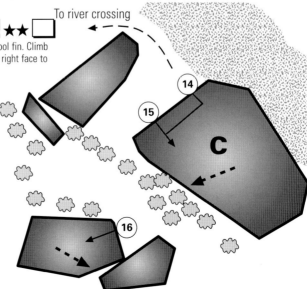

Joe's Valley

The Riverside ▼ left fork 3.1m

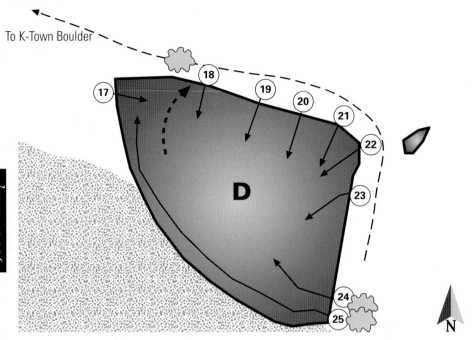

D. The Riverside Boulder ▲
Another good warm-up boulder with great moderate problems. The Riverside Boulder is about 50 feet east (downstream from the K-Town Boulder.

17. Necrophilia V0-
Climb the face just right of the arête

The next three problems are on the heavily pocketed north face. The three most-obvious, straight-up problems are described, although many eliminates are possible.

18. V1 ★★
Start in the first big hueco. Climb up and slightly left to a cruxy topout.

19. Club Tan V2 ★★
Start right of where some moron has written, "don't write on the walls." Climb straight up to a tricky mantel.

20. To Infinity V1 ★★★
Climb huecos to the left of the "don't write on the walls" graffiti. Move a little left at the top to a tricky top out.

21. Chi V3 ★★★
Start sitting under the small roof using a flat edge four and a half feet up. Climb through the roof to the arête, then follow the arête to the top.

22. Kelly's Arete V5 ★★★★
Start sitting four feet left of "Chi". Climb straight up the blunt prow. Careful up high — the finishing holds aren't as good as you might think.

23. Fire in the Hole V6 ★
Start matched on the rounded edge seven feet up. Make one hard move to a jug ledge up and left. Mantle the ledge and continue up the easy face.

24. Riverside V0 ★★★
Start at the left end of the boulder. Climb the easy face right over the river.

25. Road to Nowhere V1 ★
Same start as Riverside, but traverse the boulder to the left over the river (don't fall). A short crux comes at the end. Finish on Necrophilia.

Fiona Lloyd on The K-Town Slab, previous page.
Photo: Dave Pegg

Big Joe ▼   left fork 3.1m

Big Joe has several great problems including the superb V6 Scary Monsters. The Big Joe boulder features several steep roof problems that stay dry in the rain. Big Joe is across the road from The Riverside Area and is subject to the same parking limitations. Please use parking pullouts further up the canyon if the main area is full. Do not block the road.

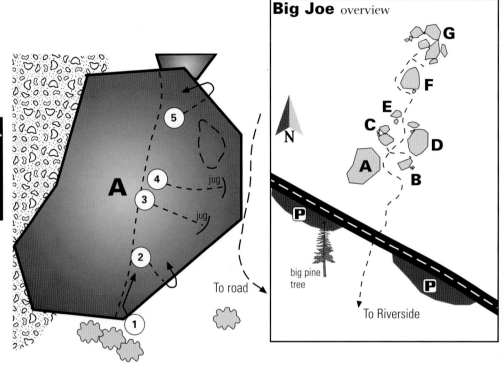

A. Big Joe Boulder ▲

A big, yawning cave with steep problems and fantastic features rarely found on the underbellies of other boulders in the canyon, Big Joe is a great place to test your strength. To locate the Big Joe Boulder, follow a trail north (up the drainage) for about 100 feet. Big Joe is the large house-sized boulder on the left. The boulder can be seen from the road, although its problems are mostly hidden from view.

1. Techno Beat V4    ★★

Sit start with both hands in pockets on the very left end of the face. Climb up and left. You can topout this climb via a tall, scary crack system. Most people jump off when they get to the big, sandy hueco.

2. Provo Gluru V10   ★

Sit start with hands in underclings. Climb up the nasty, greasy, slimy, glued crimps to the obvious sandy hole. Drop off.

3. Big Joe V7    ★★★

Sit start in the lowest jugs. Climb the flake system up and right. Pull some hard moves past the ugly drilled out hold and finish on the big left-facing jug. Drop off.
A **V10** variation **Nerve Extension** starts up Big Joe and continues via small crimps to the next obvious jug.

4. Smoking Joe V9   ★★★★

Sit start six feet to the right of "Big Joe" in two underclings. Pull off the ground and make a desperate move with your left hand. Follow crimps up and right to the jug with a small tree growing out of it. Drop off. A stellar power problem.

5. Prophet in a Ditch V10   ★

Grovel in the dirt at the very back of the cave. Sit start in two underclings and make hard, cramped moves out the roof to the lip and top out.
An enjoyable **V5 variation** starts in the middle of the roof in good-sized underclings.

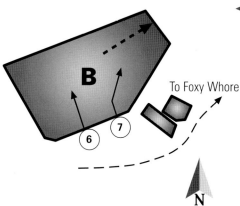

◀ B. The Bill Boulder
A small boulder with two decent problems. To locate the boulder, follow the trail northeast from Big Joe for about 60 feet. The problems are on the southeast side of the boulder, facing the road.

6. Bill Left V3

Start with your right hand in a good pocket and your left in a big sidepull. Climb straight up.

7. Bill Right V2

Start with your left hand in the pocket and right hand on edges. Climb up and right directly over the rocks at the base. Bad landing.

C. Might as Well Boulder ▶
If you're on the way to Scary Monsters, you might as well try the one problem here. The boulder is 40 feet northeast (up the drainage) from Big Joe.

8. Might as Well V2

Start sitting in the obvious pockets. Climb up and left onto the slabby face.

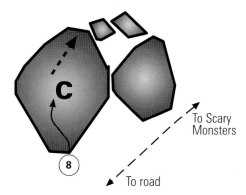

◀ D. Foxy Whore Boulder
To locate this boulder, follow the trail northeast for about 60 feet, past the Might as Well Boulder, and into the drainage. The Foxy Whore Boulder is the black boulder on the east side of the drainage.

9. Foxy Whore V8/9

Begin in underclings five and a half feet up. Climb straight up the black prow.

10. I Want to be Black V?

This climb used to be rated V8, but several holds have broken. It is now probably V10 or harder. Begin five feet to the left of Foxy Whore and climb crimps up the black face.

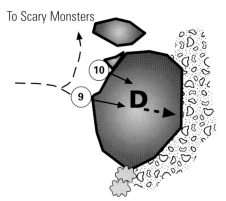

◀ E. The Funky Boulder
Located across the drainage (west) from the Foxy Whore Boulder.

11. Get Funky V4

Short but fun. Start sitting under the roof on good underclings. Climb out to the lip and follow the arête to the top.

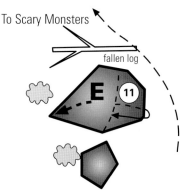

Joe's Valley

Big Joe ▾

left fork 3.1m

To Scary Monsters

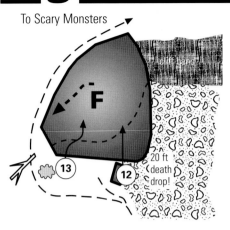

◄ **F. The Widow-Maker Boulder**
The Widow-Maker Boulder is 60 feet north (up the drainage) from the Funky Boulder. As you walk up the drainage, a small cliff band will block your way. Just to the left of the cliff band is a black boulder with a small tree at its right side. This is the Widow-Maker Boulder.

12. Widow-Maker V5
Well-named. Start just to the left of the 20-foot drop off. Climb the black face using pockets and edges. An uncontrolled fall off this one could end in disaster/death.

13. Tree Hugger V4
Begin on the left side of the face just right of a tree. Climb up and right on crimps to a hard top out.

G. Scary Monsters Boulder ▶
Home to several good problems, including the outstanding Scary Monsters, one of the best V6s in the canyon. To locate this area, follow the trail up the drainage to the small cliff band. Detour past the cliff band on the left, passing the "Widow Maker" boulder. Climb around the left side of the Widow Maker boulder. Then scramble across numerous rocks back right to the top of the cliff band. Scary Monsters boulder is in the middle of the drainage on rock slabs, about 50 feet north of the cliff band.

14. Scary Monsters V6
As good as it gets. Sit start on a big edge, move into underclings, then up the face using the left-facing layback, crimps, and a well-lubricated smear (if you can get your foot to stick). The topout is tall and harder than it looks. Photo opposite.

15. A Bobcat in the Kiparoo V4
Sit start two feet to the right of Scary Monsters. Climb crimps up and right to the arête and climb it on the left side.

16. Right Side Arete V4
Sit start on the right side of the arête and climb its right side.

17. Meat Head V1
Start on the top of the rock at the base of the boulder. Climb the left-facing crack, trying not to get killed by the choss.

18. South Slab V1
Climb the face five feet to the right of Meat Head.

19. Choss V1
Start at the very right side of the boulder. Climb the friable face.

The next problem is located on a boulder that is just to the northwest of Scary Monsters.

20. The Seven V2
Start on two small crimps, make a move to the hueco, and top out.

The last three problems are located on a boulder 10 feet northwest of The Seven.

21. Lefty Loosey V3
Start in underclings. Climb big holds up and left.

22. Righty Tighty V2
Same start as Lefty Loosey but follow big holds up and right.

23. Indecision V0
Climb the face choosing from a plethora of holds.

Joe's Valley

The scary bit of *Scary Monsters* (V6).
Photo: Dave Pegg

RIGHT FORK

The Right Fork, located in Cottonwood Creek Canyon, is the most popular area in Joe's Valley with many classic problems of all grades. Most of the boulders are within a few minutes walk from the car and can be seen from the road.

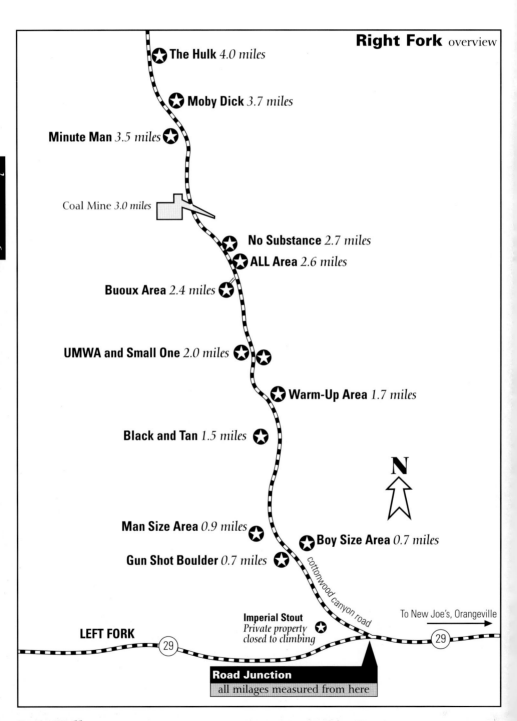

Chris Grijalva cranks *Speed* (V3), page 116.
Photo: Dave Pegg

Boy Size Area ▼ right fork 0.7m

The first area you reach as you drive up the Right Fork, The Boy Size area has a high concentration of quality climbing, mostly in the V0 to V5 range. Two harder stand-out problems are Boy Size and Golden Plates, both V7. To locate the Boy Size area, drive up the Right Fork, for about eight tenths of a mile, and park on the right (east) side of the road in a pullout next to a dry wash. Walk up the wash (east) for a few minutes, about 100 yards, until you come to a sandy boulder in the wash. This is the Alien Boulder. From the Alien Boulder a trail leaves the wash to the left and weaves through trees (east) for a few more yards to the main area.

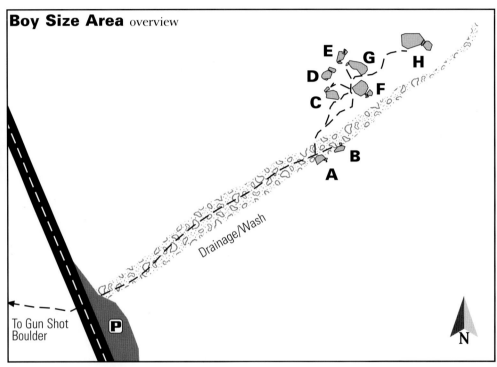

Boy Size Area overview

Joe's Valley

A. The Alien Boulder ➤
The first boulder you come to as you walk up the wash. The rock here is a little sandy, making the quality of the climbing less than that of the Main Area. That said, the problems here are decent warm-ups, and it's worth throwing down a pad and attempting a few problems as you're passing by.

1. Alien Arête V0
Sit start. Climb the Arête.

2. Rim Job V3 ★
Same start as Alien Arete. Follow the arête to the lip, then traverse the lip to the right and top out directly above the white streak.

3. V2
Sit start on two opposing side pulls. OK climbing, but very sandy rock.

4. Alien V3 ★★
Sit Start with both hands in the hueco. Climb straight up.

5. Alien Right V2 ★★
Same start as Alien, but move right.

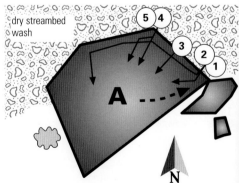

Wolverine Publishing   www.wolverinepublishing.com

B. The Butt Hugger Boulder ➤

Located about 40 feet further up the wash from the Alien Boulder.

6. Butt Hugger V5
Start with your left hand in a slopey pocket and your right hand in an under cling. Step on the rock at the base of the boulder and use it to make the first couple of moves.

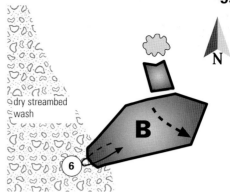

◄ C. The Sabotage Boulder

This is the western-most boulder at the main Boy Size Area. Depending on how you navigate through the trees, it can be the first boulder you come to, or you can easily pass right by without seeing it. If you pass it, and you come to the Boy Size Boulder, which is at the center of the main area and pretty much unavoidable, simply turn around and look west.

7. South Face V0
Climb the left side of the south face.

8. Sabotage V1
Climb the face in front of the almost-dead tree. This one gets a little slopey and insecure at the top.

9. V1
Sit start on two tan flakes. Climb straight up.

10. V0
Begin standing with both hands on a tan jug seven feet up.

11. Footmare V5
Begin standing using two small underclings six feet up. Thin!

12. Sole Food V0
Climb the slaby face right of "Footmare". Perfect rock.

D. Boulder ➤

The next two boulders are located just a few feet north of the Sabotage Boulder.

13. V1
Sit start using the flexing flake four feet off the ground. Follow the jugs to the top.

14. V3
Sit start using the right side of the sandy hole. Climb straight up.

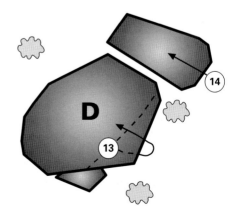

Joe's Valley

Boy Size Area ▼ right fork 0.7m

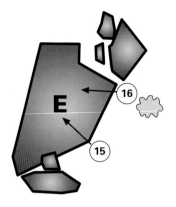

◀ **E. The Pudgy Gumby Boulder**
The easiest way to find this boulder is to locate the Golden Plates Boulder. From the Golden Plates Boulder, just walk up the hill and a few feet to the west.

15. Fat Lad V0
Start on a right-facing jug seven feet up.

16. Pudgy Gumby V4 ★
Sit start with your right hand on a good edge in the tan streak and left hand in pockets. Climb the arête and face.

F. The Boy Size Boulder ▼
The Boy Size boulder is in the center of the main area, and is easily identified by the heavily chalked slopey rail on the Boy Size problem. To find this boulder, follow the trail out of the wash past the Sabotage Boulder. Look for the Boy Size problem on the southwest face of the boulder.

17. Pocket Pool V3 ★
Sit start just right of the tree. Left hand in a deep two-finger pocket, right hand on edges.

18. V6 ★★
Sit start to the right of #17 on some incut edges. Climb to the lip, and pull onto the slab using small crimps.

19. Boy Size V7 ★★★
Sit start in an obvious right-facing hueco. Pull to the hellish, hard-to-hold sloping rail.

20. Boy Size Right V4 ★★★
Same start as #19, but move right to another hueco, then up edges to the top.

21. Point of Impact V2 ★
Sit start using edges five feet up. Climb the pocketed face then pull the hard top out. Photo page 103.

22. The Cadaver V0
Start in pockets seven feet up. Climb the face.

23. Dos Mundos V0 ★
Start in pockets six feet up. Climb the face.

24. The Bung Hole V1 ★
Begin three feet to the right of #23 in two two-finger pockets. Climb the face.

25. Flatulence V0 ★
Begin on an edge five feet up. Climb the face.

26. Deep Thoughts V1 ★★
Sit start using right facing edges. Climb straight up the face.

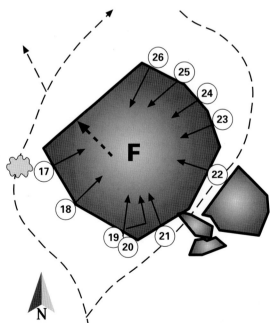

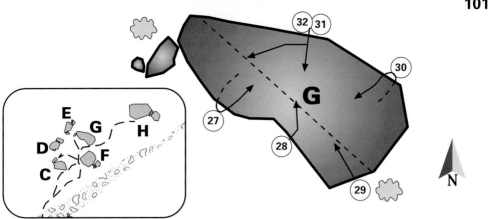

G. The Golden Plates Boulder ▲
The Golden Plates boulder is about thirty feet due north of the Boy Size Boulder.

27. Golden Plates V7  ★★★
Sit start in huecos. Climb up bad crimps moving a little right.

28 Mono E Mono V5 ★★
Start standing five feet right of Golden Plates with your left hand in a mono and right on an edge. Follow crimps up and a little left.

29. V3 ★
Sit start with your ass on the tree. Grab good edges and climb straight up.

30. Wanker V4 ★
Sit start using the ugly glued edges. Climb straight out the prow.

31. V1 ★★
Sit start in the middle of the sandy hole. Climb straight up.

32. V2 ★★
Same start as #31, but follow the rail up and right.

H. The Fit Boulder ▶
Located about forty yards to the east of the Golden Plates Boulder. Look for a clean vertical wall that faces towards the wash (south).

33. V2 ★★
Start in the hueco just left of the tree. Climb up and a little left.

34. Peep Show V1 ★★★
Begin right of the tree. Climb straight up.

35. The Fit V7 ★★
You will have to be fit to get up this one … or you might throw a fit because you can't. Begin on the right side of the face with sharp crimps seven and a half feet up. The **sit start** is **V8/9**.

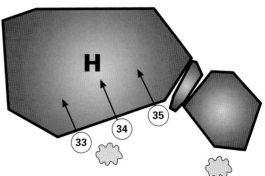

Joe's Valley

Gun Shot Area ▼ right fork 0.7m

The Gun Shot Boulder is a small isolated boulder with a few decent moderate problems. Due to its isolation and the small number of climbs, it is seldom visited, and thus a good area to visit if other areas are crowded, or if you are looking for something new off the beaten path. To find this boulder, park the same parking area as The Boy Size Area, about seven tenths of a mile up the Right Fork. Walk across the road (west) and locate a faint trail heading across the stream and into the trees. Follow this trail for about 150 yards. The Gun Shot Boulder can be seen from the road.

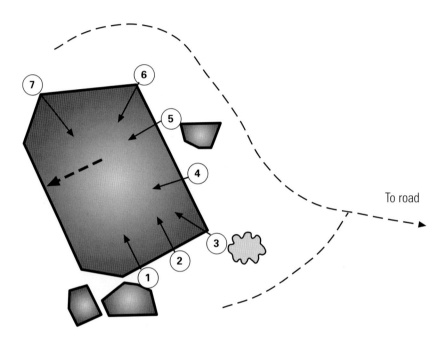

1. V0
Climb the left side of the south face.

2. V0
Climb the right side of the south face.

3. Headshot V4 ★★
Sit start. Climb the prow.

4. Faceshot V1 ★★★
Sit start in a hueco. Climb the left-facing flake.

5. Gunshot V3 ★★
Start with left hand on a side pull and right hand in an undercling two feet right of Faceshot. Climb into the bullet holes. Better get off quick if you see any rednecks with guns around.

6. Gutshot V5 ★★
Sit start with an undercling for the left hand and a crimp on the arête for the right. Climb the arête.

7. Jell-O Shot V1 ★
Climb the arête on the right side of the north face.

Joe's Valley

Fiona Lloyd looking for the *Point of Impact* V2, page 100.
Photo: Dave Pegg

Man Size Area ▼ right fork 0.9m

This classic area has a little bit of everything, from dicey highballs to burly all-out testpieces, from thin, crimpy faces to pleasant V0 slabs. No matter what your skill level you'll find challenging problems here on some of the highest quality rock in the canyon. To locate the Man Size Area, drive up the right fork for 0.9 miles and park in a large pullout on the left (west) side of the road. From the pullout locate a good trail heading west into a wash. Follow this wash for a few minutes.

A. The Man Size Boulder ▼
The first problems after leaving the pullout are found on the impressive Man Size boulder. Although most of the problems ascend good rock, the boulder is tall, and a broken hold could be disastrous, so be wary of the holds you use up high. The easiest descent is The Down Climb, problem 5. Make sure you're solid reversing V0 20 feet off the deck before you launch up this boulder!

1. The Comedian V4
Start sitting at the right side of the overhang. Climb the lip of the overhang up and left to the same top out as Finger Hut.

2. Finger Hut V10
Sit start using small crimps. Power out the overhang using small crimps and brute force. Move right then back left to the big jug on the face and top out at the point of the overhang. Photo: page 107.

3. V5
Sit start at the left end of the overhang. Right hand in a pocket under the lip, left hand in a positive dish four and a half feet up the face. Climb the lip rightwards using slopey pockets to reach jug pockets. From the jugs climb straight up the highball face.

4. It Hurts When I Pee V0
Begin standing on the rock at the base of the boulder. Climb the black rock moving right. Be careful of brittle edges on this highball.

5. The Down Climb V0
Climb the tall face three feet right of the arête. This is also the best way to get off the boulder.

6. Poricini or Portobello V6
Sit start under the roof in a hueco jug two feet off the ground. Pull hard moves out the roof then climb the arête and face to the top.

7. Michelangelo V3
A masterpiece indeed. A must-do for the highball connoisseur. Climb straight up perfect rock using edges down low and moving into shallow pockets up high.

8. Ankle Deep in Gasoline V4
Climb the face to the left of Michelangelo. Worth doing, but be careful of crispy crimps.

9. V4
Climb the face on very suspect rock. Bad landing.

10. Dave's Face V5
Start with both hands in underclings seven feet up. Slap up to the sloper, move left, then straight up the face. Bad landing.

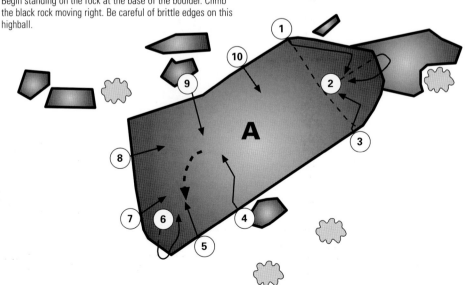

Man Size Area overview

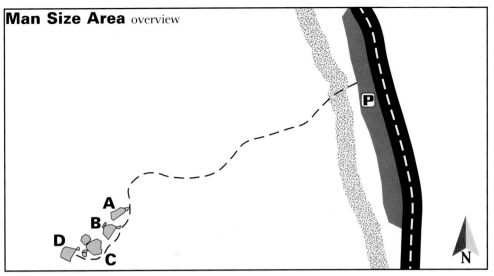

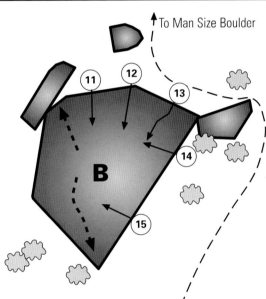

To Man Size Boulder

To The Scrawny and The Brawny

B. The Black Days Boulder ▲
A small boulder with several good easy problems 25 feet southwest of the Down Climb on the Man Size Boulder.

11. Pubic Affair V0 ★
Friction up the low-angle face.

12. Black Days V1 ★★★
Begin in the middle of the face. Climb straight up perfect rock. Bad landing

13. Sheep Dip V1 ★★
Climb up the face to the left-facing corner, layback the corner to the top. Bad landing.

14. The Clap V1
As you may have suspected the "Clap" begins in the bush, then straight up the face.

15. Itchy Crotch V0 ★
A little more fun than the name implies. Climb the face.

Joe's Valley

Man Size Area ▼ right fork 0.9m

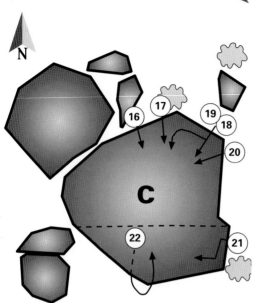

◀ **C. The Scrawny and the Brawny**
To locate the Scrawny and the Brawny Boulder continue up the trail for about 50 feet past the Black Days Boulder.

16. V9 ★ ☐
Start with two horrible slopey pockets seven feet up. Make one desperate move to good edges and the top.

17. V4 ★★ ☐
Start standing just right of where the tree leans against the boulder. Climb the face.

18. The Scrawny and the Brawny V10 ★★ ☐
Sit start using gnarly crimps four feet up. Make one desperate move to flat edges then one more move to jugs and it's all over.

19. Scrawny V7 ★★ ☐
Begin with both hands on flat edges one move up #18. Traverse right and top out on Code Red.

20. Kind of Brawny V8 ★★ ☐
Sit start with both hands on crimps. Make one hard move to blocky slopers, then jugs to the top.

21. V4 🧗 ★ ☐
Sit start with both hands in pockets. Climb good holds up and left, then make the hard top out.

22. Brawny Dyno V5 ★★★ ☐
Start standing. Grab the jugs seven and a half feet up, fire to the lip, and mantel.

D. The Triangle Boulder ▶
The Triangle boulder is about 25 feet due west of the Scrawny and the Brawny Boulder and has some great V2s and V3s.

23. Triangle Arête V2 ★★ ☐
Layback the arête up and right.

24. The Triangle Traverse V7 ★★ ☐
Begin on the arête. Traverse the face and finish on Black Gold. Sharp.

25. The Tan Streak V3 ★★★ ☐
Climb the face straight up the tan streak. Sharp.

26. The Triangle V3 ★★★ ☐
Start just right of the tan streak in the lowest crimps. Climb straight up the black face using sharp crimps and pockets.

27. Black Gold V2 ★★★ ☐
Start in the pockets. Follow pockets up and right to crimps.

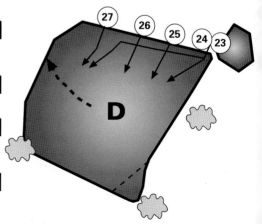

Matt Birch on-sighting *Fingerhut* (V10), page 104.
Photo: Andrew Kornylak

Black & Tan

right fork 1.5m

Comprised of many boulders scattered along the hillside, The Black and Tan area is large and varied. Consequently some of the boulders can be hard to find. To get to the Black and Tan Area, drive up the Right Fork for 1.5 miles and park in a pullout on the left (west) side of the road, just down canyon from the Warm-Up boulder. Walk back down the road (south) for about two tenths of a mile and enter the first major wash on the (west) right side of the canyon. The first boulders are a couple of hundred feet up the wash.

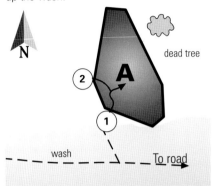

A. The First Boulder
Located in the right side of the wash, this is (duh) the first boulder you come to.

1. First V2
Sit start in the sandy hueco. Climb the pockets up and left. Good climbing but dirty.

2. Second V2
Sit start in a hueco three feet left of #1. Climb pockets up and right to join #1. Dirty.

B. The Fuzzy Boulder
The Fuzzy boulder is about 40 feet past the first boulder on the right side of the wash.

3. Fuzzy V1
Climb the corner of the boulder. A decent little problem.

4. Ace V3
Start in pockets. Climb the swirly black and tan face. Very dirty

C. The Dry Gulch Boulder
NO TOPO
A small and chossy boulder with very little appeal located about 150 feet up the wash.

5. Dry Gulched V1
Climb southeast face of the chossy blocky boulder.

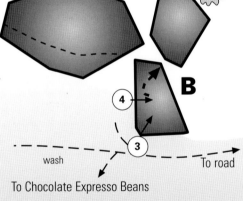

D. The Fast Twitch Boulder
To locate the Fast Twitch Boulder continue up the wash past the Dry Gulch boulder to a small cliff band that blocks the wash. Walk around the right side. Drop back into the drainage and look for the obvious clean boulder in the bottom of the wash.

6. Wake Me Up V4 ★★
Start on the vertical fin that separates the two sandy huecos. Climb the face.

7. Don't Reach Around V6 ★★★
This climbs the face just left of the small juniper that is growing out of the wash. Sit start in the hueco. Pull hard moves on small holds. An excellent problem that is well worth the walk.

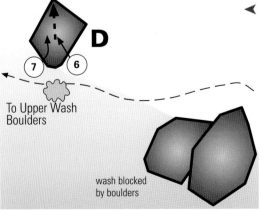

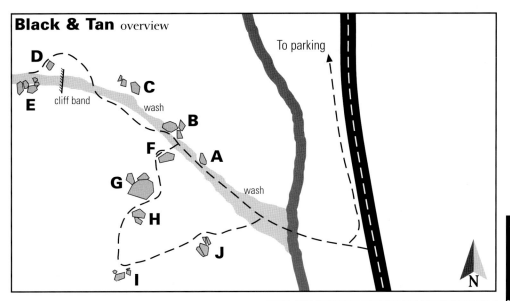

Black & Tan overview

E. The Upper Wash Boulders ▶

These boulders are located about 30 feet past the Fast Twitch Boulder. Look for a black and orange streaked north face.

8. V2
Start on the left side of the face. Left hand in a good undercling pocket, right hand in a dish. Dyno to the big dish at the lip.

9. V1
Start in the middle of the face, right hand in a good two-finger pocket, left hand in a dish. One move wonder to the lip.

10. Black Overhang V5
Climb the black overhang.

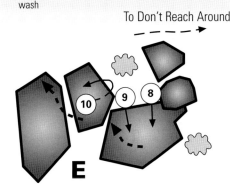

◀ F. The Java Boulder

The Java Boulder, and the remaining boulders at the Black and Tan Area, are on the hill to the right (south) of the wash. To locate the Java Boulder, follow instructions to the Fuzzy Boulder. Once at the Fuzzy Boulder, walk a few feet to the obvious black boulder on the hill south of the wash.

11. Chocolate Espresso Beans V2
Start in the middle of the face on the slopey rail. Right hand on a sloper with a thumb catch and left hand on a slopey edge. Climb the face. Bad landing

12. Java V0
Begin five feet right of #11 with both hands in pockets. Climb the face.

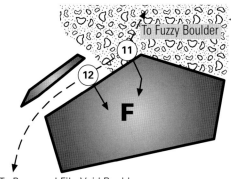

To Prow and Fila Void Boulders

Black & Tan ▼ right fork 1.5m

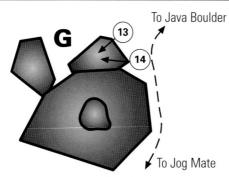

To Java Boulder

◀ **G. The Not So Bad Boulder**
The Not So Bad boulder is actually not so good. If you really want to get there, continue walking south and a little up along the hillside.

13. Not so bad V1
Climb the chossy face.

14. Quality before quantity V1
Flakes up the arête.

To Jog Mate

H. The Jog Mate Boulder ▶
The Jog mate has one good slab problem on great rock. To find this boulder continue walking up and south along the hillside.

15. Jog Mate V0 ★★
Climb the tall slabby face.

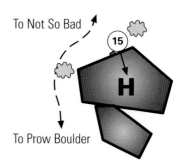

To Not So Bad

To Prow Boulder

◀ **I. The Prow Boulder**
To locate the Prow boulder, continue traversing the hillside to the south. Look for a boulder with an obvious north-facing prow.

16. V3 ★★
Sit start in the right-facing flake.

17. The Prow V4 ★★
Begin with pockets and edges seven feet up. One move to the lip followed by a hard mantel. A **V7 sit start** has been reported but seems much harder.

18. Milky Way V2 ★★
Begin left of the prow. Climb the pocketed face to a slopey mantle. Bad landing.

19. Blue Eyed V3 ★★★
Sit start in the horizontal edge three feet up. Move left hand into the first pocket. Then follow the beautiful huecoed face up and left.

To Jog Mate   To Fila Void

log

J. The Fila Void Boulder ▶
This boulder can be found by walking down the hill (east) from the Prow Boulder.

20. Fila Void V5 ★★★
Start on the arête. Move right hand to the small crimp sidepull and start slapping the slopey arête.

21. Chicks Are For Kids V1 ★★
Climb the right side of the north face. Avoid the choss to the left.

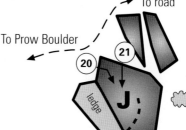

To road

To Prow Boulder

Joe's Valley

Fiona Lloyd almost making the big move on *Problem #1* (V1) at the U.M.W.A area, page 114.
Photo: Dave Pegg

Warm-Up Area ▼ right fork 1.7m

Conveniently located less than a minute from the road, the Warm-Up Boulder offers a high concentration of quality problems, including, as the name implies, many good warm ups. To locate this boulder, drive up the right fork for 1.7 miles and park in a pullout on the right (east) side of the road. The climbing is on the obvious gray boulder about 75 feet off the right side of the road. The parking area will hold a maximum of four cars. More parking can be found down the canyon on the west side of the road.

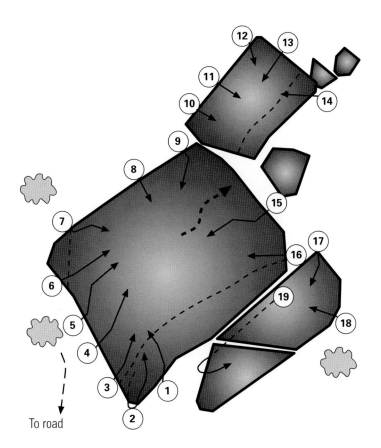

1. 3 Weeks V6 ★★★
Start standing with both hands in the bottom of the scoop. Heel hook elegantly, or grovel, into the scoop. Use spotters and be careful of the rock at your back — or you could fall backwards and split your noggin.
A **V9 variation** starts one move lower in the two small crimps below the scoop.

2. #2 Arête V10 ★★
Sit start in underclings. Slap to bad slopers and follow the arête.

3. Ian's V6 ★★
Start in pockets three feet to the left of #2 Arete. Climb up and right into the cracks. Reachy.

4. Scoopable V1 ★★★
Climb the obvious scoop in the middle of the face up and left. A mini-route.

5. Rearrange V5 ★★
Sit start in jugs just to the right of the tree. Climb up and left into the flaring crack. Follow the crack to the top and join Scoopable.

6. Better than Coffee V4 ★★★★
Climb the beautiful water-worn crack at the left end of the face. Harder to start than it looks and highball at the top.

WolverinePublishing   www.wolverinepublishing.com

Eric Cutler hoping his right foot doesn't blow on the crux mantel of *3 Weeks* (V6).
Photo Dave Pegg

7. Dem' Bones V3
Sit start on good holds on the far right end of the north face. Move up and left on sharp crimps to jugs.

8. Sling Blade V4
Sit start in good incut hold. Climb straight up on sharp crimps.

9. Who Cares? V2
Start standing just right of where the two boulders touch. Make one move to jugs.

10. Shorty Pie V2
Start standing in the rounded crack. Follow the crack to the arête, then the arête to the top.

11. Warm Up V1
Start in jugs at the bottom of the left-facing corner. Climb the face.

12. Easy Arête V2
Climb the slopey arête avoiding the jugs on the face to the right.

13. Whatever V0
Start in the jug seven feet up. Climb the face.

14. Leaving Base Camp V4
Start standing on the rocks at the base of the boulder. Swing onto the arête and face and mantle up.

15. Easy Crack V0
Climb the crack up and right.

16. Chipped V-pointless
Climb the ugly gouged out worthless holds, or better yet don't climb them and curse the brainless dickhead who would do such a thing.

17. Bitter Bite V2
Sit start on the arête. Make a couple of moves up the arête and pull onto the left face.

18. Pop Belly V2
Sit start in jugs three feet right of the tree. Climb up and slightly right.

19. Cave Man V4
Sit start in jugs at the back of the cave. Climb the jug rail to the crack, then climb the crack and around the corner to the right. Be careful of the boulder that lurks beneath the crux.

U.M.W.A

right fork 2m

Located on the verge of the highway, the U.M.W.A. area is the sine qua non of roadside bouldering. Two small boulders here host a surprising amount of quality climbing. To locate the U.M.W.A Area, drive up the right fork for 2.0 miles and park in a pullout on the left (west) side of the road. The UMWA Boulder is located next to the pullout, about 100 inches off the road.

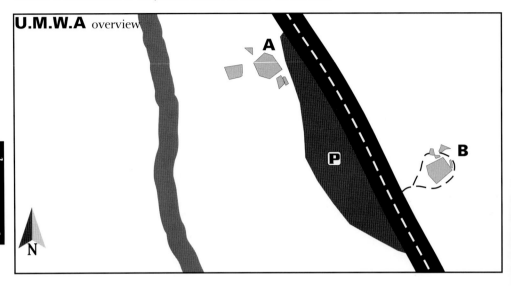

U.M.W.A overview

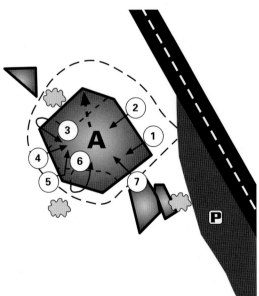

A. U.M.W.A. Boulder ▼
The obvious boulder just off the road at the north part of the pullout. The boulder is named for the graffiti scratched on its west face.

1. V1 ★★
Start with your right hand in the pocket; make one big move to jugs.

2. Smoothie V5 ★★★
Sit start in pockets three feet up. Climb up to the crappy left hand gaston then to small edges. A good technical problem.

3. Stompin' Hippies V7 ★★
Sit start on side pulls at the back of the roof. Climb out the roof to the arête, and follow the arête to the top.

4. High Ride V2 ★★
Sit start with your left hand in a good three-finger pocket and right hand on some edges. Climb the face.

5. Rug Rat V5 ★★★
Sit start in underclings. Climb huecos out the roof to the rail. Follow the rail right to the arête, and then take the arête back left to the top.

6. Walrus V5 ★★
When you get to the top out on this one, the name will make complete sense. Sit start in the sandy scoop. Follow the scoops straight up to the hard mantel.

7. Reach Around V3 ★★
Sit start in jugs. Climb the face on huecos; locate the hard to see pocket over the lip and mantle. Bad landing.

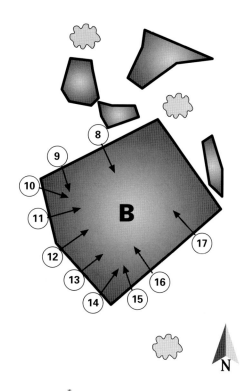

B. The Small One ▲
The Small One is a few feet south of the U.M.W.A. boulder 20 feet from the verge on the opposite side of the road.

8. Dustbuster V2
Sit start in the jug undercling. Climb the face.

9. Midget V3
Start standing three feet right of Dustbuster. Climb the face on great rock.

10. Runt V7
Sit start using edges on both sides of the arête. Climb the arête on some tricky slopers.

11. Pee Wee V4
Sit start with your right hand on a layback pinch, left hand on some edges. Climb the face.

12. Pint Size V3
Sit start by laying back on the pod and climbing into some pockets.

13 LCC V4
Sit start. Climb the finger crack. Sharp.

14. Mini V1
Start on the sandy edge five feet up; move into underclings and the top.

15. Tiny V1
Sit start in a jug sidepull. Climb up and right.

16. Small One V2
Sit start in underclings three feet up. Make one big move to the thread and mantel.

17. One Move V0
Start on flat edges five and a half feet up. Make one move to the top.

Buoux Area ▼   right fork 2.4m

The Buoux Boulder is the jewel of this small area and has a bounty of classic problems, including some sphincter-puckering highballs on outstanding rock. There's also great climbing on the other boulders. The Buoux Area is 2.4 miles up the right fork. Park on the left (east) side of the road at the beginning of a dirt road and walk down canyon (south) along the dirt road, which dead-ends at the Buoux Boulder.

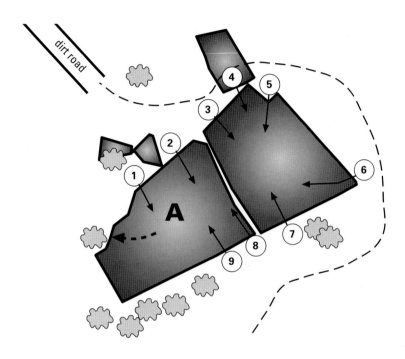

A. The Buoux Boulder ▲
The Buoux Boulder is the first boulder you come to as you walk down the dirt road.

1. V1 ★★
Sit start with both hands on a flat edge three and a half feet up. Climb the face to the right of the rocks at the base of the boulder.

2. The Complete Guide to Economic Theory V4 ★★
Start with a right-facing flake and pockets. Pull the heinous slopey mantel..

3. The Buoux Problem V3 ★★★★
Climb the awesome pocketed face just left of the crack.
A **V7 Variation** ★★★ sit starts with your left hand in a sidepull crimp and right hand in the lowest pockets.

4. Tradesque V4 ★★★
Climb the obvious crack/seam on the left side of the face. Quite tall and quite insecure at the top. Yikes!

5. Possession With Intent V1 ★★
Climb the dihedral. Highball and scary at the top.

6. Thin Ice V0 ★
Climb the flakes up the left side of the face trending rightwards. Cleaner than it looks, but you should still be very careful of what you pull on. Tall. Bad landing

7. Prendre La Fuite V2 ★★★
Start in the tree to the right of the crack. Climb the tall face moving right to top out. Very tall.

8. The Buoux Crack V2 ★★★★
A must do on the highball tick list. Climb the left edge of the crack and face. The crux comes at the very top — about 25 feet above the ground.

9. Speed V3 ★★★
Climb the highball face to the left of The Buoux Crack. Move left to top out. The crack is off.

WolverinePublishing   www.wolverinepublishing.com

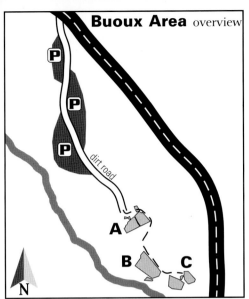

B. The Bowling Ball Boulder

To locate the Bowling Ball Boulder, follow a trail south from the Buoux Boulder for about 80 yards.

10. The Bowling Ball V4 ★★★
This great problem starts with your left hand in the three monos and right hand on a small gaston crimp. Climb straight up the face.

11. Bowling Ball Arête V2 ★
Climb the arête on the left side of the face.

12. V4 ★★
Sit start with both hands on a triangular block. Climb straight up the face to the hard mantle top out.

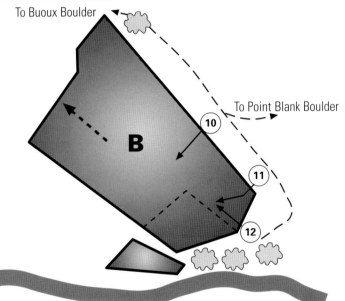

C. Boulder

This boulder is located about 30 feet east (towards the road) from the Bowling Ball Boulder.

13. V4 ★★
Sit start just to the right of the prominent tan streak. Climb the black prow.

14. V2 ★
Sit start with both hands on a crimpy edge below the lip. Fire to the lip and top out.

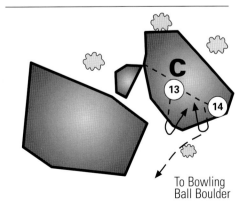

Joe's Valley

ALL Area ▼   right fork 2.6m

Comprised of several small boulders, the ALL area offers more roadside problems, mainly short but worthwhile. Water Paintings is an area classic. To locate the ALL Area, drive up the right fork 2.6 miles. Park in a pullout on the left (west) side of the road directly across from a sign that reads "Motorized Vehicle Travel Restricted to Designated Roads and Trails."

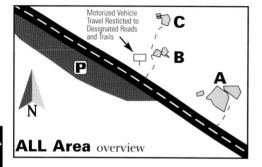

ALL Area overview

A. The ALL Boulder ▼
The ALL Boulder is located about 50 yards down the road (southeast) from the travel-restriction sign. It is a large boulder 15 feet off the side of the road.

1. Water Paintings V7
Sit start using sidepulls in the back of the roof. Climb out the roof to the rail, pull the lip and mantel. A Beta-intensive classic.

2. Domestic Violence V5
Sit start with both hands on sharp crimps under the roof. Make one hard move out to the lip, then up the face.

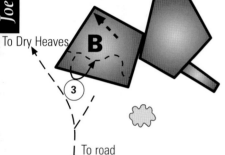

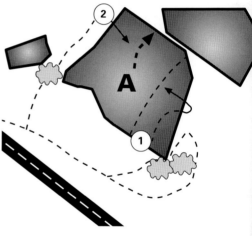

B. The Marker Boulder ▲
The Marker boulder is located about 20 feet from the travel-restriction sign.

3. Marker V4
Sit start matched in an incut flake three feet left of the big sandy hole. Slap to the lip and pull the slopey mantle top out.

◀ C. The Dry Heaves Boulder
To find the Dry Heaves boulder, walk behind the Marker boulder, away from the road, for about 25 yards. The climbs face the road.

4. Fat Lip V1
Sit start on the right side of the face. Climb the lip up and left to the summit.

5. Dry Heaves V4
Sit start under the roof with both hands on the flake four feet up. Climb to the lip and top out the same as Fat Lip.

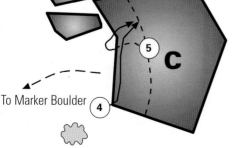

Joe's Valley

Peanut gallery at *No Additives* (V11), page 120.
Photo: Dave Pegg

No Substance ▾ right fork 2.7m

The No Substance area is home to a couple of well-known and often attempted problems: No Substance and No Additives. Two hard, impressive and on perfect rock. You'll also find several good moderates here. The No Substance area is 2.7 miles up the right fork. Park in a small pullout on the left (west) side of the road. The boulders are just down-canyon from the mine.

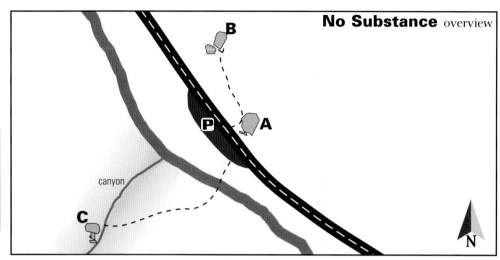

No Substance overview

◀ A. No Substance Boulder

The No Substance boulder is located just off the east side of the road; the No Additives side of the boulder faces up canyon, towards the mine.

1. J-Rad V2 ★★

Climb the pocketed face, move a little left to top out. Don't fall. Bad landing.

2. No Non-Séance V7 ★

Start standing with your hands on the lip. Traverse the lip left to the apex of the boulder and topout.

3. No Additives V11 ★★★★

Start standing with your left hand in a positive undercling and your right hand in the pair of tiny dimples. Power up to the slot on the face, and top out as for No Substance. Photo page 118. The **sit start** is **V13**.

4. No Substance V8 ★★★★

Another ultra classic. Easy or impossible, this one depends on your ability to hang big, rounded slopers. Having paws the size Shaquille O'Neil will help. Begin in the see-through ring at the left end of the face. Traverse the rounded lip to the apex of the boulder, and top out on its right side. Get a good spot on this problem as the marginal holds can spit you off on your back.

5. Scuzlocks ★★

No grade on this one. Slither through the ring at the left end of the face. Don't get stuck.

WolverinePublishing   www.wolverinepublishing.com

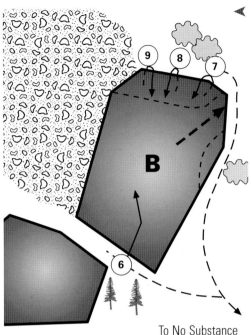

◀ B. The Thriller Boulder

A large boulder of perfect rock with a tall, crack-littered face that is visible from the road. To reach the Thriller Boulder, start at the No Substance Boulder and traverse gradually uphill up-canyon (north) for about 200 feet.

6. Thriller V0

Climb the numerous cracks up the tall face seen from the road. Bad landing. A fall from the top could be very serious.

7. V2

Sit start with right hand in the two-finger pocket and left hand in a side pull just above the tan scoop. Pull the bulge.

8. V3

Begin standing using two left-facing sidepulls one foot to the right of the two-finger pocket on problem #7.

9. V4

This would be a four-star classic if it was a little taller, but it is still damn good. Sit start with both hands on the jug knob. Climb the bulge on immaculate gray stone.

To No Substance

Joe's Valley

C. The Maxi Pad Boulder ▶

The Maxi Pad boulder is located in the canyon directly opposite the No Substance Boulder. More problems have been done in this canyon, however most are isolated, hard to find, and have long approaches. For this reason, only the Maxi Pad Boulder has been described. If you feel like doing some adventure-type climbing, explore the potential that exists further up canyon. To reach the Maxi Pad boulder walk up the canyon directly opposite the No Substance Boulder for a few hundred feet. The boulder is in the bottom of the wash.

10. Ross's Chosses V2

Climb the sandy right-facing corner to a slabby mantle.

11. V3

Climb the face straight up into the shallow groove. Bad landing.

12. V3

Climb the face up and right, and finish the same as #11. Bad landing. Highball.

13. Maxi Pad V6

Start on the lowest edges under the roof. Climb up and right to the prow. Follow the prow to the highball finish.

14. Bit o' Honey V1

Begin standing just left of the ten-foot drop off. Climb the slab.

15. Reeces Pieces V1

Climb the slab up to the large right-facing flake. This is also the best way to get off the boulder.

16. JB's Arête V1

Climb the slab and arête.

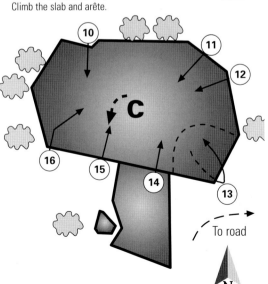

To road

N

Joe's Valley

Minute Man ▼   right fork 3.5m

There are many boulders at the Minute Man area, but few of them offer good problems. The exception is the excellent Minute Man. Just a Minute and A War on Nature, two neighboring problems are also worth doing. To locate the Minute Man area, drive up the right fork for 3.5 miles and park in a pullout on the right (east) side of the road. Walk across the road and locate a faint trail leading west into the small stream. Cross the stream, walk up the hill and go a little down-canyon (south) for about 150 feet. The Minute Man Boulder can be seen from the north end of the parking pullout.

◀ A. Minute Man Boulder

1. Just a Minute V2 ★
Start standing, climb the arête.

2. Minute Man V6 ★★★
Start low on the left-facing flake. Climb the flake and get the pocket with your right hand. Continue to the lip and a hard mantle. Could be bad if you blow the top out.

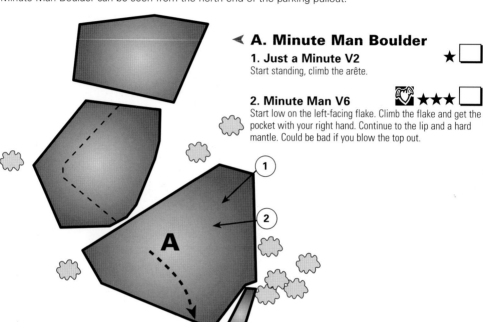

B. War with Nature Boulder ▼
This boulder is about 20 feet southwest of the Minute Man Boulder. It has one problem which faces the road.

3. A War with Nature V5 ★★
Quite good. Climb the black swirly face. Rocks at the base keep things spicy. Don't blow it at the top.

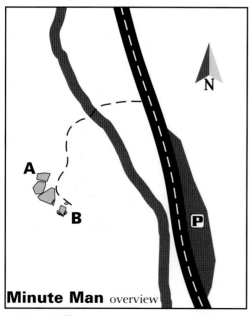

Minute Man overview

Joe's Valley

Eric Cutler feasts on *Frosted Flakes* (V4), page 128.
Photo: Dave Pegg

Moby Dick ▼   right fork 3.7m

These south-facing boulders get lots of sun and have several quality problems, ranging from moderate to truly desperate. The Moby Dick area is 3.7 miles up the right fork. Park in the large pullout on the right (east) side of the road below the boulder-strewn hillside.

There are many boulders, and some established problems on the hillside between Moby Dick and The Hulk area (page 128). The area is worth exploring, but since the bouldering is widely scattered and of variable quality it has not been described in this guide.

◄ A. The Roadside Arête Boulder
This is the first boulder on the hill, about 30 feet from the road.

1. Roadside Arête V6 ★★
Climb the arête and face staying on the right side of the arête. Be careful of loose rock up high.

2. V2 ★★
Climb the black face with many edges.

3. The Face Left V1 ★
Climb the black face right of the trees.

4. The Face Right V0 ★
Climb the face left of the crack.

5. Easy Crack V0
Climb the crack.

B. The Runnel Boulder ►
This boulder is located about thirty feet up the trail; the climbs are on the dirty-looking rock that faces the road.

6. Runnel V1 ★★
Sit start. Climb the face just left of the corner and finish in the water runnel.

7. Runnel Left V2 ★
Sit start in jugs just right of the big sandy hole.

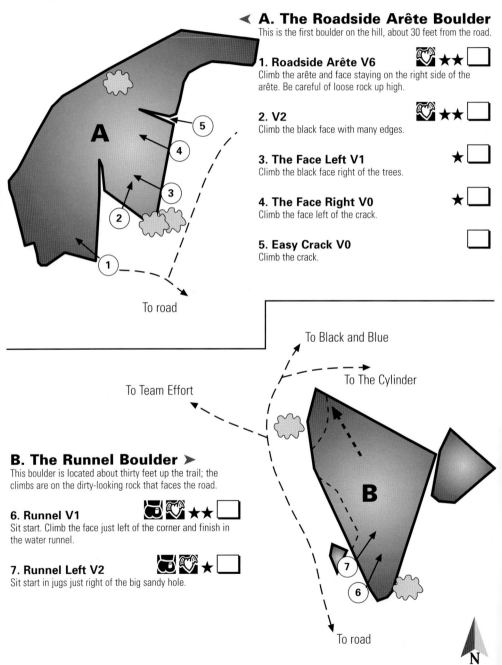

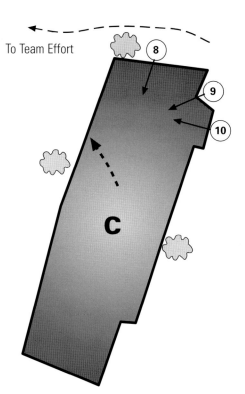
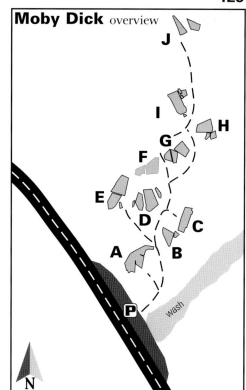

C. The Cylinder Boulder

The Cylinder boulder is behind (south) of the Runnel boulder.

8. The Cylinder V1
Begin in big pockets five feet up just left of the small pine tree. Climb into the big slot and mantle. Great rock. Tall!

9. Corner Crack V0
Climb the crack in the corner.

10. V6
Sit start in jugs. Slap up both corners, get your right hand in the pair of shallow pockets on the right face, and fire for the lip. The crack is off.

D. The Team Effort Boulder

Easily recognizable by the large bulging prow that faces down hill, this boulder is about 30 feet uphill from the Runnel Boulder.

11. Team Effort V8
Start standing with left hand on a knobby pinch seven feet up and right hand on a side pull six feet up. Huck out the dramatic prow with a long powerful lock-off to finish. Well placed spotters should be able to stop you tumbling down the hill. A good **V9 sit-start variation** begins with both hands in the flake four feet up. Climb into Team Effort.

12. V2
Climb the face three feet left of the sit start to Team Effort. Very bad landing.

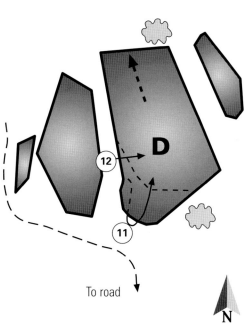

Joe's Valley

Moby Dick   right fork 3.7m

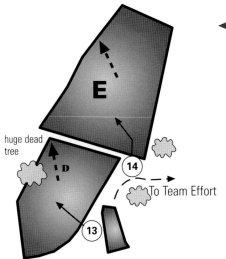

◄ E. The Dead Tree Boulder
Located about 25 feet past the Team Effort Boulder, this boulder forms the beginning of a small cliff band, and is distinguishable by a huge dead tree on top.

13. Dead Tree V0   ★ ☐
Climb the tall slab directly beneath the dead tree. The rock is better than it looks.

14. Badlands V2   ★★ ☐
Begin on the left side of the arête. Climb the arête and face staying on the left side of the arête.

F. The Black and Blue Boulder ►
A classic boulder with perfect rock, good landings, and three great problems. To find the Black and Blue boulder traverse the hill eastwards from the Dead tree boulder for about 30 feet.

15. Hooters V9   ★★★ ☐
No honking jugs on this one. Small crimps up the pretty face left of the prow. An exercise in finger power and deadpoint accuracy.

16. Black and Blue V6   ★★★★ ☐
Sit start. Climb the obvious prow. Ultra classic.

17. Skins Game V3   ★★★ ☐
Sit start on blocky jugs right of the prow. Climb huecos and edges to the top.

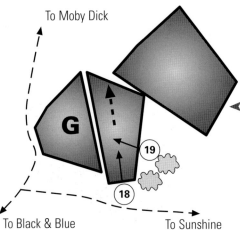

◄ G. The Sandy Hueco Boulder
This boulder is 20 feet right (east) of the Black and Blue Boulder. The climbing is OK on somewhat sandy rock.

18. Good One V0   ★ ☐
Climb the face on the left side of the arête.

19. Sandy Hueco V1   ★ ☐
Begin on the right side of the arête. Climb into the sandy hueco.

Wolverine Publishing   www.wolverinepublishing.com

H. The Sunshine Boulder ▶

To find the Sunshine Boulder, traverse right (east) along the small cliff band, at the end of the cliff band scramble up blocks to the boulder with the killer juggy face.

20. Sunshine V1  ★★★★ ☐
Sit start. Climb the perfect juggy face. Bad landing; if you were to fall from the top, it could become a dark day.

21. Todd's Problem V4  ★★ ☐
Sit start on the horizontal flake, move left to the crimp on the face then fire for the crack. Top out on the big see-through threader. Bad landing.

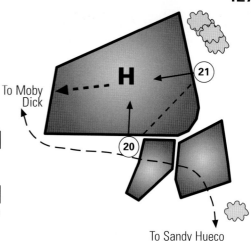

I. The Moby Dick Boulder ◀

This boulder has several good moderate problems and the classic Moby Dick. To find it, walk uphill from the Sunshine boulder for about 30 feet. Look for the big boulder with a small roof that faces towards the road.

22. Moby Dick V6 ★★★★ ☐
This climb is located just right of the small roof. Start in the lowest pockets and mount the perfect gray bulge. If you don't find the right finishing holds you might find yourself floundering like a beached whale.

23. Little Tree V0 ★ ☐
Climb the face left of the little tree growing out of the boulder.

24. Water Groove V0 ★ ☐
Climb big pockets up the obvious water groove. A little dirty.

25. T-bone V1 ★★★ ☐
Just left of the lichen patch is a hueco with a cool-looking cactus growing in it. Climb the face eight feet left of the cactus. Good moves on great rock.

26. V0 ★ ☐
Climb the arête and face.

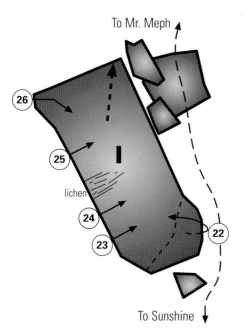

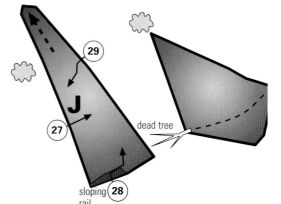

J. The Mr. Meph Boulder ▶

Although this is the furthest boulder at the Moby Dick area, the three problems here are worth the walk. To find the Mr. Meph boulder, continue past Moby Dick for a couple hundred feet.

27. V0 ☐
Climb the slabby juggy face.

28. Mr. Mephosropholies V6 ★★ ☐
This climb faces the parking area. Sit start on a slopey rail. Climb right and slap the two arêtes to the top. Some crimps on the face are useful as well.

29. V1 ★★ ☐
Sit start on a jug. Follow the right-facing rail to the top on quality rock.

Joe's Valley

The Hulk
right fork 4m

The Hulk is the final area up the Right Fork, and one of the best. A good proportion of the dozen or so climbs here are three- to four-star classics. To locate the Hulk Area, drive up the right fork for 4 miles and park in a small pullout on the left (west) side of the road. You can see The Hulk boulder from the parking area.

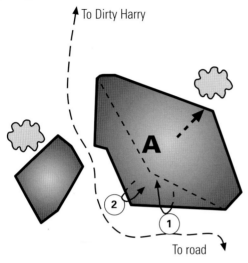

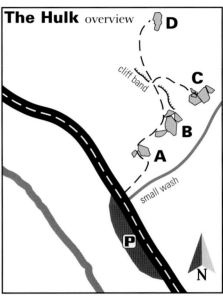

A. The Hulk Boulder
The hulk boulder is the first boulder at this area. It is located to the east, just off the road.

1. Frosted Flakes V4 ★★★★
Climb the obvious crack and pockets.

2. The Hulk V9 ★★★★
Sit start on the right facing flake. Climb into two bad underclings and move right aiming for the big jug at the lip. Burly!

B. The Dirty Harry Boulder
To locate the Dirty Harry Boulder, walk around the left side of the Hulk Boulder, then up the hill for about fifty feet.

3. Dirty Harry V8 ★★★
Start with a juggy tan flake. Climb shallow pockets straight up the face to exciting exit moves. Don't chicken out and grab the small tree when topping out. Tall!

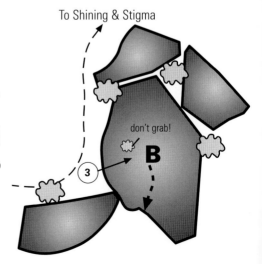

Wolverine Publishing   www.wolverinepublishing.com

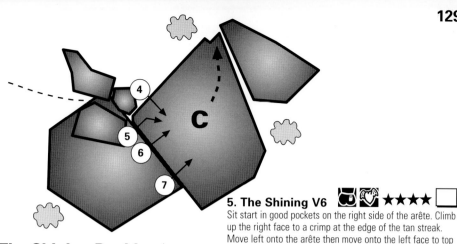

C. The Shining Boulder ▲

The best way to approach the Shining Boulder, is to walk from Dirty Harry up the hill to the small cliff band. Traverse the cliff band left (north) to a break. Climb through the break and traverse the top of the cliff band back right (south) to the obvious black and tan boulder with the beautiful arête.

4. V1
Start in the big sandy pocket. Climb the face.

5. The Shining V6 ★★★★
Sit start in good pockets on the right side of the arête. Climb up the right face to a crimp at the edge of the tan streak. Move left onto the arête then move onto the left face to top out. Totally classic, a must do. Bad landing.

6. Profound V6 Gratitude ★★★
Start the same as The Shining. Climb straight up the face. A little sandy and a lot scary. Tall with a bad landing.

7. Project
The face four feet right of Profound Gratitude.

D. The Stigma Boulder ▶

This boulder is well worth the time and effort the approach demands. The Stigma Boulder is fairly tall with beautiful black rock and great features. The climbs face north (up canyon) and are shaded most of the day. To locate this boulder walk from Dirty Harry up the hill to the small cliff band. Traverse the cliff band left (north) to a break. Climb through the break and continue up the hill while traversing to the left (north) for a couple hundred feet. You can see The Stigma Boulder from Dirty Harry.

8. All You Sinners V6 ★★★★
Another total classic. Start matched on a blocky jug five and half feet up. Climb the steepest part of the face staying in the tan steak. Get the gaston flake with your right hand and throw to the jug at the lip.

9. Antaeus V5 ★★★
Start matched in pockets in the middle of the gray/green streak. Climb numerous pockets straight up the face. Top out to the left on the big sandy block or make harder but cleaner moves to jugs on the right.

10. Stigma V7 ★★
Start with your left hand in a good gray/tan-colored sidepull pocket and your right hand in the crack. Climb the arête. Move left to top out.

11. Wicked Garden V4 ★
Begin in the crack/seam three feet to the left of Stigma. Climb the face just right of the small tree growing out of the crack.

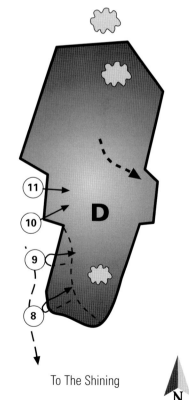

To The Shining

The Innumerables

The Innumerables is one of the newest editions to Joe's Valley. It is situated high on a mesa, offering splendid views of the canyon below and unobstructed vistas of buttes and plateaus far to the east. In addition there are hundreds more boulders scattered along the hillside, and for the willing climber the potential is huge. The Innumerables can be a good choice on hot days as the area receives afternoon shade. The parking for the Innumerables is on an oil-well platform. Camping and fires of any kind are prohibited.

To locate The Innumerables, drive west on highway 29 out of Orangeville to the intersection with highway 57. From the intersection with highway 57 continue west another 2.4 miles on highway 29, and turn left (south) onto a dirt road with a green gate. From the gate, drive over the bridge and turn right (west) after passing the first oil well. Continue driving the dirt road (west), passing a couple of left turns, to a fork in the road. Take the left fork and head uphill. The parking is located at the highest oil well 1.8 miles past the gate. To reach the boulders, follow a trail northwest from the parking lot, across three washes, for about 500 yards

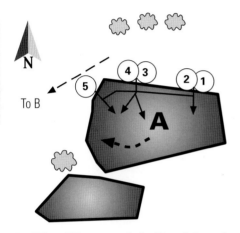

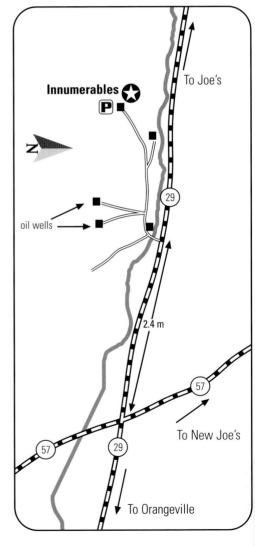

A. The Warmupish Boulder

Although this is the first and eastern most boulder at the Innumerables, it is difficult to see from the trail, and the first-time visitor will likely pass it on the way to the main area. From the Innumerables Boulder, walk down hill about 20 yards. Look for a large black boulder. Five quality moderate climbs make the Warmupish boulder a good warmupish place.

1. Wonder Hole V1 ★★
Start standing in the obvious wonder hole five feet up.

2. Bowling for Dollars V3 ★★
Start in the wonder hole. Traverse the face right and finish on #5.

3. Jug Rash V3 ★★
Sit start in jugs two and a half feet off the ground. Climb into a jug then follow sloping pockets to hard top out.

4. Swine Boy V2 ★★★
Sit start at the same point as #3. Climb right into good holds.

5. Happy Slab V0 ★★
Climb the slab. The big sandy to the right is off. Good rock.

Wolverine Publishing   www.wolverinepublishing.com

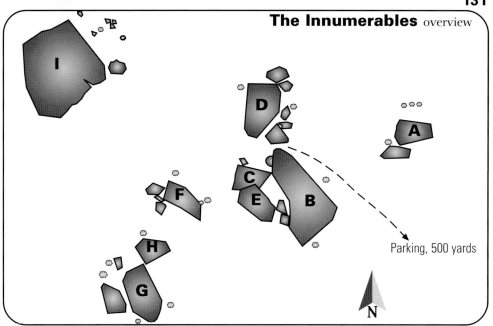

The Innumerables overview

B. The Innumerable Boulder
This 25-foot-tall boulder is impossible to miss, and is the best landmark for describing the location of the remaining boulders.

6. V1
Climb the low-angle face above the slab. Bad landing

7. V0
Climb the corner and face just left of the tree.

8. You Have Done Well V3
Sit start at the left end of the roof. Locate a good incut crimp in black rock for the right hand and a tan rail for the left. Climb out the roof and continue up the tall slab.

9. Techno D-Day V4
Sit start under the roof in a head-sized hueco that is good as an undercling. Climb out the roof moving a little to the right and finish up the tall slab.

10. Creatine Roof V4
Sit start in good holds under the roof at the corner of the boulder. Climb out the roof and top out on the corner.

11. Creatine Roof V7 Right
Same start as #10, but at the lip traverse right, use the two knobs in the orange streak, and top out the same as #12.

12. Home Boy Bumping V3 Beef Snack Sticks
Start standing using a good dish and a cool knob six feet up. Climb straight up. At about mid height it is best to traverse left onto the south face to top out.

13. The Birth of Venus V5
Sit start using the lowest good gray knobs. Climb the knobby protrusions left and finish on #12.

14. Deformation V6
Begin at the right side of the huge overhang on a jug six feet up. Climb the tall face on slopey and insecure holds. Outstanding but scary.

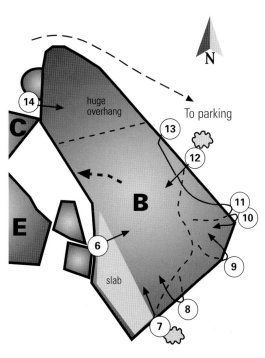

Joe's Valley

The Innumerables

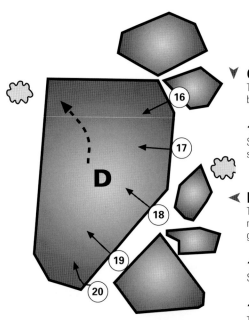

▼ C. Dyno Boulder
This small boulder is located next to problem #14 on the main boulder and has one OK problem on its north face.

15. Obligatory Dyno V2
Sit start on the big brown flake, grab an undercling in the small black streak, and punch to the lip.

◄ D. Horse Tooth Boulder
This beautiful tan-colored boulder is located just a few feet north of the Main Boulder's huge overhang. It has several good problems including the classic Horsetooth Simulator.

16. R.K. Arise V1 ★★★
Start in the jug dish six feet up. Great rock.

17. Halloween V2
This is a great climb, and should perhaps have three stars, but the hollow holds are a little scary and detract from the overall quality. Climb the obvious flakes.

18. Horsetooth Simulator V5
Start on a good protruding edge. Climb the face to a hard mantle. A fall from the mantle would suck. Bad landing.

19. V4 ★
Climb the hollow flakes four feet left of #18.

20. Fin V1 ★★
Layback the left-facing corner.

◄ E. The Throne Boulder
This boulder is located just west of the Main Boulder, and lies on top of the Dyno Boulder. Two classic, although short, V4s scale great rock on the north face.

21. The Throne V4
Sit start in pockets four feet up. Climb straight up the black bulge.

22. The Throne Traverse V4
Same start as #21, but traverse the sloping rail left. Top out on the arête.

23. The Moat V4
Start on horizontal edges directly above the worst possible landing. Careful what you grab.

24. V2
Sit start in the right-facing flake. Cruxy top out.

25. V1
Sit start on a flat edge four and a half feet up. Climb up and left, avoiding bad rock to the right.

F. Pocket Line Boulder ▶

This short black boulder is located about 25 yards uphill (west) from the Main Boulder.

26. Pocket Line V7 ★★★ ☐
A good short power problem. Start in pockets five feet up, place your left foot on the only available hold and power up shallow pockets to a hard mantle.

27. Yort V4 🎒★★ ☐
Sit start using the awkward pocket and edges. Mantel into the sloping scoop.

28. Short V1 🎒★ ☐
Sit start with edges four feet up. Climb up and a little left.

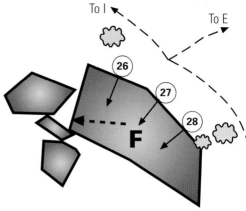

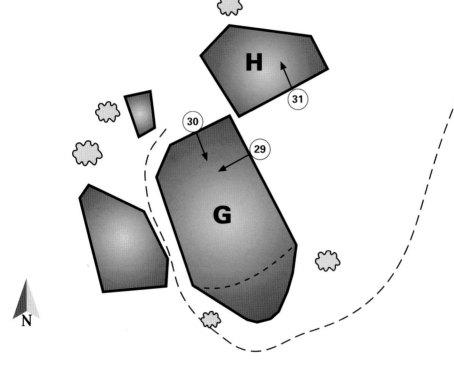

G. The Glide Boulder ▲

The Glide boulder is located 45 yards uphill and a little towards the wash (southwest) from the main boulder. Two cool V3s make this boulder worth visiting.

29. Glide V3 ★★ ☐
Start five feet left of the Sister Sarah boulder. Climb the face. Harder than it looks.

30. Lowball Productions V3 🎒 ★★★ ☐
Sit start on horizontal edges three feet off the ground. Climb straight up the face.

H. Sister Sarah Boulder ▲

This small boulder touches the Glide Boulder on its northeast corner.

31. Kinda Like Sister Sarah V0 ★ ☐
Start in the big brown scoop. Climb the face.

Joe's Valley

The Innumerables

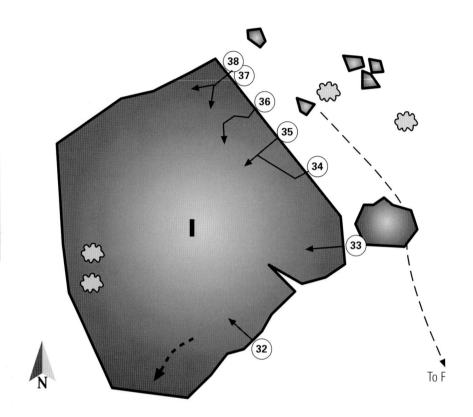

I. The Centerpiece
For such a large boulder, the Centerpiece is surprisingly difficult to find. To locate this boulder, walk north from the Main Boulder, past a small faint wash, and then walk west (uphill) for a total of about 60 yards. The top of this boulder can be seen as you approach from the Main Boulder, and its impressive east face is unmistakable.

32. Bold and Bald V3 ★
Start eight feet left of the obvious crack in the face.

33. Stitches V4?  ★★
Sit start in the hueco. Climb up the right-leaning crack.

34. Posterized V8  ★★★
Start in the obvious basketball-sized hueco in the middle of the face. Climb straight up shallow pockets to about mid height then move right and top out the same as #35.

35. Center Piece V6  ★★★
Sit start on left-facing crimpers four feet right of #34. Climb straight up the face on sharp crimps. Awesome.

36. San Jose V7  ★★
This climb begins seven feet right of #35 on an edge seven feet up. Climb up and right on sharp holds then traverse back left on the horizontal flake.

37. The Royal Coachman V2 ★★
Sit start in the big hueco at the right end of the face. Climb up and left.

38. Mi PC V1 ★
Same start as #37, but climb up and right.

NEW JOE'S

Bouldering doesn't get much better than at New Joe's. This classic area has some of the finest, hardest, and most famous boulder problems in Joe's Valley. It also has a high concentration of superb moderate climbs. The boulders are scattered among pinon and juniper trees on a south-facing hillside, and because they get a lot of sun, New Joe's can be an ideal place to climb on cold winter days.

To get to New Joe's, drive west out of Orangeville on Highway 29 to the intersection with Highway 57. Take a right (north) on Highway 57 and follow it for 3.2 miles to a dirt road on the right (east) side of Highway 57, just past a large fenced in area. Follow the dirt road down into a ravine, then uphill, and park at the oil well. Please respect oil-company workers, drive considerately — and do not camp or light campfires.

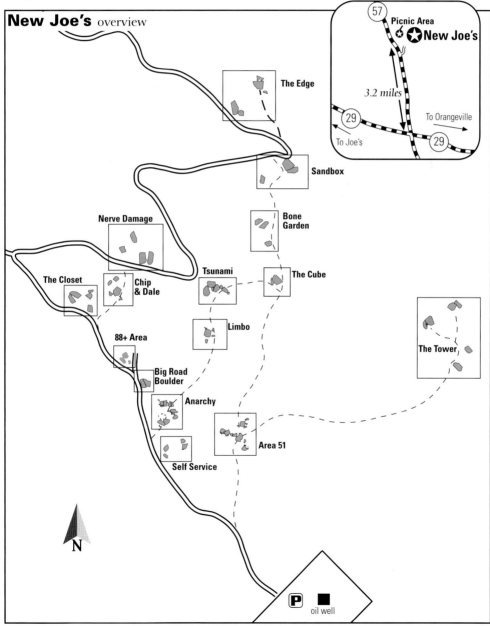

Joe's Valley

Area 51

New Joe's

Area 51 is probably the most popular area in all of Joe's Valley, and for obvious reasons. Some of the most famous boulder problems in the country are located here, as well as a high concentration of not so famous but no less classic lines. The downside is that it's often the most crowded area in all of Joe's too. To locate this area follow the old mining road from the oil well for several hundred feet. Look for a well-worn trail and cairns leading north, up the hill. Follow this trail to the obvious group of four large boulders.

A. The Scotty Boulder ➤

The Scotty Boulder is the western-most boulder at area 51, and is easily recognized by the juggy southeast face, which has several great warm-ups on sandstone so good it could be mistaken for limestone.

1. Warm Me Up Scotty V1
Follow the obvious jugs up the left side of the southeast face. Perfect rock.

2. Getting Warmer V2
Same start as #1 but traverse the lip left and finish on #3.

3. Get Shorty V3
Sit start matched on a good edge under the roof. Pull to the lip and mantle.

4. Nitty Gritty V1
Start matched in the low horizontal crack. Climb the face. Bad landing.

5. Blind Nights V3
Sit start with left hand on a good positive edge and right hand on the bottom of the scoop.

6. Sun in My Eye V4
Sit start matched on the slopey rail. Make a big move up and left to a jug at the lip and mantle.

7. Sun in My Eye V6 Traverse
Same start as #6. Traverse the rail right to sharp crimps, then onto the arête.

8. V1 ★★
Start on small crimps. Layback the right-facing flake.

B. The Evil Boulder ➤

The centerpiece of Area 51, the Evil Boulder sports great rock and classic problems spanning a wide range of difficulty on all faces.

9. Stand Up V8
Start in the good holds seven feet up. Climb up aiming for the orange blob over the lip.

10. Resident Evil V10
Start on two small crimps. Climb pockets following the overhanging black arête up and right; move to the big pocket on the face and top out.

11. Black Lung V13
A famous testpiece. Start with your right hand on the positive crimp and left hand on the pinch. Climb straight up the perfect black prow. Photo page 1.

12. Scary V3
Climb the left-facing, hollow-sounding flake. Good climbing, but quite scary.

13. Snake Bite V4
Start in two underclings four and a half feet up. Move right into the obvious line of pockets.

14. Super Sloper V3
One of the best V3s at Joe's. Same start as #13, but move left to the slopers and up the face.

15. Slab-a-riffic V2
Sit start on the corner of the boulder. Pull onto the slab and climb left of the slopers.

16. V6
Sit start with both hands in the crack. Follow pockets on the lip up and left. Top out the same as #17.

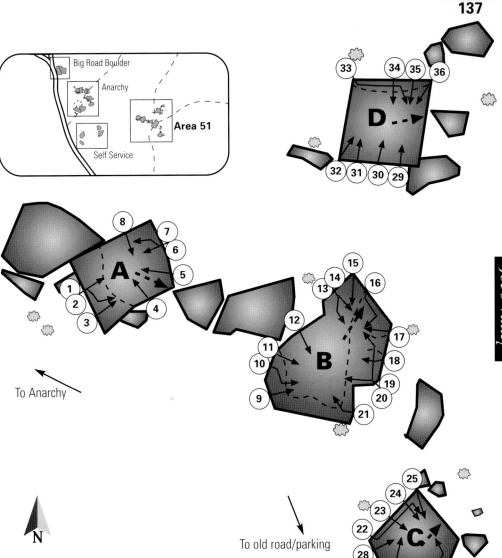

17. Big Boy V7
Big Boy is big fun — absolutely classic. Sit start matched in the good edge under the roof. Climb out the roof up and right.

17a. Two-Finger V9 Variation
Same start as Big Boy, but get the two-finger pocket with your right hand and move straight up.

18. Freak V10
Sit start in the back of the roof on a right-facing side pull. Power straight out the roof.

19. Phony V7 Baloney Traverse
Another must-do on the Evil boulder. Sit start in an undercling and slopey ledge. Climb up the prow, and then traverse the holds below the lip right all the way to the crack just left of Big Boy.

20. Phony Baloney V5
Begin the same as #19. Climb the slopers up the prow and corner, then finish on the big ledge.

21. Slap Me Silly V4
Sit start six feet left of #20. Climb up the edges into the crack.

Joe's Valley

Area 51

New Joe's

C. The Cake Boulder
TOPO PAGE 137

Another example of stellar Joe's Valley rock, the Cake Boulder is located a few feet southwest of the Evil Boulder.

22. Shagadelic V9 ★★ ☐
Traverse the crack from right to left.

23. Marble Cake V9  ★★★ ☐
Sit start with two bad crimps. Make one sick hard move to the crack and top out in the corner.

24. Spam V7 ★★★ ☐
Start with both hands in the crack. Mantle onto the face right of the arête. The arête is off.

25. Crash Landing V2 ★ ☐
Climb the arête. Bad landing.

26. Stumblebum Traverse V5 ★★ ☐
Sit start on a right-facing blocky edge. Traverse the boulder to the right, and top out on the corner of the east face.

26a. Stumblebum V2 Variation ★★ ☐
Begin on the corner, in middle of the Stumblebum Traverse.

27. Joe Cool V3 ★★★★ ☐
Begin the same as #26. Follow the line of jugs straight up great rock to a difficult and scary top out. Excellent.

28. Sharpie V4 ★ ☐
Climb the arête.

D. The Goatee Boulder
TOPO PAGE 137

The northern-most boulder at Area 51, the Goatee has several quality moderate problems on good rock.

29. Chit V4 ★ ☐
Start on a crimper just right of the crack/seam. Make one move to jugs.

30. Suck That V2 ★ ☐
Start with your right hand in the three-finger pocket high on the face. Climb straight up.

31. Huge Mama V2 ★★ ☐
Start with your left hand in an undercling seven feet up and right hand on a fin in the seam. Climb into the great pockets on the black face.

32. Goatee Arête V1 ★ ☐
Climb the arête.

33. Goatee Traverse V2 ★★★ ☐
Sit start at the right end of the face. Traverse the jugs left and top out on #35.

34. Goat Milk V3 ★★ ☐
Start in the tan jugs in the middle of the face. Climb straight up.

35. Goat Cheese V2 ★★ ☐
Begin with left hand on a sidepull pocket and right hand on a small crimp.

36. Goat Droppings V0 ☐
Climb the short and easy arête.

Joe's Valley

Lisa Rands on *The Phoney Balony Traverse* (V7), page 137.
Photo: Wills Young

Self Service ▼   New Joe's

The Self Service area comprises two small boulders offering a few OK problems and Self Service, a total classic. Locate this area by walking up the old mining road for several hundred feet, passing the trail to Area 51 and a small drainage. Look for a short, slabby boulder about 25 feet off the right (east) side of the road.

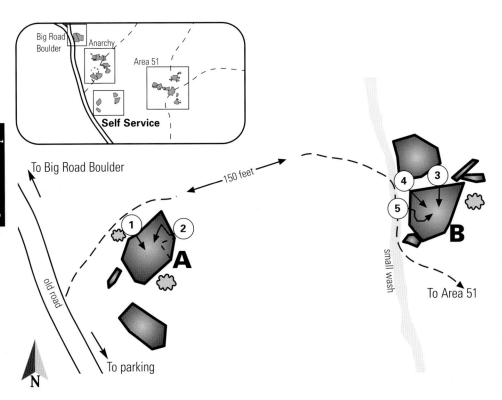

A. Boulder ▲
The short, slabby boulder about 25 feet off the road has a couple of decent problems.

1. V0   ★
Layback the shallow left facing corner just left of the small tree.

2. V2   ★★
Sit start on a big flat ledge. Climb the juggy crack up and right, move onto the arête and top out.

B. The Self Service Boulder ▲
The Self Service Boulder is east of Boulder A in the small wash.

3. DIY V2   ★★
Get the two-finger pocket with your right hand. Climb the slabby face. Bad landing.

4. Whopper V2
Climb the arête. Dirty. Bad landing.

5. Self Service V5   ★★★★
A fantastic problem with fun, thuggy moves and great rock. Sit start, climb the steep prow up and right. Big moves with bad feet.

Dave Schmidt fires *Pocket Rocket* (V6), page 142.
Photo: Tim Kemple

Anarchy

New Joe's

The Anarchy Area is a good sunny area with many moderate problems. To locate this area walk up the old mining road past the Self Service Area. Look for a group of boulders about forty feet off the right side of the road. This area can also be reached by walking northwest from Area 51.

A. Mob Rules Boulder
As you approach the Anarchy Area from the mining road, the trail goes between two boulders. The left boulder is the Anarchy Boulder, the one on the right is Mob Rules.

1. Mob Rules V1
Sit start matched on a hollow-sounding edge four feet up. Climb the small bulge.

2. Pervert V0
Climb the face.

B. Anarchy Boulder
Home to the classic Pocket Rocket, the Anarchy Boulder has the best climbing at this area. The Anarchy Boulder is on the left as you approach from the road.

3. V2
Sit start. Climb the lip up and right to join #4.

4. Idiot Man V4
Sit start on the juggy flake three feet off the ground. Climb up and a little left.

5. Easy V2
Same start as #4 but move up and a little right.

6. Scary Baby V4
Sit start with hands on edges on both sides of the arête. Make one hard move to jugs.

7. Pocket Rocket V6
A very good problem with cool features and perfect rock. Begin with your right hand in the two-finger pocket and left hand on the side pull. Dyno to the lip and move left to top out. Photo previous page.

C. Happy Mantel Boulder
Although super short this boulder offers one entertaining problem. The Happy Mantel boulder is about thirty feet east of the Anarchy Boulder.

8. Happy Mantel V3
Sit start with two pockets under the lip, heel hook left foot, go to the lip, and mantel.

D. Conman Boulder
Located just north of the Happy Mantle Boulder, this rock has a few easy but not-so-good problems on its north face.

9. Conman V1
Sit start in the left side of the flat scoop. Climb left.

10. What Where? V2
Sit start in the middle of the scoop. Climb straight up.

11. Warm-Up V0
Face.

12. Ex Con V0
Sit start. Follow the lip of the groove up and left.

E. Smokin' Boulder
Located in a small group of trees about forty feet north of the Anarchy Boulder, the Smokin' Boulder has a couple of problems that are worth checking out.

13. Smokin' V4
Climb the black streak between the two tan scoops. Scary top out. Bad landing.

14. V0
Climb the slabby north face.

F. Grip Tape Boulder
This boulder touches the west side of the Smokin' boulder and has one good problem on its overhanging west face.

15. Grip Tape V2
Sit start in good holds. Climb out the bulge.

143

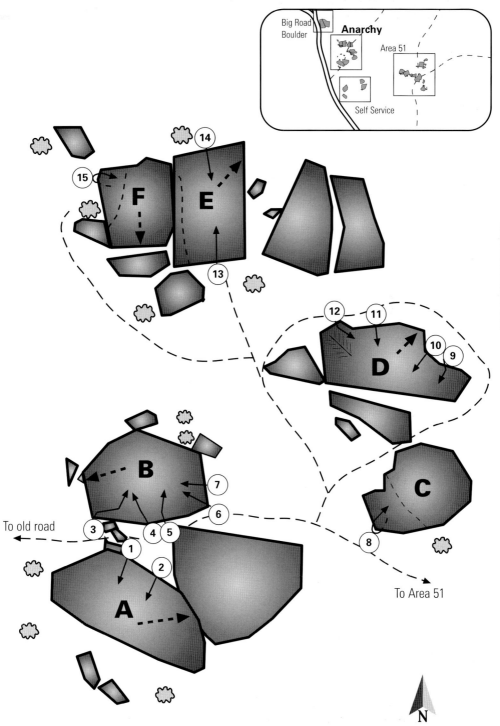

Joe's Valley

Big Road Boulder ▼ New Joe's

144

The Big Road Boulder is a large black boulder lying just off the right side of the old mining road. Although somewhat chossy looking, many good problems can be found on all sides of this boulder, and a hard project or two as well. Locate this boulder by walking up the mining road to the obvious black boulder on the right (east) side of the road.

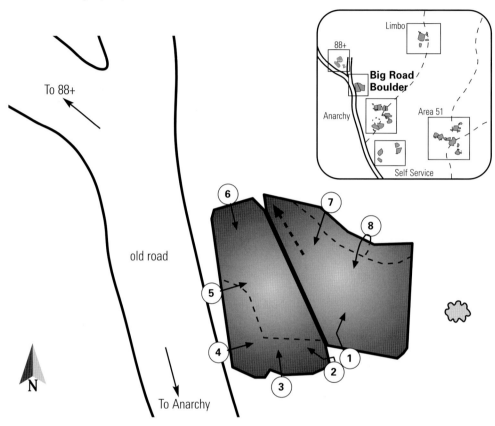

1. V1
Start in the crack. Climb the face to the right.

2. Mad Man V3 ★
Begin just left of the crack. Climb the rounded lip up and left.

3. Poopy V1
Start in the jug seven feet up. Make one silly move into the groove.

4. High V3 ★★
Sit start right hand on a blocky edge four and a half feet up and left hand on a positive side pull. Climb up into a sandy mantle.

5. On the Road Again V2 ★★
Begin five feet left of #4. Climb the tan rock. Better than it looks.

6. V0 ★
Climb the slabby face right of the crack.

7. V3 ★★
Sit start five feet left of the crack, mantle onto the slabby face then straight up.

8. Dark Hole V2 ★★
Sit start with both hands on big holds at the lip. Mantle into the scoop.

Wolverine Publishing   www.wolverinepublishing.com

88+

New Joe's

To reach the 88+ boulders continue up the mining road past the Big Road Boulder. After walking up the road for a few feet, you will come to a fork. The 88+ boulders are located between the two forks. Another boulder with numerous V0s (not shown on the topo) is located east of the 88+ boulders by the right fork in the road.

1. Not so Hot V2
Not so hot ... and not so good. Climb the arête.

2. Contact V6 ★★★
There are many different ways to do this problem. The best is to begin on the slopey knob left of the crack. Climb the out the slopers and crimpy face avoiding the crack and everything right of it. Using the crack and features to the right, which even yields a no-hands kneebar, makes the problem significantly easier.

3. V4 ★
Climb straight out the scoop to the right of the crack. Hard top out. Bad landing.

4. Crusty V4 ★★
Sit start on a positive knob four and a half feet up. Climb the face and left arête.

5. Attention V6 ★
Start standing with a left-facing sidepull. Move right to the corner. Scary top out. Bad landing.

6. Project

7. V3 ★
Sit start with both hands on the left-facing flake. Surmount the bulge.

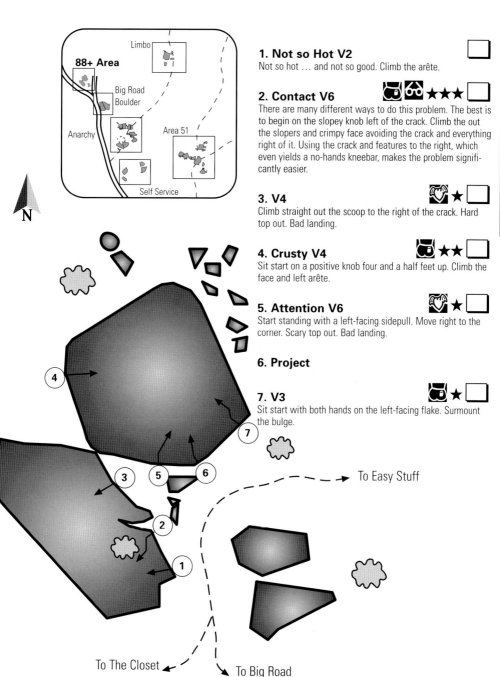

Joe's Valley

The Closet — New Joe's

With 11 great problems, from V0 to V5, The Closet is a great place to warm-up, finish off the day, or just send some classic problems on perfect rock. Most of the climbs here have good landings, and on cold blustery days, the area is often sheltered from the wind. Locate The Closet by continuing up the mining road, past the 88+ Boulders, looking for a cluster of boulders on the right (north) side of the road. The entrance to the Closet is in a faint drainage, and is obscured by trees.

A. Desperate Boulder ➤
The Desperate boulder is the first boulder at the Closet; it is located just off the mining road with the west face in the trees.

1. V1
Climb the face and blunt corner up and left. Bad landing.

2. Roll the Dice V5
Climb straight up the dimpled face. Ultra technical and a little spooky. Bad landing.

3. Desperate V2
Climb the arête and left face. Great climbing up superb rock. Bad landing if you fall leftwards.

B. Bad Genes Boulder ➤
Duck through the trees past the Desperate Boulder and you'll see the beautiful Bad Genes boulder. Killer features criss-cross the overhanging south face offering the best climbing at the Closet.

4. Bad Genes V3
Sit start with both hands on the good hold four feet up. Climb straight up and mantel.

5. Pimpin' Jeans V4
Totally classic. Same start as #4, but climb up and left on perfect rock.

6. V2
Start on a right-facing jug, move left to jugs around the corner, and finish on the corner.

C. The Rainbow Boulder ➤
Located just west of the Bad Genes Boulder, the Rainbow Boulder offers a couple of good problems on its multi-colored south face. Look for two boulders that form a small alcove. The Rainbow Boulder is the northern boulder.

7. Sunshine V2 on a Rainy Day
Sit start on a pointy flake three feet up. Climb the face where the black and tan rocks meet.

8. Reading Rainbow V5
Begin four feet left of #7 in two very shallow dishes; make a hard stab to another dish on the face and punch for the lip.

D. The Sphere Boulder ➤
The Rainbow Boulder's southern neighbor is a fine piece of stone with several good easy slab climbs.

9. V1
Start with both hands in the big undercling flake. Climb straight up the face.

10. V1
Step onto the slabby face and work your way to the right-facing flake.

11. Sphere V0
Layback the arête in the right side.

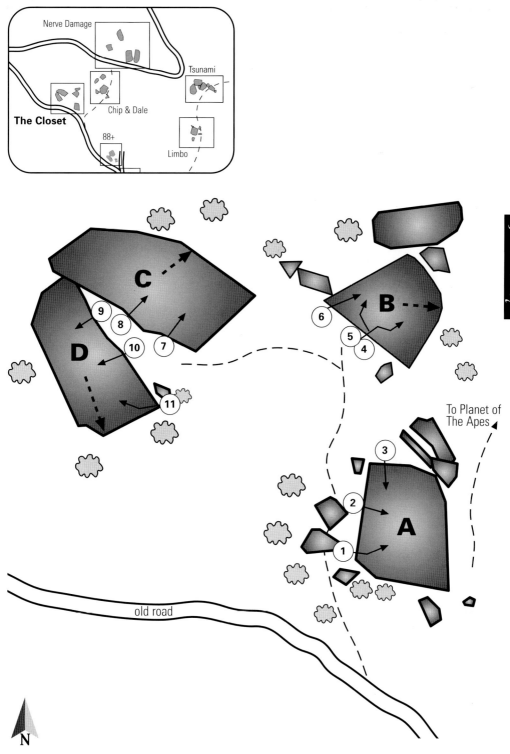

Chip & Dale

New Joe's

The Chip and Dale Area is comprised of two boulders, and offers several great problems ranging from V4 to V7. Many more boulders are scattered around the area and could perhaps yield more climbs, although of lesser quality. To locate the Chip and Dale Area walk up the mining road. Just before you reach The Closet, look for a faint trail heading north off the right side of the mining road. Follow this trail for about a 100 feet to the large boulder with an obvious overhanging southeast face.

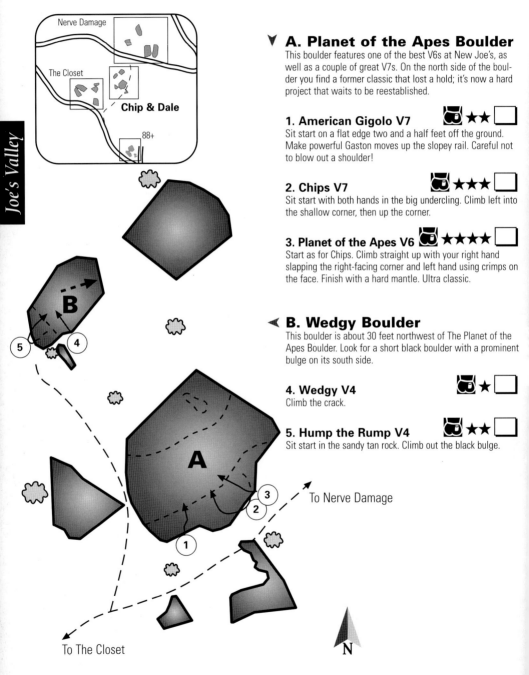

▼ A. Planet of the Apes Boulder
This boulder features one of the best V6s at New Joe's, as well as a couple of great V7s. On the north side of the boulder you find a former classic that lost a hold; it's now a hard project that waits to be reestablished.

1. American Gigolo V7 ★★
Sit start on a flat edge two and a half feet off the ground. Make powerful Gaston moves up the slopey rail. Careful not to blow out a shoulder!

2. Chips V7 ★★★
Sit start with both hands in the big undercling. Climb left into the shallow corner, then up the corner.

3. Planet of the Apes V6 ★★★★
Start as for Chips. Climb straight up with your right hand slapping the right-facing corner and left hand using crimps on the face. Finish with a hard mantle. Ultra classic.

◄ B. Wedgy Boulder
This boulder is about 30 feet northwest of The Planet of the Apes Boulder. Look for a short black boulder with a prominent bulge on its south side.

4. Wedgy V4 ★
Climb the crack.

5. Hump the Rump V4 ★★
Sit start in the sandy tan rock. Climb out the black bulge.

Joe's Valley

Not New Joe's!
Chris Grijalva fishing for holds on the classic *Angler* (V2), Riverside Area, page 88.
Photo: Dave Pegg

Nerve Damage ▼   New Joe's

Nerve Damage is yet another classic Joe's Valley area. Tall and intimidating, it offers superb and committing bouldering high above the valley floor. Facing south, the area gets sun all day. Due to its exposure, it can be windy. The Nerve Damage boulder is located literally inches off the old mining road. Walk up the mining road until you come to a switchback shortly after passing the Closet. After the switchback, the road heads east. Two large boulders (C & D) loom over the left (north) side of the road. The Nerve Damage area can also be approached by thrashing up the scree from the Chip and Dale area.

A. Boulder ➤
A large black boulder with numerous projects on its gently overhanging dimpled faces, and a couple of moderate climbs on its heavily featured, although chossy, slabby ones. The boulder is about 60 feet west of the main area, set back in the trees, north of the road.

1. V1
Begin on the rock at the base of the boulder. Climb the south face.

2. V4
Start in the undercling flake, move onto the corner, then make a scary and committing dyno. Bad landing.

B. Peach Schnapps Boulder ➤
Another boulder with some hard projects and a couple of moderates. Locate this boulder by walking north from the main area for about 60 feet.

3. Peach Schnapps V3
Start left of the arête. Follow ramps to shallow pockets. Bad landing.

4. Hot Toddie V1 ★★
Climb the arête on the right side.

C. Nerve Damage Boulder ➤
The Nerve Damage Boulder has the best and the biggest concentration of climbs at the area, including one of the best — and most photographed highballs — in the state. Easily identified by the beautiful face looming above the road, the Nerve Damage boulder is well worth the hike.

5. V0 ★★
Climb the slabby face.

6. Chichenish V1 ★★
Climb the face with your left hand on the corner.

7. V2 ★★★
Begin at the left edge of the cave. Climb the face up great rock.

8. Sex Machine V8
Horizontal climbing out a huecoed roof make this an unusual climb for Joe's. Sit start in deep pockets at the back of the cave. Climb out the roof and onto the face.

8a. Variation V3 ★★
Start in the hueco at the lip.

9. Thriller V1
Begin on the right side of the big white flake. Traverse the flake to its end, then up the face where the black and tan rock meet.

10. Nerve Damage V6
Ultra classic, one of the best highballs in the state. Begin in horizontal cracks. Follow pockets out left to the prow, pull the crux at 18 feet ... and mantel.

11. The Dude V5
Sit start in sandy side pulls four feet up. Climb up good holds, then move left round the corner and into a short crack.

12. The Big Lebowski V3
Same start as # 11, but keep moving right.

D. Sherpa Boulder ➤
The large boulder just east of Nerve Damage boulder has one scary, hard highball on its south face, as well as several other potential highballs on its west face.

13. Sherpa's Pie V7
Climb the intimidating, overhung face above the road.

Wolverine Publishing   www.wolverinepublishing.com

151

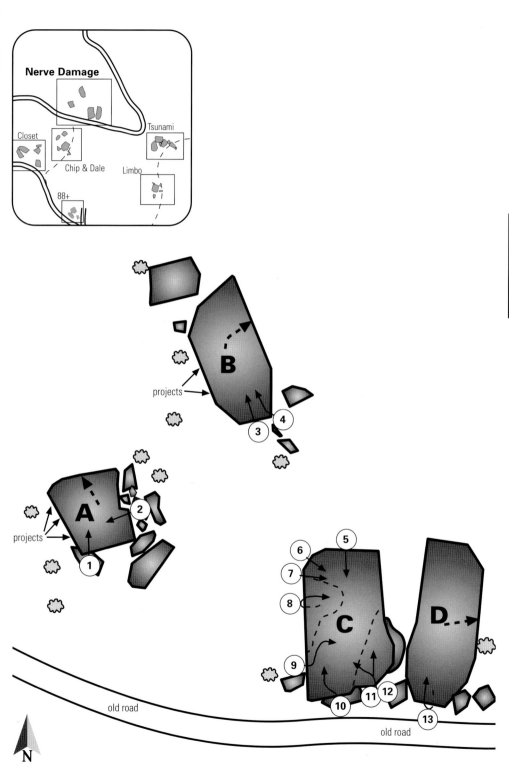

Joe's Valley

Limbo & Tsunami ▼ New Joe's

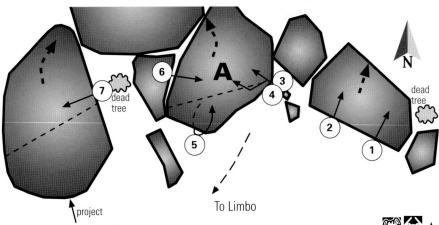

To Limbo

A. Tsunami Area ▲

The Tsunami Area is tucked away amongst the trees in the middle of New Joe's. However, in this case, the middle is not easy to find, as all the trails seem to go around this little gem. The best way to approach the Tsunami area is to follow directions to the Limbo Boulder. From the Limbo boulder, continue north to an obvious boulder shaped like a cresting wave with a tan underbelly and a black top. You can find this area in several other ways, including walking due east from the Cube Boulder.

1. Don't Leave Thirsty V1 ★★★
Climb the line of jugs up a tan streak on the well-featured south face.

2. Cherry Coke V1 ★★★
Climb the black face six feet left of #1.

The following problems are on the breaking-wave boulder that forms the centerpiece of the Tsunami Area.

3. Sex Thing V1 ★
Climb jugs on the arête. Bad landing.

4. Snook V4 ★
Same start as #3, but move left to the pod on the face, get a heel hook, match, control the swing and top out. Bad landing.

5. I'd Rather V6  ★★★★
Be Climbing Her
Start on holds five feet up. Climb out left to the jug; get the two-finger pocket with the left hand and finish up the black face.

5a. Variation V7  ★★★
Same as #5, but get the pocket with the right hand.

6. V2 ★
Start in a jug six feet up. Climb into the scoop.

The large boulder at the east end of the tsunami area has one good V0 and perhaps a project or two in the cave at the south side of the boulder.

7. V0 ★★
Climb the slab in front of the dead tree. Bad landing.

To Tsunami ▲

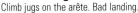
To Anarchy

◀ **B. Limbo Boulder**

The Limbo Boulder offers a couple of decent problems, and although the rock is less than perfect, it is good enough to pay a visit on your way to or from the Tsunami area. Difficult to find, The Limbo Boulder is just that, in limbo, without any close neighbors, or obvious landmarks. The best way to locate this boulder is by walking due north from the Anarchy Area; look for a medium-sized boulder surrounded by trees. The climbs are located on the east face. If you reach the Tsunami area, or the road, you have gone to far.

1. Cactus V1
Sharp as a cactus and rather chossy. Climb the arête and face.

2. Tanks V2 ★★
Sit start on some edges four and a half feet up. Climb the center of the face. A little sharp, but otherwise, quite good.

The Cube

New Joe's

Although large and impressive looking from a distance, the Cube Boulder offers a disappointingly limited amount of climbing. To locate this boulder, walk north (uphill) from Area 51, for several hundred feet. Look for a large boulder with a tall black south face and a deep cave on its north side.

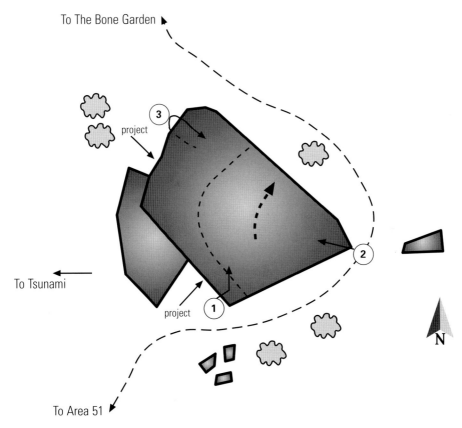

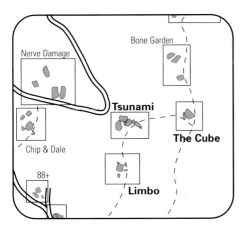

1. Johnny Copper V7
Start in a slanting crack just left of the arête. Climb up more cracks on the left face and pull the airy topout.

2. The Cube Arête V2
Sit start. Climb the arête on the left side. Kind of fun until the rock gets bad. Best to top out on the right face at the second horizontal seam.

3. Pitbull V6
Sit start down in the cave, matched in an undercling. Climb out the cave to the left and mantel.

Joe's Valley

Bone Garden ▼ New Joe's

Located north (uphill) from The Cube, the Bone Garden is another small area. One of the problems here is a classic V6 that should not be missed. Most of the climbs face south, making this a good venue on cold days.

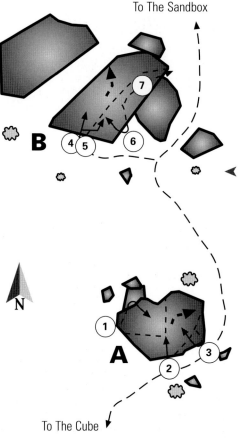

▼ **A. The Jenny Boulder**
The Jenny Boulder is the first boulder you arrive at as you approach from The Cube. It is a small boulder with a golden south face. Although short and a little sandy, several OK problems can be found here.

1. V1
Sit start matched in jug crack. Climb the crack left and pull the bulge. Bad landing.

2. The Example V1 ★★
Climb the short golden face.

3. Shorty's Revenge V2
Sit start matched in the right-slanting crack; pull the bulge onto the nasty crumbling top out.

◀ **B. The Bone Garden Boulder**
Named for the many animal bones strewn around the area of the massive rodent's nest, the Bone Garden boulder has the best bouldering in the area. This boulder is located about 40 feet north of the Jenny boulder.

4. Bowtie V2 ★
Climb the center of the face.

5. Life Ender V5
Same start as #4 but move right to the crack/seam and follow it to the arête. A little tall, but not as bad as the name might imply.

6. Roll the Bones V6 ★★★★
Another amazing V6. Sit start in jugs right of the arête. Climb pockets on the overhanging black face up and left onto the arête. Finish on the arête.

7. Worm Hole V6
Same start as #6. Climb right, through the tunnel on rat-shit coated holds, step off some where in the vicinity of the rodent nest. Might be a good way to catch Hanta virus.

The Sandbox ▼   New Joe's

Despite the long walk uphill, the Sand Box is a quality area with good climbs at all grades. The area can be reached two ways. First, and perhaps easiest, is to stay on the old mining road to the fourth switch back. The B boulder of the Sand Box is located just south of the fourth switch back. Alternatively, the Sand Box can be reached by walking north from the Bone Garden. This way is shorter, but it makes finding the Sand Box a little more difficult.

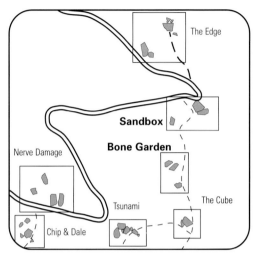

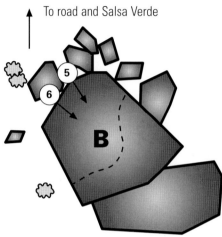

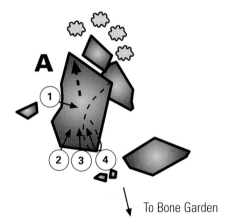

3. Wills V4
Climb the middle of the south face. Bad landing.

4. Playtime is Over V9 ★★★
Sit start in the wide crack under the roof. Climb out the roof moving left to the lip, mantel and finish on the tall slab.
Variation: V4 ★★ Start standing at the lip.

A. Playtime Boulder ▲
The Playtime boulder is the southern-most boulder at the Sand Box. It offers several okay problems, and one good V9. The climbs face south and are exposed on the hillside, making this a good place on cold days, although it can be windy.

1. John Tesch is a Smurf V2 ★

Climb pockets and edges up and left on the west face.

2. Sandy Choss V2
Climb the arête.

B. The B Boulder ▲
The B boulder is a large boulder located just south of the mining road. Two good V0s on the north face are worth checking out, and perhaps others await discovery.

5. B Sides V0 ★★★
Start between two rocks at the base. Climb killer jugs up the black bulge.

6. Miss B V0 ★★
Climb the face four feet right of #5.

Joe's Valley

The Tower ▼   New Joe's

The Tower, like many other areas at Joe's, has a large number of boulders, but most are small, and only a few have good climbs on them. Locate the Tower by walking north and a little east from the oil well. This area can also be reached by walking east from Area 51, over the small ridge.

Joe's Valley

A. The Tower Boulder ▶
This boulder is the main attraction of the area. Good moderate climbs scale all sides, including one super-classic V4, Fuchsia. Easily identifiable, the Tower Boulder stands alone and is the tallest boulder in the area.

1. Orange Flakes V1 ★★★
Climb up the orange rock. A little dirty low, but improves higher up. Bad landing.

2. Stellar V2 ★★
Climb straight up where the orange and black rock meet.

3. What is This? V3 ★★★
Start matched in a sandy hueco five and a half feet up. Climb left onto the prow. Suspect edges on top.

4. Fuchsia V4  ★★★★
Sit start in two good pockets. Climb straight up beautiful rock using the corner with your left hand. Totally classic.

5. V2 ★★
Sit start using sandy holds. Climb the corner and left face.

6. V2 ★★★
Sit start four feet left of #5. Climb straight up the face, joining the down climb at the top.

7. Tower Down Climb V0 ★★★
This is the best way to get off the boulder. It also makes a great way to get up. Start at the left end of the face. Climb up until your hands are in the jugs at the bottom of the scoop. Take the jugs up and right to the top.

8. V1 ★
Climb the small dihedral.

9. V4 ★★
Sit start matched on a flat edge four and a half feet up. Move your right hand to a pocket on the face and start slapping with the left.

B. Boulder ▶
This small boulder is located about 20 yards northeast of the Tower Boulder. One short problem climbs out its black roof.

10. V6 ★
Sit start with a right-facing edge under the roof; make a stout move to the lip and mantel.

C. The Juniper Boulder ▶
The Juniper Boulder is located about 60 yards north of the Tower Boulder. Three good climbs ascend its south and east faces.

11. Juniper V5 ★★★
Start with right hand in slopey sidepull and left hand in the lowest pocket. Climb up the bulge. Good climbing on sharp rock.

12. Mud V2 ★
Sit start matched in a tan colored dish. Climb up and right. Some of the grips are a little crispy.

13. V0 ★★
Climb the slab up the south face.

D. The Island Boulder ▶
The Island Boulder is a small black and tan boulder lying at the bottom of a small drainage. The climbs face south, and can be reached by walking northwest from the Tower Boulder. Enter a small wash, and follow it for about fifty yards. Look for an obvious boulder on the west side of the wash.

14. Good Energy V3 ★
Begin with your left hand in a two-finger pocket six feet up, right hand on whatever. Climb the face. Seems best to move right to top out.

15. Calcite V3 ★★
Climb the vertical right-facing edge.

16. Down Shift V8? ★★
Perhaps something has broken off this recently, as it seems harder than its reported grade of V7. Climb the crimpy face right of the tan streak.

17. Nectarine V2 ★★
Begin just right of the hole at the base of the boulder. Climb the tall slab.

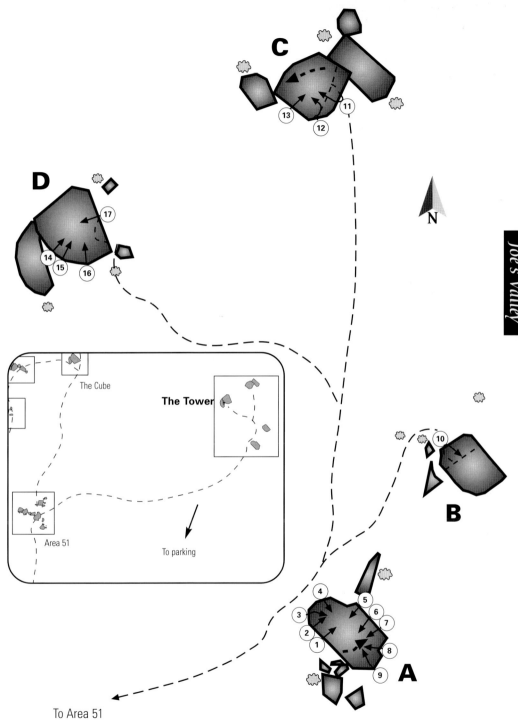

The Edge

New Joe's

Getting to The Edge requires a long uphill trek, but the rewards — panoramic views, good climbing, and an isolated, wild feel — are worth it. Although The Edge is the furthest area at New Joe's, it's quite easy to find. Walk up the old mining past the fourth switchback, look for an obvious black boulder on the north side of the road; this is the Salsa Verde Boulder. You can also reach this area by walking due north from Area 51, intersecting the mining road just past the Sand Box.

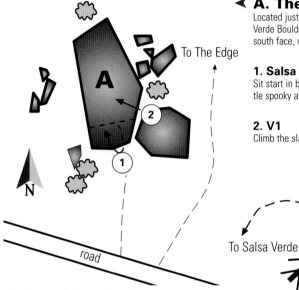

◄ A. The Salsa Verde Boulder
Located just off the north side of the mining road, the Salsa Verde Boulder is easily identified by it's black overhanging south face, which has a very good V4.

1. Salsa Verde V4 ★★★★
Sit start in big holds, climb the overhanging south face. A little spooky at the top.

2. V1
Climb the slab on the east face, between two bushes.

B. The Edge Boulder ►
This lone boulder is located about 30 yards uphill (north) from the Salsa Verde Boulder and has several good moderate problems on great rock.

3. Panic Waves V4
This problem ascends the south face over the worst possible landing. Poor rock quality makes this problem even more intimidating.

4. The Edge V2 ★★★
Climb the arête on the left side. The crux comes at the top.

5. The Edge Right V1 ★★
Climb the arête on the right side.

6. Smear Test V2 ★★★
Start between the two rocks at the base. Friction up the slab on perfect rock.

7. Down Climb V0 ★★
Climb up or down the right side of the north face.

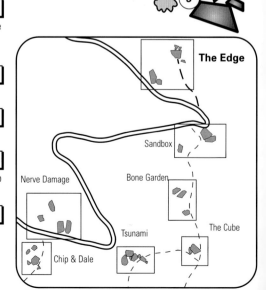

Wolverine Publishing — www.wolverinepublishing.com

The Picnic Area ▼   New Joe's

Located at the bottom of a wash on the banks of a lazy stream, the Picnic Area is a good place to chill and escape the crowds. Although technically part of New Joe's, the Picnic area has its own parking area, separate from the main parking. To locate this area continue along Highway 57 past the main New Joe's turn off for about one mile. Park in a pullout on the right (northeast) side of the road just beyond a "Do Not Pass" sign. From the parking area, follow cairns for several hundred feet northeast and descend into the large wash. The boulders lie next to the stream and the problems face the parking.

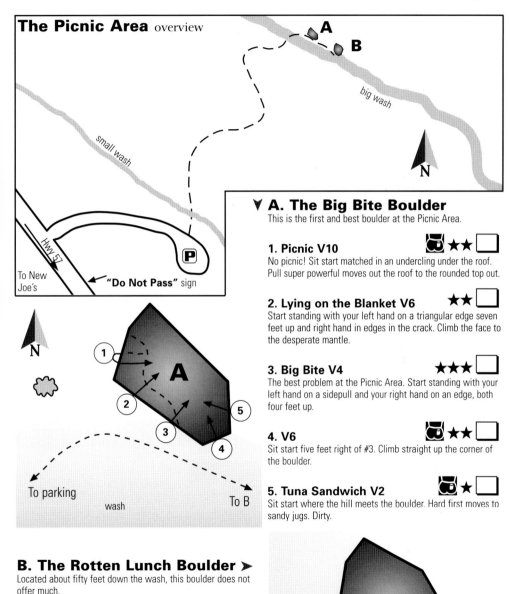

▼ A. The Big Bite Boulder
This is the first and best boulder at the Picnic Area.

1. Picnic V10 ★★
No picnic! Sit start matched in an undercling under the roof. Pull super powerful moves out the roof to the rounded top out.

2. Lying on the Blanket V6 ★★
Start standing with your left hand on a triangular edge seven feet up and right hand in edges in the crack. Climb the face to the desperate mantle.

3. Big Bite V4 ★★★
The best problem at the Picnic Area. Start standing with your left hand on a sidepull and your right hand on an edge, both four feet up.

4. V6 ★★
Sit start five feet right of #3. Climb straight up the corner of the boulder.

5. Tuna Sandwich V2 ★
Sit start where the hill meets the boulder. Hard first moves to sandy jugs. Dirty.

B. The Rotten Lunch Boulder ▶
Located about fifty feet down the wash, this boulder does not offer much.

6. Rotten Lunch V2 ★
Climb the sandy jugs in the middle of the boulder.

Joe's Valley

Don't let the night end your day.

ZIPKA

ZIPKA Tiny, lightweight, incredible burn time (150+ hours). For alpine starts or putting the wraps on a day of bouldering—stretch your day into night.

for a dealer near you
www.petzl.com or 801-926-1500

Photo: Olivier Anoourcheux

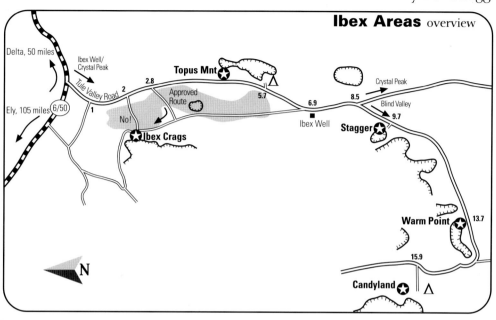

Ibex Areas overview

INTRODUCTION

Ibex is huge. If it were close to Salt Lake City, or anywhere for that matter, it would likely be the biggest bouldering area in Utah. Imagine a tract of land several times the size of Hueco Tanks on which every hillside is dotted with brown, orange, and white quartzite blocks. Summing up the potential in an article for *Rock & Ice* magazine, Ibex activist the late Michael Mott wrote: "This place is sick, unlimited ... Like you could swim around forever and still find stuff."

Unfortunately, or fortunately, depending on your viewpoint, Ibex lies in the remote western Utah desert. Even for the closest locals getting there involves driving for at least two and a half hours. Perhaps that's why most visitors get no further than Ibex Crags, the closest area to the highway and the one with the greatest concentration of problems. This leaves the rest of this vast area virtually untouched. Perfect for those seeking a wilderness bouldering experience/ vision quest. In keeping with the adventurous nature of the climbing at Ibex, only the most popular areas — Ibex Crags, Topus Mountain, and the Stagger Boulder — are described in detail here. On page 179 you'll find overviews of Warm Point and Candyland, two other Ibex areas that are good starting points for further exploration.

Another distinctive feature of Ibex is the rock. The boulders are made of quartzite, some of the hardest and most solid stone on the planet. It's difficult to image a more unbreakable hold than a fused quartzite crimp. The downside of quartzite is its poor friction. The aforementioned crimp may be harder to hold than a greased piglet — especially if you try to grab it on a hot day in the sun. Expect every problem to be a couple of grades harder than it looks!

GETTING THERE

Ibex is located in the western Utah desert, just south of Highway 6/50, about 50 miles west of Delta, Utah, and 105 miles east of Ely, Nevada.

From Delta: Drive west on Highway 6/50. After about 48 miles the road will pass through a road cut and start to go downhill. At the bottom of the hill, just before mile marker 39, take a left on a dirt road signed "Ibex Well and Crystal Peak." Zero your odometer here.

Shane Carignan at sundown on *Way Cows* (V2), page 164. Photo Dave Pegg

To reach the Ibex Crags, drive south from Route 6/50 on the dirt road (Tule Valley Road). After 2.1 miles, when you're directly opposite the big cliffs on the other side of the dry lake bed, you'll see a rough road on the right that leads directly across the lake bed towards them. Please do not use this road — it is heavily rutted and encroaching on vegetation as people try to avoid the ruts. Instead continue to another dirt road on the right at the 2.8-mile mark. Take this and continue west across the lake bed to a dirt road on the far side. Follow this back north to the big cliffs. The boulders at the base of the cliffs comprise the Ibex Crags area.

To reach the other areas continue south on Tule Valley Road. For details see the area descriptions in the following pages.

From Ely: Drive east on Highway 6/50 for about 105 miles. Turn right onto a dirt road at the *second* sign that says "Ibex Well and Crystal Peak," which is located just after mile maker 39. (Before reaching this turn off you'll pass another sign for "Ibex Well and Crystal Peak" and one for "Blind Valley.") This dirt road is Tule Valley Road. From here follow the directions above.

SEASON

October through April. Although Ibex is often touted as a winter area, the popular Ibex Crags area goes into the shade in the early afternoon in winter and can be extremely cold. If you're stymied by the temps, try Topus Mountain, Warm Point, and Candyland, which get better afternoon sun.

ACCESS

The desert ecosystem is fragile. Pack everything in and pack it out. Bring your own firewood. Drive only on existing roads and walk on existing trails. Don't disturb plants and wildlife.

CAMPING

The best and most sheltered camping spots are at Topus Mountain and Candyland. You can camp on the dry lake bed at Ibex Crags (this can be one of the windiest places on earth so anchor your tent well) but please don't camp among the boulders themselves.

DESERT SURVIVAL

You'll need to bring all the food — and water — you need for your trip. Make sure you have enough gas (the nearest services are 45 miles east on the outskirts of Delta) and that your car is in good shape; it would be a bummer to break down way the hell back in there at Candyland. Although the roads described here are usually good enough for two-wheel drive vehicles, it's a good idea to carrying a shovel in case you need to dig yourself out. Delta has the nearest grocery stores and motels.

The best of IBEX

V0
- [ ] Bovinity ★★★ *page 164*
- [ ] Tub Thumper ★★★ *page 172*
- [ ] Belly Slaps ★★★ *page 172*
- [ ] Scary Monsters ★★★ *page 173*
- [ ] 25-Foot Ronald ★★★★ *page 176*

V1
- [ ] Defused ★★★ *page 170*
- [ ] Andre The Giant ★★★ *page 176*
- [ ] The Hamster ★★★ *page 179*
- [ ] Way Cows ★★★★ *page 164*

V2
- [ ] Right Bouncer ★★★ *page 166*
- [ ] Stagger Slab ★★★ *page 178*
- [ ] Weigh Cattle ★★★★ *page 164*

V3
- [ ] Captain Choss ★★★ *page 168*
- [ ] Warm-Up Traverse ★★★ *page 172*

V4
- [ ] Super Creeps ★★★ *page 173*

V5
- [ ] Left Bouncer ★★★ *page 166*
- [ ] The Blob ★★★ *page 172*
- [ ] Mouse-cateers ★★★ *page 179*
- [ ] Topus Right ★★★★ *page 176*

V6
- [ ] Butt Mantel ★★★ *page 166*
- [ ] Tranced Out and Dreaming ★★★ *page 174*
- [ ] Topus Left ★★★ *page 176*
- [ ] Auganile ★★★★ *page 179*

V7
- [ ] The Thing ★★★ *page 172*
- [ ] Stagger and Lurch ★★★ *page 178*
- [ ] The God Nodule ★★★ *page 179*
- [ ] Blue Flowers ★★★★ *page 166*
- [ ] Ju ★★★★ *page 166*
- [ ] Bigger Is Better ★★★★ *page 172*
- [ ] Red M&M's ★★★★ *page 179*

V8
- [ ] Jesus ★★★ *page 179*
- [ ] Big Gulp ★★★★ *page 166*
- [ ] White Arete ★★★★ *page 172*
- [ ] Bigger is Better sit start ★★★★ *page 172*
- [ ] Meat and Potatoes ★★★★ *page 172*

V9
- [ ] The Bomb ★★★ *page 170*
- [ ] #60 Ibex Crags ★★★ *page 172*
- [ ] Mouse on Mars ★★★ *page 179*
- [ ] White Arete sit start ★★★★ *page 172*
- [ ] Tic Tac Toe ★★★★ *page 176*

V10
- [ ] Atomic Bomb ★★★ *page 170*
- [ ] Bruce Lee ★★★★ *page 166*

V13
- [ ] Bruce Lee Center ★★★★ *page 166*

Ibex Crags

This is the best area at Ibex, with the highest concentration of quality problems. The boulders lie at the base of the tall cliffs visible from Route 6/50. If you're new to Ibex, or your time is limited, the Ibex Crags should be the first stop on your tour. (For approach, camping, and climate information, see page 161.)

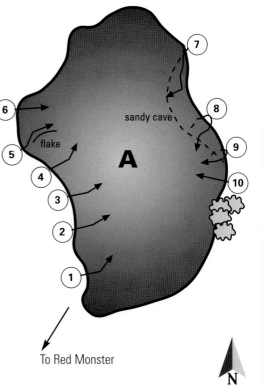

A. Way Cows Boulder ➤

This squat, rounded boulder sits on the shore of the dry lake at the north end of the Main Area. From a distance it looks a bit like a giant lump of cow dung. But the shitty appearance is deceptive. The west face of the Way Cows Boulder is a great place to warm-up, with the best moderate (V0-V2) problems at the Main Area, including the must-do classics *Way Cows* and *Weigh Cattle*.

1. Bovinity V0 ★★★
Start in a cave at the right side of the west face. Bridge up and pull leftwards around the lip.

2. Way Cows V1 ★★★★
Start in huecos six feet left of #1. Pull through the bulge using an undercling.

3. Weigh Cattle V2 ★★★★
The classic central line of the west face. Start in some sloping "huecos," stretch up to a long thin crimp, and finish slightly leftwards around the bulge.

4. V1 ★★
Start six feet left of Way Cows Left and pull through the bulge.

5. V0 ★
The layback flake just left of #4.

6. V0 ★
Start at the left end of the west face with your right hand in a good sidepull five feet off the ground. Climb the chocolate-colored slab.

The next four problems are on the fringes of the scooped-out east face of the Way Cows Boulder (facing the dry lake bed).

7. V3
Hand traverse the right bounding lip of the friable cave as far as you dare.

8. V0+ ★
Start in the back of the cave and climb up and left on sometimes friable jugs, exiting leftwards. Be careful of what you pull on near the top.

9. Ice V5 ★★
Start low, at the left edge of the cave, with your hands in sideways-facing underclings three and four feet off the ground. Surmount the bulging using small sharp crimps and bad feet.

10. V2 ★
The thin dark-brown slab just left of Ice. Harder than it looks.

Wolverine Publishing   www.wolverinepublishing.com

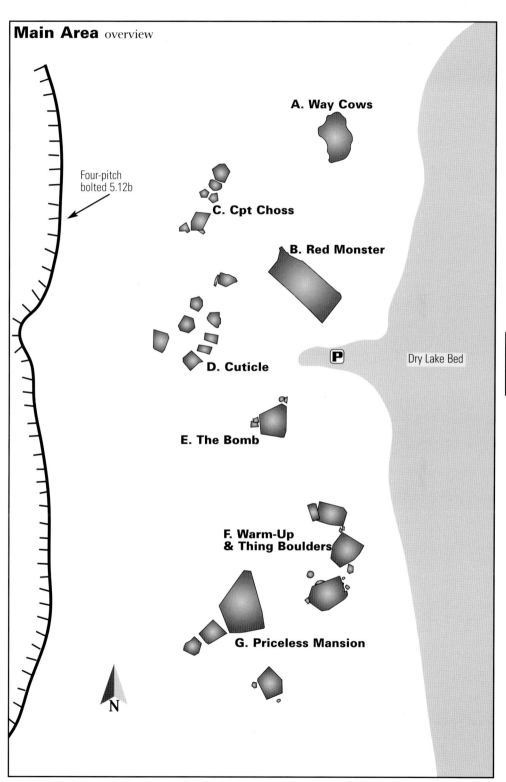

Ibex Crags

B. Red Monster Boulder ▶

The Red Monster's southwest face, an 80-foot-long wave of 30-degree-overhanging stone, has one of the highest concentrations of hard quality bouldering in North America. The main lines on the face — *Right Bouncer, Big Gulp, Bruce Lee, Blue Flowers, Ju, Left Bouncer* — are all classic. There's also lots of scope for hard link-ups, sit starts, and eliminates, some of which are described here. All the problems are tall and many have hard moves turning the lip. Fortunately the ground below the face is flat and sandy; you couldn't ask for a better landing. In spring and fall, the face stays in the shade until about 12:30. It's a good idea to get an early start if the temperatures are warm.

11. Down Climb V0-
The highball south-facing slab. Make sure you can reverse the problem — it's the easiest way down.

12. Right Bouncer V2
The easiest line on the wall, but still no push over. Climb the crack at the right end of the face, using face holds on the right to pull the bulge.

13. Big Gulp V8
Start seven feet left of Right Bounder. A big move gains an obvious pocket. Another big move is required to finish. The **sit start** is **V9**.

14. V12?
Start just left of Big Gulp and climb up and left.

15. Bruce Lee V10
Start with your left hand in a good incut sidepull; you may need a cheater stone to reach this hold. Move up to a good righthand sidepull/pocket and punch leftwards to finish in the runnel/crack. **A V10 variation** takes the pocket with your left hand and finishes rightwards around the bulge. Holds may have broken making this finish harder.

16. Bruce Lee Center V13?
Sit start below the Bruce Lee finishing crack and climb straight up. This project may not have been done. A **V9 variation** starts standing; you may need a cheater stone to reach the first good holds.

17. Bruce Lee Left V9
Start just right of Blue Flowers on a double-toothed edge; you'll probably need a cheater stone to reach this hold. Muckle rightwards to finish up the Bruce Lee crack.

18. Blue Flowers V7
Start above the bush with your left hand in an incut sidepull seven feet up. Short people will need a cheater stone to reach this hold. Climb straight up around the bulge. A **harder variation** traverses into this problem from the start of Ju.

19. Ju V7
(a.k.a Red Monster)
One of the best V7s in Utah. Low in the grade. Start on a huge left-facing jug. Climb the faint depression, moving right at the top past two eye-shaped pockets to an intimidating mantel. A **V10 variation** uses a blocky pinch to pull the finishing bulge direct.

20. Left Bouncer V5
(a.k.a Crack Addict)
Old-school bouldering! Climb the thin crack on fingerlocks, then layback the seam above to highball exit moves. The topout is easier if you stay left.

21. Butt Mantel V6
Start with your hand on the small ledge on the arête. Make a hard mantel and finish rightwards up the face toward the top of Left Bouncer. A **harder variation** climbs into this problem from a sit start at the right side of the roof.

22. Bigger Than Sheep V4
Start around the corner in juggy pockets. Make hard moves to get your feet established above the bulge. Continue up the ultra-highball face or jump off (probably wiser).

23. Good Woman V0
A mini-route. Start just left of Bigger Than Sheep. Climb delicately up and left into a scoop and follow it back rightwards to the top. Be careful of what you pull on near the top — and don't fall off.

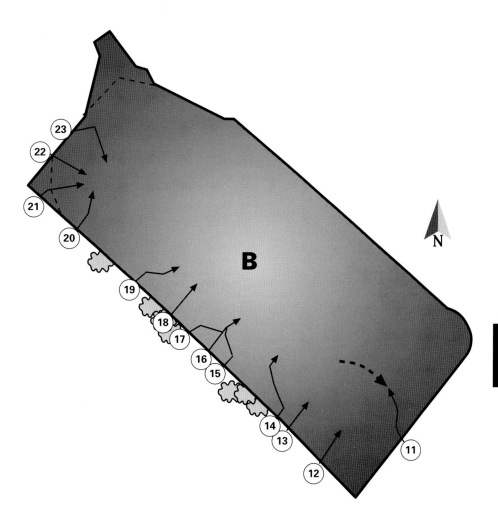

Ibex Crags

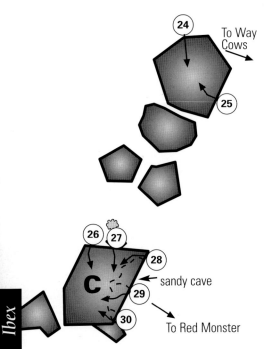

◀ C. Captain Choss Boulders

This group of small boulders is located several yards west (toward the cliff) from Way Cows. The distinctive Captain Choss Boulder looks like something has taken a huge bite out of its east face, leaving a sandy, hollowed-out cave.

24. V0-
The easy blocky north face of the boulder a few yards northeast of Captain Choss.

25. Blocky Dihedral V0 ★
Climb the white blocky dihedral facing Way Cows. Fun but sandy.

The following problems are on The Captain Choss Boulder itself.

26. V0 ★★
Start on good pockety edges on the right side of the north face. Pull into the hanging crack and topout on the left.

27. V0- ★
Step off the boulder and pull leftwards onto the slab.

28. V0- ★
Start on an incut finger jug just right of the hollowed-out face.

29. Captain Choss V3 ★★★
A fun, thuggy problem. Start with a pistol grip and scalloped crimp under the roof in the middle of the sandy, hollowed-out section. Pull through the roof; it's easiest to exit leftwards.

30. Toxic Avenger V1 ★★
Sit start on a big undercling at the left side of the cave. Climb straight up.

D. The Cuticle Boulders ▶

Another group of small boulders spread out between Red Monster and the Main Cliff. The easiest problem to identify is #33, The Cuticle, a small, low square-cut roof facing the Red Monster Boulder.

31. V2 ★
Start with a small, sharp right-hand gaston/crimp at head height and climb the center of the brown diamond-shaped face.

32. V1 ★
The short bulging arête left of #31.

33. The Cuticle V4 ★★
Sit start under the low roof with your right hand in a short crack. Power up the face just left of the crack.

To reach problems #34 and #35 walk west (towards the cliff) from The Cuticle for about 20 yards.

34. V0 ★★
Start sitting at the right end of the face with your hands in a good thread undercling. Pull onto the juggy shelf and up the face above.

35. V0 ★
The shallow crack on the left side of the face.

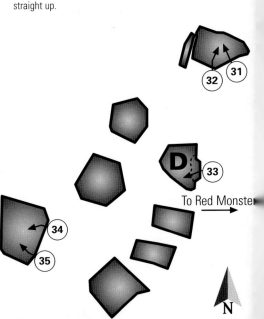

Jerry Gillingham directing traffic while Shane Carignan climbs *Captain Choss* (V3).
Photo: Dave Pegg

Ibex Crags

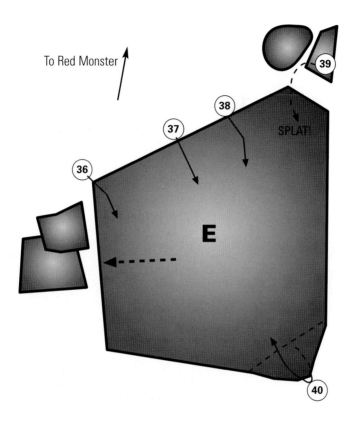

E. The Bomb
The Bomb Boulder is due south of the Red Monster Boulder. Two classic problems, at opposite ends of the difficulty spectrum, scale its bulging north face on immaculate stone.

36. The Bum V1 ★
The arête right of The Bomb topping out on the right. Bad landing.

37. The Bomb V9 ★★★
The classic central line of the bulging north face. Using two small crimpy sidepulls, explode for the sloping top of the boulder. Variation: **Atomic Bomb V10**, start sitting.

38. Defused V1 ★★★
A short, sweet problem on superb stone. Start three feet left of The Bomb with your left hand in a good incut edge. Make a long reach to another good incut and pull over the top.

39. Slap Happy and Stupid  ★★
No grade on this one! Jump from the small adjacent boulder onto The Bomb boulder. Good entertainment when your tips are shredded.

40. Too Small V4 ★
Sit start and climb the short, overhanging finger crack.

Lisa Rands reaching for *Blue Flowers* (V7), page 166.
Photo: Wills Young

Ibex Crags

F. Warm-Up Boulder ➤
This rectangular, flat-topped boulder has some decent lowball problems and the excellent Warm-Up Traverse. Chuck a lap or two on this pumpy problem to get warmed up for the hard classics on the neighboring Thing Boulders.

41. V3
Start crouched awkwardly above the bushes on the left side of the tiny cave with your left hand in a good sidepull three feet off the ground. Climb straight up.

42. Mr. Sit and Spin V3 ★★
Sit start in a good flake at the right side of the tiny cave. Climb straight up on slick, sloping edges.

43. Warm-Up Traverse V3 ★★★
Start at the top of Mr. Sit and Spin and traverse rightwards along the lip. Finishing around the corner. Pumpy.

44. V2
Sit start with both hands in a horizontal crack at the left end of the face, and climb the blind crack. A hidden undercling helps at the start.

45. V4 ★★
Make a crunched sit start in the middle of the face with your left hand in a big, pocketed edge and your right in the lowest diagonal slot. Climb straight up.

46. The Melon V5 ★★
Sit start on two blobs in the back of the roof.

G&H. Thing I, Thing II ➤
Along with the Red Monster, these twin blocks are the proudest boulders at Ibex. Thing I and Thing II bear an uncanny resemblance to each other, with hard testpieces on their overhanging northeast faces and less steep but often intimidating highballs on their flanks. The main faces of both boulders are in the shade from noon onwards — a perfect compliment to the main face of the Red Monster Boulder which bakes in the afternoon sun.

G. Thing I
47. The White Arete V8 ★★★★
Climb the tall right arête on its left side to a committing finish. The **sit start** is **V9**.

48. Project? ★★★★
The seam just left of the arête. Arete is off.

49. The Thing V7 ★★★
Climb the center of the face past a big flat sidepull. Hard to start, especially if you're short. The **sit start** is **V11**.

50. The Blob V5 ★★★
Start with your right hand on a good pinch and your left in a sidepull dish. Climb the face moving right to the same finish as The Thing. Bad landing.

51. V6 ★★
Start low, crimping an edge 3.5 feet off the ground. Climb the left side of the face moving left to topout at the notch on the arête. The **high start** with your left hand in a good sidepull at 7 feet is **V3**. Another **good variation** (**V6** or **V3**, depending on the start) traverses right to the top of The Thing.

Several lines are possible on the slabby south face of Thing I. Only the most obvious have been described.

52. V1 ★★
The slabby left side of the bulging arête.

53. Tub Thumper V0 ★★★
The line of weakness in the right side of the slab.

54. Belly Slaps V0 ★★★
The line of faint dishes just left of center.

55. V3 ★
Between Belly Slaps and the left arête past a sandy white edge at half height.

56. V0
Climb the crest of the slabby left arête.

57. V0 ★★
The crack in the north face of the boulder.

H. Thing II
58. Bigger is Better V7 ★★★★
Climb the left side of the right arête, moving right at the top. The **sit start** is **V8**.

59. Meat and Potatoes V8 ★★★★
Start just left of Bigger is Better and the climb up and left on sloping holds to finish in the middle of the face.

60. V9? ★★★
Step off the boulder and climb the left side of the face on small sharp crimpers.

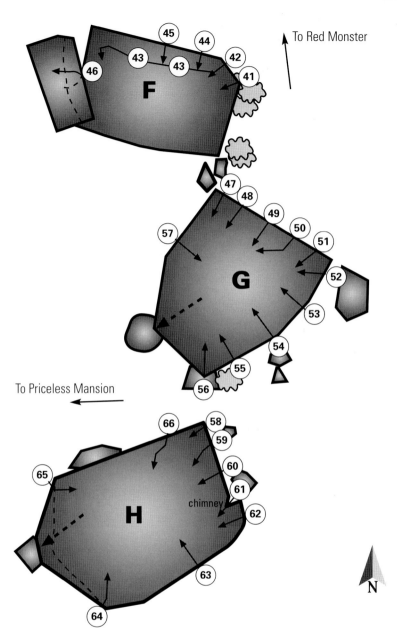

61. For Rectal Use Only V0  ★
The fissure/chimney.

62. Queen Elizabeth V6 ★★
Start on the big jug. Climb the bulging face left of the chimney.

63. Not A Warm-Up V5 ★★
Start in the pocket and climb the gnarly-looking highball face. Several other frightening problems may be possible on this tall face.

64. V0 ★★
Pull into and climb the fissure. A harder sit start is possible.

65. Scary Monsters V0 ★★★
Start on a big jug. Haul your feet around the roof and finish up the tall but easy dihedral on fantastic stone.

66. Super Creeps V4 ★★★
Start on a big flat jug 4 feet off the ground and climb diagonally rightwards up the highball face.

Ibex Crags

Priceless Mansion Group ➤

The Priceless Mansion is the Main Area's biggest boulder. It's massive, looming east face has two 5.13+ crack climbs. Although the Priceless Mansion is too tall for bouldering, several other blocks in the neighborhood have fun problems, especially in the easier V0-V2 grades.

I. Boulder

67. V0+ ★
Climb the right side of the face, tricky at the top.

68. V0 ★
Climb the left-slanting diagonal seam.

J. Boulder

69. Tranced Out and Dreaming V6 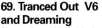 ★★★
Sit start low with a right-hand pinch and left-hand crimp. Climb straight up on cool pinches, then move right on slopers to finish on the arête. The **standing start** is a fun **V2**.

70. V1
The thin crack just left of Tranced Out and Dreaming.

71. Big Job V0 ★★
This problem is 30 yards west of Tranced Out and Dreaming on a boulder leaning against the cliff band. Climb the blocky south face of the boulder.

K. Magic Roundabout

This squat, round flat-topped boulder is 20 yards south of the Priceless Mansion. It has a high concentration of good moderate bouldering.

72. V0 ★
Mantel onto the shelf on the blunt arête facing the Priceless Mansion and topout.

73. Magic Roundabout V1 ★★
A fun little problem. Start matched on good incuts 6 feet up. Pull up right to a sidepull and topout.

74. V0 ★
Climb the thin crack in the blunt arête. A hard sit start is possible but unpleasant.

75. V1 ★
Start on a good incut edge 5 feet up. Rock up onto the slab, reaching for another good incut, and finish straight up.

76. V0 ★
The seam in the blunt arête just right of #75.

77. V1 ★
Climb the scoop on thin crimps. Beware friable holds. Bad landing.

78. V0+ ★★
Start on good incuts 4 feet up and climb the bulging arête.

79. V1  ★★
Sit start. Climb the juggy hollow flake. A fun steep problem.

L. Lone Boulder

As the name suggest, this boulder stands by itself at the south end of the Main Area. The three thuggy problems on its steep south face are worth the short walk. They are described from right to left:

80. V2  ★★
Sit start and climb big sandy jugs out the steepest part of the arête to a tricky topout.

81. V5 ★★
Sit start with your right hand in a pocket and your left on a gaston/crimp. Climb the thin seam.

82. V2 ★★
Sit start. Climb the flake 3 feet left of #81.

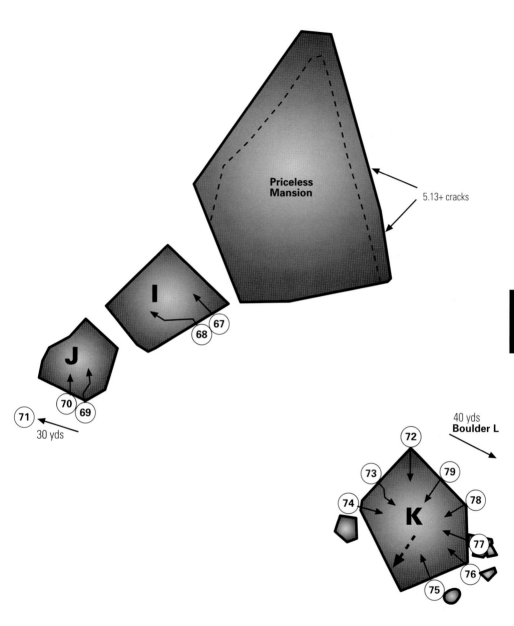

Topus Mountain

Topus Mountain is a rocky mound at the southwest end of the dry lakebed. There's just one heavily developed boulder here, but it has a high concentration of good, often highball problems. *Topus Right* V5, one of the steepest problems at Ibex, and the mini-route *25-Foot Ronald* V0/R alone are worth the five-minute walk.

To reach Topus Mountain drive Tule Valley Road south from Highway 6, ignoring the right turn across the dry lakebed to the Main Area. At 5.7 miles take a left turn onto a short dirt road that leads to the south (far) end of Topus Mountain and an excellent, sheltered campsite nestled into a hollow. Park here, and follow a trail north for five minutes to Topus Boulder, the big block on the northwest side of Topus Mountain.

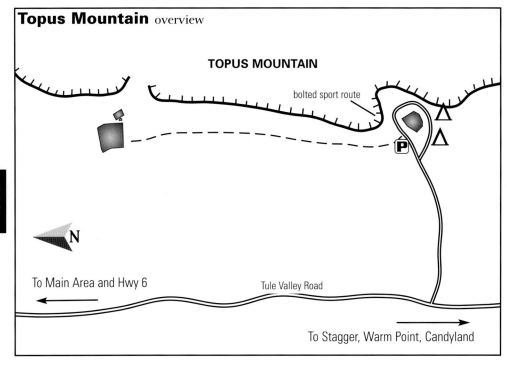

1. 25-Foot Ronald V0
Climb the prominent, blocky, low-angle arête. Not very hard, but so tall that spotters and crash pads are pretty much irrelevant at the top.

2. Andre The Giant V1
The tall right-facing dihedral in the west face.

3. V5?
A scary-looking V5 problem has been reported that starts up #2 and climbs leftwards out the seam to finish on the blunt prow.

4. Topus Right V5
The slick, compact quartzite rock of Ibex doesn't produce many ultra-steep problems. This ship's-prow arête is a notable exception. Start on a huge undercling and make big moves on good holds to a tricky exit. Outstanding!

5. Topus Left V6
Start on two good crimps just left of the arête and follow the seam up and right to the finish of Topus Right or, harder, finish direct. Bad landing.

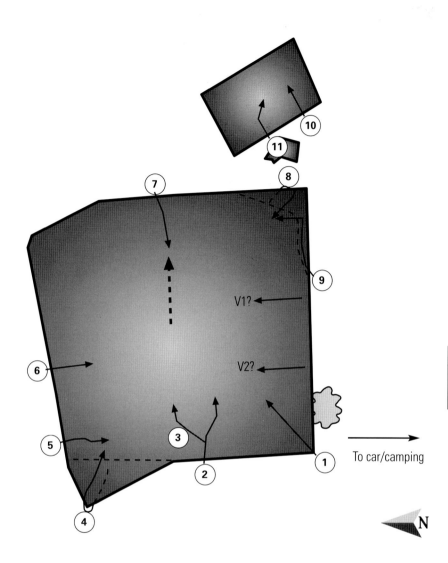

6. Tic Tac Toe V9
Climb the center of the tall, proud, blank-looking north face. Yes, it goes!

7. Down Climb V0-
Make an awkward starting move and climb the center of the tall but easy slab. This is also the easiest way to get down from the boulder.

8. V7
Sit start on a good flake under the roof. Climb out on small crimps to finish on the arête.

9. Grimace V4
Start sitting. Hand traverse and heel hook rightward along the lip to finish on the arête.

Two scary looking problems, V1 & V2, have been reported on the 25-foot tall south-facing slab. We chicken out. Good luck!

The last two problems described here are on a small separate block at the southeast corner of the Topus Boulder.

10. Welcome to Quartzite V0+ ★★
A short fun problem up the right side of the face.

11. V0 ★
Start sitting on a boulder and climb the left side of the face, moving slightly right at the lip to topout.

Stagger Area

Although only a handful of problems are described, the Stagger Boulder has some of the best quality rock at Ibex, and is worth stopping for an hour or two, especially as it's right by the road on your way to Warm Point and Candyland. You'll find more climbing on the boulders just north of the Stagger Boulder, which aren't described here.

To reach the Stagger Boulder drive south on Tule Valley Road, past Topus Mountain, to a fork in the road at 8.5 miles. Take the right fork, signed "Blind Valley," and continue for 1.1 miles until you see a small hill and some boulders on your right. Continue past these boulders for another 100 yards or so to a short dirt track on your right that leads to a big boulder with a staggeringly smooth golden face. This is the Stagger Boulder.

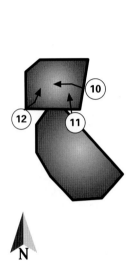
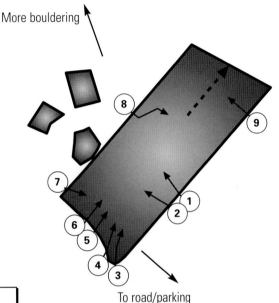

1. Project V?
Start from a sidepull jug in the center of the golden face and climb the diagonal seams up and right.

2. Stagger and Lurch V7 ★★★
Start on the sidepull jug in the center of face and climb up and left.

3. V0 ★★
Climb the left arête.

4. V4 ★
Sit start on a good edge three feet off the ground just left of the arête. Climb the face using small crimps and sloping edges just left of the arête. The arête is off.

5. V1 ★
Climb the crack.

6. V3 ★★
Start crouching with your left hand on a small crimp at 2.5 feet and your right in the lowest hold in the crack. Move left to a bad pinch and finish straight up on good flat face holds finishing over the bulge left of the crack.

7. V0- ★
Climb just left of the arête using a juggy flake.

8. Stagger Slab V2 ★★★
A thin, technical problem on superb stone. Start in the center of the slab and teeter up and leftwards to finish. Several harder variations are possible.

9. V0 ★
Start on a juggy undercling and pull onto the top of the boulder on jugs.

10. V1 ★★
A fun highball up the center of the face.

11. Project V? ★★
Sit start in the gap between the boulders with a good right-hand crimp in a horizontal slot and a left-hand pinch. Climb out the bulge.

12. Stagger and Stem V3 ★
Sit start. Climb the dihedral and face.

Other Ibex Areas

WARM POINT

This area has a good concentration of worthwhile problems, especially in the easier (V0 to V3) grades. It is in an open sunny location and can be warm on winter afternoons when the Ibex Cliffs fall into icy shade. Few problems are classic enough to warrant topos, but you can have a fun-filled day exploring here, and since the boulders are clustered together and close to the road the good stuff isn't hard to find.

Three of the best and hardest problems at Warm Point are on a boulder about 80 yards north of the parking area, identified by a smooth, golden 20-degree-overhanging south face (facing the parking area and road). **Auganile V6** ★★★★ ☐ climbs the center of the face with a hard jump start from a good right-hand tooth to catch a diagonal left-hand edge. **Mouse on Mars V9** ★★★ ☐ climbs the left side of the front arête. **Mouse-cateers V5** ★★★ ☐ climbs a shallow groove in the east face, just right of the Mouse on Mars arête. About 100 yards east of the main group of boulders is another cluster of boulders by a juniper tree. You'll find more fun bouldering here. One standout problem is on the east face of a boulder on the northeast side of the cluster: **The God Nodule V7** ★★★ ☐ starts with a no-hands twin kneebar in a huge undercling and uses small crimps to climb diagonally rightward out the face.

Approach: From Route 6/50, drive south on Tule Valley Road for 8.5 miles to a fork in the road. Take the right fork signed "Blind Valley." Zero your odometer and drive a further 5.2 miles to a big pullout on the right. See location map page 161.

CANDYLAND

This is a good area with around 80 established problems, including some proud highballs. It is also one of the best camping areas at Ibex with several primitive sites in a grove of juniper trees. The boulders are spread out to the north of the campground. The first big one is the Loaf Boulder. This tall block has several highballs, notably the right arête of the south face (facing the campground): **Red M&M's V7** 🎱 ★★★★ ☐. Continue north from here for about 300 yards, staying near the valley floor (don't get suckered up the hillside to your left) and passing the triple-sliced Wonder Bread Boulder, and you'll reach Upper Candyland. This area has a good concentration of bouldering. Its most prominent landmark is the big triangular southeast face of the Pyramid Boulder. Just downhill from here you'll find the bizarre **Hamster V1** 🎱 ★★★ ☐, which starts with a jump for a hole in the capping roof of a boulder and finishes with a desperate squirm for freedom. North of here you'll find a boulder with big white roofs on its east and west faces. **Jesus V8** 🎱 ★★★ ☐ starts sitting and climbs out the right side of the roof on the west (uphill-facing) side of the boulder; the **standing start is V6.**

Approach: From Route 6/50, drive south on Tule Valley Road for 8.5 miles to a fork in the road. Take the right fork signed "Blind Valley." Zero your odometer and drive until the road splits at 5.6 miles. Stay right and continue to a dirt road on the left at the 7.4 mile mark. Take this and drive for a few hundred yards to the camping and parking area. See map on page 161.

Ibex

BIG BEND

By Noah Bigwood

INTRODUCTION

The boulders at Big Bend are somewhat of an anomaly in the desert. They are giant chunks of Wingate sandstone that have tumbled from the cliffs above and found their resting place on the level ground along the outside of a "Big Bend" of the Colorado River. The rock is solid, the landings are mostly flat, and with a backdrop of sandstone walls and towers, the aesthetics of the area are incredible. Throughout the years climbers have been drawn to these boulders for the quality and difficulty of the problems, their easy roadside access, and great winter temperatures. Many of the first ascents at Big Bend were done by such climbers as John Sherman, Chris Jones, and Dan Osman. Yet many of the area's classics have no recorded first ascent, name, or grade, and have remained in obscurity for years. More recently climbers from around the world have visited and left their marks with first ascents, flashes, and as often as not a piece of their egos and some unfinished business. Moab locals like Tom Gilge, Tait Rees, Eric Decaria, and Noah Bigwood have persistently worked on the area's testpieces and have managed to add many difficult new problems. Such new classics as *Hellbelly* V11, *Barracuda* V10, *Scoopula* V10, and the sit start to *Phantom Fighter* V11 have drawn a whole new crowd of bouldering's strongest to test themselves against these improbable lines.

A note on ratings: The grades at Big Bend are notoriously stiff. Expect to work harder for your numbers here than at some other areas in this guide.

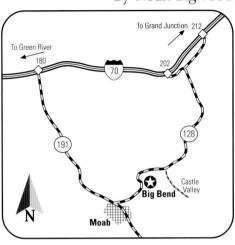

GETTING THERE

From I-70 (Colorado): Take the Cisco exit and follow Highway 128 for approximately 45 miles to the boulders which are on the left side of the road across from the Big Bend campsite.

From I-70 (Green River): Take the Crescent Junction exit and head south on Highway 191 until it crosses the Colorado River then turn left on Highway 128 and drive 8 miles to the boulders which are on the right side of the road across from the Big Bend campsite.

From Moab: Take Main Street (Hwy 191) north for about 2.5 miles. Just before the Colorado River turn right on Highway 128 and drive 8 miles to the boulders which are on the right side of the road across from the Big Bend campsite.

WHEN YOU GOTTA GO ...

If you need to go to the bathroom, please use the facilities just a 100 yards or so across the road at the Big Bend campground.

SEASON

The best time to visit is between October and April when temperatures allow slopers to feel sticky and skin to remain tough. Expect daytime temps between 30 and 70 degrees and evenings a chilling 10 to 40 degrees. If you come when the temps are high, avoid climbing in the sun as the black rocks absorb heat and have been known to blister even the most callused tips.

CAMPING/ACCOMODATION

Camping at the Big Bend campsite is easy and puts the boulders a stone's throw from your tent. Sites cost $10 a day and are almost always available during the winter. For those who want more deluxe accommodations, many hotels in Moab offer off-season discounts. The Adventure Inn 435-259-6122 is an inexpensive clean hotel run by a couple of nice climbers. For those who just can't stomach the idea of paying for a spot to crash, the desert is full of back roads, hidden canyons, and commando-camping opportunities. I won't wreck the thrill by pointing out any specific spots.

EATS & TREATS

For all of your climbing needs while in Moab you can go to Pagan Mountaineering 435-259-1117 or Gearheads 435-259-4327. For groceries go to City Market, Boomers, or the local health- food store Moonflower Market (located opposite the Post Office). The movie theater is located behind McDonalds and the Moab Brewery generally stays open all winter for pool, beer, and brew-pub-style food.

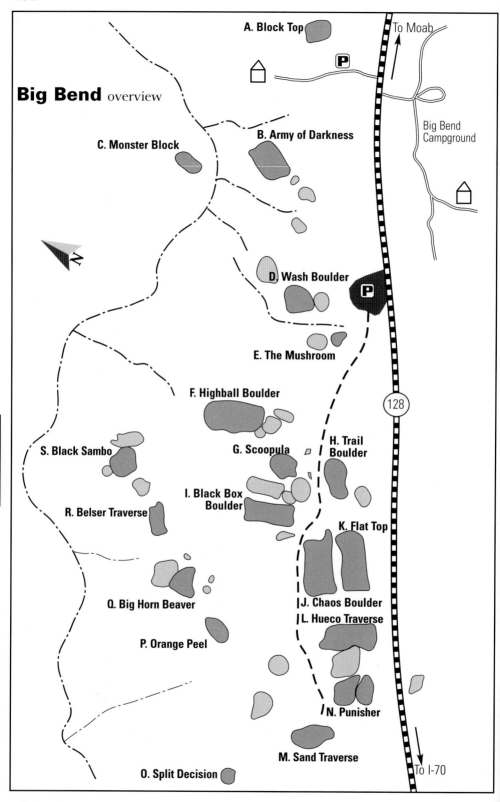

The best of BIG BEND

V0
- [ ] Leftover Lover ★★★ page 192
- [ ] Block Top Descent ★★ page 184

V1
- [ ] Black Box Center Start ★★★ page 189
- [ ] Hueco Finish ★★ page 194

V2
- [ ] Middle Man ★★★ page 188
- [ ] Slots of Fun ★★★ page 189
- [ ] Washing Machine ★★ page 186
- [ ] High Step ★★ page 188
- [ ] Mr. Trujillo's Big Day ★★ page 192
- [ ] Sand Traverse ★★ page 195
- [ ] The Punisher ★★ page 195
- [ ] Orange Peel ★★ page 196

V3
- [ ] Black Box Arete Left Side ★★★★ page 189
- [ ] Black Box Arete Right Side ★★★ page 189
- [ ] Trail Traverse ★★ page 188
- [ ] Black Box Center Direct ★★ page 189
- [ ] Silly Wabbit ★★ page 192
- [ ] Aunt Jemima ★★ page 196

V4
- [ ] Brown Power ★★★ page 184
- [ ] Washed Up ★★★ page 186
- [ ] Circus Trick ★★★ page 190
- [ ] Drunkula ★★ page 185
- [ ] Double Crimp ★★ page 192
- [ ] Blankety Blank ★★ page 195
- [ ] Black Slab ★★ page 196
- [ ] Black Sambo ★★ page 196

V5
- [ ] Block Party ★★★ page 184
- [ ] Army of Darkness ★★★ page 185
- [ ] Basketball Diaries ★★★ page 185
- [ ] Wussula ★★★ page 188

- [ ] Black Box Arete Left Side Dyno ★★ page 189
- [ ] Grim Reacher ★★★ page 190
- [ ] Black Box Shorter Traverse ★★ page 189
- [ ] Circus Trick Right ★★ page 190
- [ ] Belser Traverse ★★ page 196

V6
- [ ] Slappin The Block ★★ page 184

V7
- [ ] High Balls ★★★ page 186
- [ ] Nazi Traverse ★★★ page 192
- [ ] Hueco Traverse ★★★ page 194
- [ ] Left Hand of Darkness ★★ page 185
- [ ] Frankenspark ★★ page 185
- [ ] Big Huck ★★ page 188

V8
- [ ] Chaos ★★★★ page 190
- [ ] Standula ★★★ page 188
- [ ] Phantom Fighter Stand Start ★★★ page 190
- [ ] Hellbelly Standing Start ★★★ page 190
- [ ] Right Hand of Darkness ★★ page 185
- [ ] 1000lb Caboose ★★ page 192

V9
- [ ] Blue Light ★★★★ page 189
- [ ] Five-Finger Discount ★★★ page 184
- [ ] Block Box Arete Left Side Sit Start ★★ page 189

V10
- [ ] Scoopula ★★★★ page 188
- [ ] Barracuda ★★★ page 189
- [ ] Big Horn Beaver ★★★ page 196
- [ ] Return of The Jedi ★★ page 185
- [ ] Skinless Dyno ★★ page 192

V11
- [ ] Phantom Fighter Sit Start ★★★★ page 190
- [ ] Hellbelly ★★★★ page 190
- [ ] Good Day Bad Day ★★ page 190

Big Bend

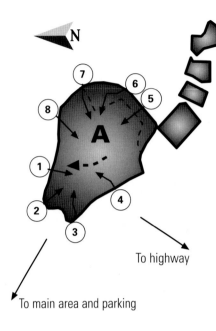

To highway

To main area and parking

◄ A. Block Top
As you approach Big Bend from Moab, you'll see a small dirt road directly across from the main Big Bend campsite, and an obvious square boulder that sits alone on a flat plain on the right side of this road. The Block Top boulder has a concentration of classic problems on perfect chocolate-colored rock with great landings and easy top outs.

1. Descent V0
On the side facing away from Hwy 128, a shallow dihedral with an obvious crimp ladder is a great problem done up or down.

2. Slappin The Block V6
Start five feet right of the descent corner with your left hand on a blunt arete and a very high left foot.
A **V10 variation** starts sitting a little left, then climb into the stand up.

3. Block Shock V2
Just right of #2. Start on an arete with holds on both sides, hard moves off the ground lead to slopers and the top.

4. Block Pock V1
Start on good holds on the right side of the west face, go up to the big pocket mid-face and then the top.

5. Brown Power V4
Start in an obvious long horizontal crack on the left side of the south face and go to a left hand sidepull; beautiful sculpted pockets lead to the top. Photo page 193.

6. Five-Finger Discount V9
Start on the right end of the same horizontal crack as #5. Go up and right, ending with incredible moves on the right arete. As of writing this problem was unrepeated and may be harder than the grade.

7. Block Party V5
Begin under the right side of the big roof on deep slots and pockets, then go straight up finishing with some mighty thin crimp matches.

8 Whodunnit? V8
Just 5 feet right of #7, start with tiny awkward holds high on both sides of the arête; a jump start to a right hand crimp gets it going. The problem was done from a **sit start** to the right **(V9)** long before some wanker tried to bolster his ego with this weak jump start and scratched "V-9" and a big arrow into the rock below. The sit start begins at the base of the descent and moves left then up using tiny crimps and tricky footwork.

B. The Army of Darkness ➤

Tucked into the folds of a gully between the Block Top and the main cluster of boulders, this big black boulder is best approached from the main parking area. Walk east (toward Block Top) for several hundred yards then angle up (left) toward the hillside. The Army of Darkness has several classic problems on great rock which are well worth the short walk, and because this boulder is off the beaten path, it is usually a bit less crowded.

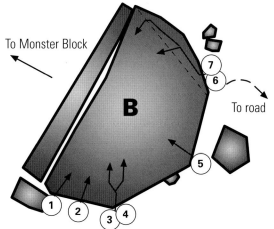

1. Left Hand of Darkness V7
On the far left end of the downhill side of the boulder, start on a good sidepull and an undercling, then go straight up. Beware the flat rock to the left, as falls tend to go in that direction. You can also start this from the flat rock with high hands for a significantly reduced difficulty.

2. Project V-hard
The black face between 1 and 3 has a series of tiny crimps and conspicuously absent feet which have almost been connected ... but not quite!

3. Army of Darkness V5
In the center of the downhill side of the boulder. Start with high edges for the hands and some tricky footwork, then move up to the left. When it starts to feel really tall move back to the right and top out. This is a real highball with large rocks around the L.Z. so pad and spot accordingly!

4. Right Hand of Darkness V8
Start the same as #3 but move right into a shallow scoop after the first move, then straight up to the top. The top is easier than #3 but the landing is worse. Using several pads can make it much better.

5. Basic Training V0
About 10 feet right of #'s 3&4 is a black slab with good rock and an easy but high top out.

6. Basketball Diaries V5
Located on the uphill side of the boulder. Start on slopers on the far left end and traverse low and right to a point about midway across the face where you can go up to good holds and continue right to top out.

7. Return of the Jedi V10 ★★
Start as for #6 but stay low where #6 goes up. Small edges set you up for a big right-hand throw to the edge of the boulder and go up. You can use the wide crack to the right to finish, or avoid it for a slightly stouter finish. Staying off the ground at the crux can be tricky.

C. The Monster Block
NO TOPO

To get to this small and rarely visited boulder, go to the Army of Darkness boulder and then hike directly uphill for a hundred yards to the first plateau. The boulder is vaguely triangular in shape and all of the problems are on the east side.

1. Drunkula V4
The angling left arete on the east side of the boulder. Start nearly sitting with slopers for the hands, and move up and right to the top.

2. Frankenspank V7
Start sitting, just right of #1. Move up and a little left using interesting pockets and edges to gain the top.

3. Quasi-Mono V4
Start standing about 10 feet right of #2 with a tiny mono and an even tinier crimp. Step up and dyno for the top.

Big Bend

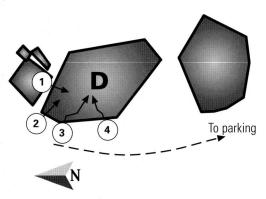

◀ D. The Wash Boulder
This boulder is invisible from the parking area, about 100 feet up a small wash. Though it doesn't have many problems, the ones it does sport are quite fun.

1. Slab V3
Located on the side facing away from the road. Start off a couple of boulders that form a ledge in the wash, use small crimps and difficult feet, then go up. Though this is short and has an easy top out, the landing is uneven so watch out!

2. Washing Machine V2
On the left arete of the downhill side of the boulder, start on big holds and go straight up. Bad landing.

3. Washed Up V4
Just right of #2, start at the bottom of a sloping right-angled hand ramp and move up. The sloping mantel at the top adds to the fun.

4. Queen of Clean V6
On the right end of the same side as #'s 2 & 3, start on a bad crimp rail and move up and left.

E. The Mushroom
NO TOPO
Just a few feet up the wash from the bumper of your car is a four-foot high mushroom of rock. There is just one problem here, and you have to be in the right mood to try it.

1. Shroom Traverse V-silly
Traverse the lip with hands and heels — good luck keeping your butt off the ground.

F. Highball Boulder ▼
This is one of the biggest boulders at Big Bend and can be seen clearly from the parking area, presenting a huge roof which leads to an even bigger slab.

1. Low Ball V3
On the side facing away from the parking, start sitting in a depression with a flat floor on positive holds at about three feet. Go straight up to a low mantle then step off.

2. Satelite 1 V3
This problem is located on a smaller boulder leaning against the Highball Boulder on the side facing away from the parking. Start on small crimps at about five feet and go up.

3. Satelite 2 V3
About 10 feet right of #2 between two boulders is a steep crack. Start at the bottom and go out finishing near the top of #2.

4. High Balls V7
On the downhill side of the boulder, start about 10 feet right of the left edge of the big roof on a good right-hand sidepull and move straight up. The start is hard, but the slab is the real business. This problem is huge ... and the rock is not perfect ... and it's not over until you're over the top!

5. Project V?
Start under the roof just right of #4 on small breakable sidepulls (the lowest start was broken by an ambitious Frenchman who tried this problem after a rainstorm). Ascend to slopers at the lip then up to finish on the big slab.

6. High Desert Drifter V1
Start near the right side of the big roof and traverse to the left then go up. The topout is high and insecure, and the landing is quite bad.

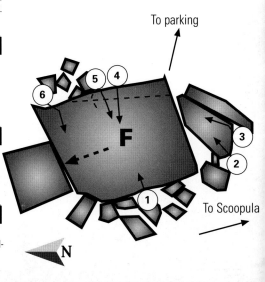

Emma Medara on *Trail Traverse* (V3), page 188.
Hobbes on the trail.
Photo: Dave Pegg

Big Bend

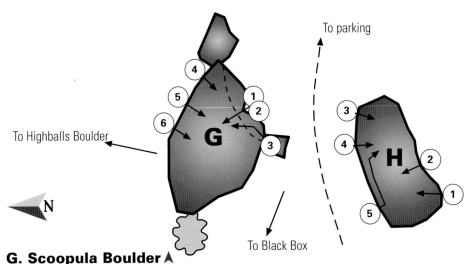

To parking

To Highballs Boulder

To Black Box

G. Scoopula Boulder
Straight ahead of the parking area the first big boulder on the right side of the trail, presents a scooped black face with one obvious crimp in its center.

1. Scoopula V10 ★★★★
On the side facing the road is an obvious scoop with one crimp at its center. Start as low as possible with both hands on an awful sloper (which feels best at about 30 degrees Farenheight) and a hidden toe hook underneath the boulder. Go up on crimpers to gain the left arete then to the top. This problem is classic and hard, but beware because falls on the last move can send bodies flying in unexpected directions.

2. Standula V8 ★★★
Start in the same spot as the Scoopula but standing with the good right-hand edge near the bottom of the scoop. Finish as for #1.

3. Wussula V5 ★★★
Start with your feet on the boulder just left of the start for #'s 1 & 2, reach around to the crimp in the scoop and get going. Finish as for #1.

4. Left V3 ★
Around the corner to the right of Scoopula on the side facing the parking. Start as low as possible on a jug and go up to the left. Staying off the boulders to the left can be tricky.

5. Center V4 ★
Just right of #4 in the center of the face. Sit start on two pockets and go up.

6. Right V1
On the right side of the same face as #'s 4 & 5. Start in a big pocket and go up.

H. Trail Boulder
Opposite the Scoopula on the left side of the trail from the parking, this plain-looking boulder has some great problems.

1. High Step V2 ★★
On the left arete of the side facing the road. Start with your left hand on the arete and a foot that seems impossibly high. Go straight up.

2. Trail Mix V0
Just right of #1 is a chossy scoop that can be climbed in several spots.

3. Big Huck V7 ★★
On the left arete of the side of the boulder facing the Scoopula and away from the road. Start with your left hand on the arete and your right on one of several sidepulls, then step up and jump!

4. Middle Man V2 ★★★
Just right of #3, start sitting with hands in the big huecos. Go straight up. Height is a huge factor in this problem and shorter people have suggested much higher grades. A popular variation starts on #4 and traverses right through #5 to finish on a sloping mantle.

5. Trail Traverse V3 ★★
At the far right side of the same face as #'s 3 & 4. Start sitting with crimps for hands and dishes for feet. Go up to a horizontal crack about one foot below the lip and traverse left topping out on Middle Man. Photo previous page.

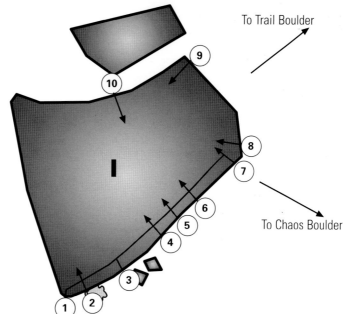

To Trail Boulder

To Chaos Boulder

I. Black Box Boulder

From the parking walk the trail until it passes between the Scoopula and Trail boulders then take a right to the big Black Box. This has some of the best rock at Big Bend and lots of great problems. On really hot days, the black rock on these crimpy problems can actually blister your skin.

1. Long Traverse V9
On the long black side facing away from the parking. Start at the left arete and — avoiding the top of the boulder — traverse to the right arete 30 feet away. A super hard move down, after moving about 10 feet right, is the crux. The rest is just hanging on for the ride.

2. Slimper V3
It's a sloper ... It's a crimper ... It's a slimper! Start five feet right of #1 with two high slimpers. Go straight up.

3. Shorter Traverse V5
Start on a big flake jug about 15 feet right of #1. Traverse right for about 20 feet staying fairly low to finish on #7.

4. Slots of Fun V2
Start on two obvious greasy horizontal slots near the center of the black face. Step up and reach right to a vertical seam, then straight up to the top.

5. Center Start V1
Start on a foot-long crimper to the right of #4 and move right and up. There are many ways to finish this problem including an option to traverse right into #7.

6. Center Direct V3
Start just right of #5 on two small sharp crimps at eye level, move straight up avoiding the long ledges to the left.

7. Arete Left Side V3
Either start on #5 and traverse in (short people) or at the base of the right arete on the same side as #'s 1 to 6. Spring up to a six-inch-long, half-pad crimper at eight feet, then use the arete to gain the top.

7a. Variation V5
From the crimper at 8 feet dyno to the top.

7b. Variation V9
Start sitting with a deep undercling and get tricky and tall to go up to the crimper at 8 feet, then dyno to the top.

8. Arete Right Side V3
Just to the right of #7. Start on the right side of the arete with a good right-hand crimper and go straight up.

9. Blue Light V9
On the undercut right arete of the side facing the road. Start with a good right hand on the arete and jump to get your left hand as high as you can. Then go straight up.

9a. Barracuda V10
Do the first two moves of Blue Light then traverse left on small holds that all seem to face the wrong way until you can finish on #8.

10. Black Alley V0
On the side facing the parking and in a corridor between two boulders, start in the middle of the face and finish at the left side of a small flat roof. If you fall high up, you may ping-pong down the alley.

Big Bend

Big Bend

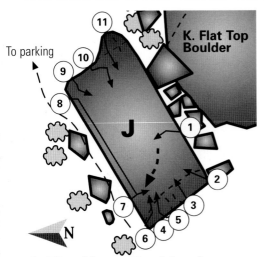

J. The Chaos Boulder ▲
This boulder is the king of Big Bend. It is the biggest, has the best rock, and the hardest problems. From the parking area go straight ahead into the main cluster of boulders, if you miss it … get your eyes checked!

1. Rampage V3
On the side facing the road is a striking right-angling ramp going from the bottom to the top of the boulder. Start just left of the base of the ramp and follow it about halfway up, then reach left to a sketchy keyed-in block and go straight up to the lip. The whole problem rises above a hideous pile of rocks and a fall from anywhere could send you to the hospital!

2. Hanging Tight V1
Ten feet left of Rampage on the right arete of the steep west face. Start on good holds from a diving-board-shaped boulder and go up to a tricky mantle. Falls from anywhere on the problem can land you on the start boulder with bad results!

3. Phantom Fighter V11
This line follows a series of obvious low sloping edges to a vertical crack. Originally done from a **standing start (V8)**, the low problem starts almost sitting with a left hand crimp and right hand in a tiny sharp one- or two-finger pocket/edge. The last moves can be done using the original fingerlock Beta or the new-school dyno for the lip.

4. Circus Trick Right V5
Just right of Circus Trick, starting with the right hand on a good two-foot-long vertical sidepull about 4 feet off the ground and the left hand on any hold you can reach out left. Go one move left then dyno way right to a sloping dish at the right side of the lip. Mantle anywhere you can.

5. Good Day Bad Day V11
Start sitting way under the boulder below Circus Trick Right with your left hand in a drilled (D.O.T blast hole) two-finger pocket and your right hand on a hideous sloper. Finish on #4.

6. Circus Trick V4
The left arete of the overhanging west face of the boulder. Start sitting with good holds, move up and right to the two good holds about 7 feet above the ground, then make a committing move to the lip and mantle.
Variations: Start on the good holds at 7 feet and go up as for the normal problem. This move has also been done as a dyno, one hand — or both.

7. Descent V0
Just left around the arete from Circus Trick is a slightly slabby line of holds going up and right to a scooped-out dish at the top of the boulder. It's not too hard to go up but watch out because it is a little harder to descend — and this is the easiest way off of the boulder.

8. Death Flakes V2
The ground below the north face of the boulder is littered with the death flakes that used to plate this entire side of the boulder. This traverse can be done in either direction from arete to arete. There are many tempting flakes up high, most lead to scary loose rock, and none make for an easier crossing so try staying fairly low. The old flakes on the ground make perfect ankle-breakers so get a spotter!

9. Grim Reacher V5
This is some serious highball action! Start on slopers at about seven-feet above the ground near the right side of the east (facing the parking lot) side of the boulder. Move up and right to a huge keyed-in block at about 15 feet, then keep going up and right to the top.
Easier Variation: Start on the right side of the arete and follow flakes and edges to the same finish.
Harder Variation: Follow Grim Reacher to the big sloper before the keyed-in block, then go out left to a harder and much scarier finish.

10. Chaos V8
This incredibly classic line starts matched on high slopers in the center of the east face just right of the overhanging prow. Move up and left through the shallow dihedral into an obvious scoop on the left side of the dihedral. Finish by climbing a little right out of the scoop to a crack, two challenging moves lead to increasingly easy terrain. See cover photo.
Harder Variation: Start sitting at the base of the right arete, traverse left and up into the normal start.

11. Hellbelly V11
Start sitting at the bottom of the huge overhanging prow on the left side of the east face. Slap, grunt, and tug up the prow, then at the lip, move either left up a sharp arete or right through sloping scoops to finish in the scoop and top out as for Chaos.
Easier Variation (V8): Start standing with the left hand on a huge flake and the right hand as high as possible on the arete, go up then right or left at the lip.

Fiona Lloyd on *Leftover Lover* (V0), page 192.
If this seems a little tame, go try the Lighthouse and
Dolomite Towers (top right).
Photo: Dave Pegg

Big Bend

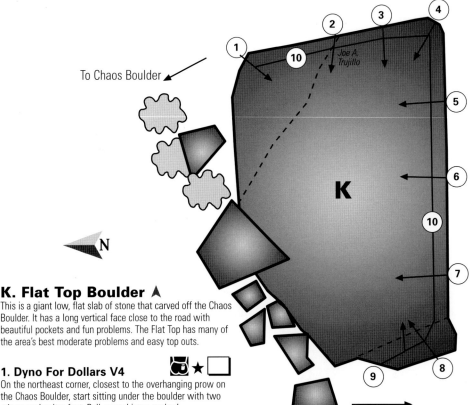

K. Flat Top Boulder
This is a giant low, flat slab of stone that carved off the Chaos Boulder. It has a long vertical face close to the road with beautiful pockets and fun problems. The Flat Top has many of the area's best moderate problems and easy top outs.

1. Dyno For Dollars V4 ★
On the northeast corner, closest to the overhanging prow on the Chaos Boulder, start sitting under the boulder with two crimps and paltry feet. Pull on and jump sucker!

2. Mr. Trujillo's Big Day V2 ★★
Start under the boulder just right of Trujillo's name. Move out and up.

3. Double Crimp V4 ★★
Near the left side of the east face, start with both hands on a short thin crimp about four feet above the ground. Pull on and move up.

4. Silly Wabbit V3 ★★
The left arete of the east side. Start low or high and go straight up the arete. **Variation:** Start the same but go right and finish up Double Crimp.

5. Kick Start V0 ★
Ten feet left of Silly Wabbit, start as high as you can (or jump for the big hueco) and go up.

6. 1000 lb Caboose V8 ★★
In the center of the south (facing the road) side of the boulder, start sitting with small strange pockets for your hands. Go up on really tiny edges to a break in a thin vertical seam. It is possible to traverse right or left to easier holds, instead try to go straight up.

7. Leftover Lover V0 ★★★
Near the left side of the south (facing the road) side of the boulder is an obvious line of pockets and edges that lead to the top. Start as low as you like (even sitting) and go straight up. **Variation:** Start just left on blocks and flakes then go right to finish on Leftover Lover. Photo previous page.

8. Skinless Dyno V10 ★★
You will need to donate some skin to this one! On the right arete of the west face, start with a high two-finger crimp for your right hand and a small crimp just right of a shot hole for your left hand. Step on and let your skin fly.

9. Nazi Traverse V7 ★★★
Near the left end of the west face, start matched on a sloper about three feet above the ground. Move right through two drilled holes (DOT blast holes) until your left hand is in the rightmost hole, then launch for the lip. **Variations:** You can go to the lip with your right hand in the rightmost hole, or with your left hand in the leftmost hole.

10. Lip Traverse V-Fun ★★★
Start on either corner of the boulder and traverse nearly 100 feet keeping your hands on the lip.

Emma Medera at the crux of *Brown Power* (V4), page 184.
Photo: Dave Pegg

Big Bend

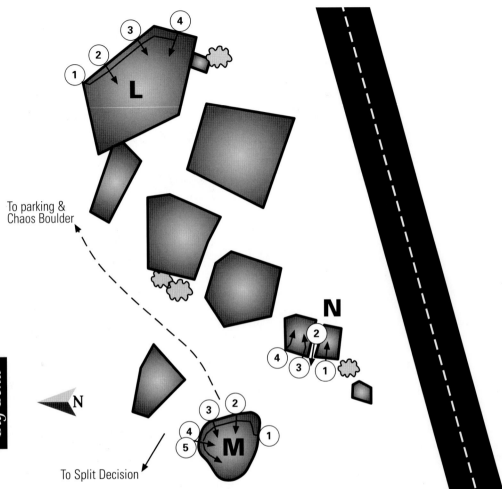

L. Hueco Traverse Boulder ▲
This boulder sits close to the road and presents an obvious line of low pockets and huecos facing back toward the Chaos and Flat Top Boulders. The namesake traverse on this boulder is a great problem even though it is a bit of a butt-dragger, and the crux, where the traverse gets closest to the road, is desperate. There are also several easier problems (some of Big Bend's easiest) which go straight up from various points along the traverse.

1. The Hueco Traverse V7 ★★★
Start at the right side of the east face on a blunt undercut arete (you can push it a bit more to the right if you want) and traverse leftward staying low. The crux comes where the traverse drops down near the road and a desperate undercling match sets you up for the final ascent. You can step off left to another boulder after the final straight-up problem instead of climbing worsening rock to the top.

2. Upwardly Mobile V0 ★
Start a few feet left of the start of the Hueco Traverse, either low on two softball-sized huecos or high on sidepull flakes, and go straight up. The topout is high with some loose rock. Fortunately, the climbing gets easier the higher you go.

3. Ranger Bob V2
Near the left side of the east face, start in the center of a long, flat horizontal rail about four feet above the ground. A strange mantel gains a shallow seam that leads to the top.

4. Hueco Finish V1 ★★
Start on the side closest to the road (a low start adds some difficulty) and climb straight up. You can exit left by stepping onto another boulder; this avoids a high topout and some bad rock.

Dave Pegg getting sandbagged on the *Sand Traverse* (V2+). Photo: Fiona Lloyd

◄ M. The Sand Traverse Boulder

This boulder looks like a giant mushroom and sits at the terminus of the main trail through the boulders. The Sand Traverse is a fun problem with big holds and many variations.

1. The Sand Traverse V2 ★★
Start on the side closest to the road and traverse left to right on slopers, jugs, and anything else below the lip. You can exit at any point, or continue all the way around the boulder until it gets too low to keep on going.

2. Middle Exit V0 ★
In the middle of the east face, start on any good holds you can reach (the lower you start the harder) and climb straight up to the top where a sloping mantel awaits.

3. Right Exit V1 ★
At the right side of the east face, start on a big edge and high lefthand sidepull. Go straight up to a fairly easy topout.

4. Rollout V1 ★
Same start as #5. Go straight up.

5. Rollover V3 ★
On the north side (facing away from the road), start as low as possible under a roof and move out and right on slopers and edges to a rollover topout.

◄ N. The Punisher Boulder

This boulder sits between Sand Traverse and the road. The Punisher is a classic bizarre desert chimney. This and the other problems on this boulder are well worth the effort.

1. Short Stuff V1
This problem is on a boulder that leans against The Punisher. Start sitting with decent sidepulls and go up.

2. The Punisher V2 ★★
Between the two boulders is a chimney. Start at the back end and come out. The exit can be done several ways, some make the problem much harder.

3. Blankety Blank V4 ★★
The obvious right arête. Start with a bad right-hand pinch and left-hand crimp. Step on and go up.
Variation: Start sitting with sidepulls and slap your way up for a significantly harder grade.

4. La Derecha V2 ★
The left arête starts with whatever holds you can reach and follows an obvious line of holds to the top.

Big Bend

O. Split Decision Boulder
NO TOPO

This boulder lies 25 yards northwest of the Sand Traverse Boulder and has an orange face split by a crack that faces the road. Although Noah omitted this boulder from his original topo on the grounds that it was chossy, it does have one decent problem.

1. Split Decision V1
Climb the crack using face holds on the left.

2. V7
Climb the right arete on suspect rock. A **V4 variation** traverses right from the start of #1 and finishes up the arete.

P. Orange Peel Boulder ➤
This boulder sits alone on the hillside above and a bit east of the Sand Traverse and presents a clean tan face facing the road. The landing below this problem is not great, but the rock and the climbing is.

1. Orange Peel V2
Start on the lowest crimps and go up on good edges.

Q. Big Horn Beaver Boulder ➤
This boulder sits on the hill above and a bit west of the main cluster of boulders and presents a dark brown face with an obvious rail. No trail yet leads to this boulder, but the short scramble up the hillside is rewarded by the excellent quality of the problems.

1. Wynona's V5
Start on a sidepull crimp and a sloper on the left side of the downhill (facing the road) side of the boulder. Go straight up on slopers to a precarious top out with a potentially hazardous landing.

2. Big Horn Beaver V10
Traverse the incredible sloping rail from right to left, and top out on the smooth slab above. The topout is not too high, but you can fall in some very bad positions and the landing has some hazardous rocks.

3. Brown V1
On the east side of the boulder (right of #2), start wherever you like and go up.

R. The Belser Traverse Boulder ➤
This boulder sits directly uphill from the Black Box Boulder and has one really fun problem on its uphill side.

1. Belser Traverse V5
Start on the left end of the uphill side on good holds and traverse to the right end on edges and slopers staying below the lip. In 2001 several hundred tons of rock from the hillside above smashed into this problem. Although a couple of holds were scarred, the problem remained.

S. Black Sambo Boulder ➤
This boulder rests up on the hillside just east of the Belser Traverse, and has excellent problems on some of the most perfectly varnished stone at Big Bend.

1. Black Slab V4
On the far right side of the scooped black face, start on great holds and move up to the sloping top edge. A good spot can prevent falls from ending up in a cave below a nearby boulder.

2. Black Sambo V4
Start just right of the big scoop on a huge foot ledge and move up and left to an airy topout on excellent rock.

3. Aunt Jemima V3
Just under the leaning arête on the left side of the scooped face, start on edges and go up the arête until you can mantel around onto the slab and finish as for #2.

Wolverine *Publishing*   www.wolverinepublishing.com

197

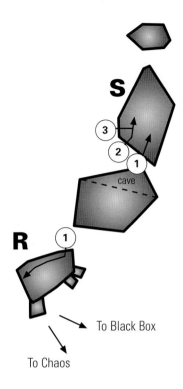

To Black Box

To Chaos

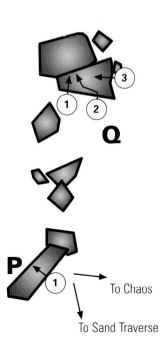

To Chaos

To Sand Traverse

Big Bend

Big Bend

BECAUSE IT'S A LONG WAY DOWN

DRY CORE™ MARATHON

STERLING ROPE
THERE IS A DIFFERENCE
www.sterlingrope.com
tel: 207.885.0330 fax: 207.885.0033

Dave Graham - Jaws 5.14c Photo: Erik Mushial

OGDEN

Chris Grijalva

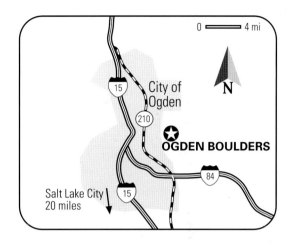

INTRODUCTION

It's a mystery why more people don't climb at the Ogden boulder field. This is a killer area with hundreds of boulders in a beautiful setting, and because non-locals rarely visit, you can often have a pleasant solitary experience. Maybe Ogden is ignored because its well-featured quartzite yield mostly moderates — problems in the V1 to V4 range. However, the area has problems up to V9, and because the hard problems tend to be on the best and most striking pieces of stone, they are, without exception, killer. This guide only describes the natural lines, but because the rock is so featured it caters well to eliminate-style bouldering. With a little creativity, you can make up thousands of problems at whatever grade you desire. Another great feature of Ogden is that it's warmer in winter than most other areas on the Wasatch Front. The boulder field gets sun from 11 a.m. till dusk, and you can be climbing here when your neighbors in Salt Lake City are digging their driveways out from under feet of snow.

GETTING THERE

The Ogden boulder field is situated at the eastern edge of the city of Ogden, no more than 10 minutes from downtown and 15 minutes from the Interstate. There are three parking areas for the boulder field. The first parking lot is located at the end of 22nd Street, which marks the head of the Bonneville Shoreline trail. Keep in mind that this parking lot closes at dusk. The second parking area is at the end of 27th Street. Park in the street and walk east into the foothills to locate the Bonneville Shoreline trail and the boulders. This is the closest and most convenient parking area. The third possibility is a parking lot at the end of 29th Street; although this parking area is the furthest from the climbing and seldom used by climbers. The best ways to reach the parking areas and the boulder field are as follows:

From the north, exit I-15 at the 12th Street exit. Follow 12th Street east (towards the mountains) to Harrison Blvd. Turn right on Harrison and drive south to 22nd, 27th, or 29th street.

From the south, exit I-15 at the Riverdale Road exit. Drive east on Riverdale Road through numerous traffic lights, to the intersection with 36th street. Turn right on 36th street and follow it to Harrison Blvd. Turn left on Harrison Blvd., and drive north to 29th, 27th, or 22nd Street.

SEASON

The best time to visit the Ogden boulder field is between October and April. Great winter climbing is one of this area's most appealing characteristics. The west-facing hillside gets sun by 11 a.m., and winter temperatures can rise to the 50s — perfect for sticking the slick quartzite crimps. After a storm, snow usually melts quickly from the boulders, although the landings can remain muddy. Forget climbing here in the summer. The small oak trees offer little to no shade and temperatures often reach the high 90s.

ACCESS

Most of the Ogden boulder field lies on public land and access is not an issue. However, the area is popular with many types of users including high-school kids looking for a place to party. Consequently, it suffers from abuse like trash, vandalism (spray paint on the rock), and people creating unofficial trails. In addition to the Bonneville Shoreline trail, which traverses the entire boulder field from north to south, dozens of small shoot-off trails crisscross the hillside linking all the main trails and boulders. While climbers are not to blame for all these trails scaring the land, we are responsible for a significant number of them. When visiting this area please stay on well-established trails. All of the boulders have trails leading to them, so if you find yourself bush whacking, act responsibly, and take a few extra seconds to back up and locate the proper trail. The trash left in the boulder field is not from climbers, but from irresponsible nitwits who can't be bothered to pick up their rubbish when they leave. Pick up all your trash, and if you're feeling virtuous, pick up someone else's as well.

CAMPING

The closest campground is Anderson Cove, located east of Ogden, just off highway 39 on the shore of Pine View Reservoir, but this is closed November 1 through May 15. Sites are $14 per night and reservations can be made by calling 1-877-444-6777. More campgrounds are located along the south fork of the Ogden River, and can be found by continuing east on Highway 39, past the small town of Huntsville. You'll find unlimited free camping in the mountains about 30 miles east of Ogden. Simply drive east on Highway 39 towards Monte Cristo Peak and head up one of many forest roads. The downside of this option is that the area receives heavy snowfall in winter.

SURVIVAL

Ogden is not the bustling metropolis of Salt Lake City, nor does it have the decadent nightlife of Las Vegas, but you will find everything you need for climbing, camping, traveling — and, yes, even for a fun night out. Harrison Blvd. is a main thoroughfare and has several grocery stores, restaurants, gas stations, and just about everything else you might need, including a liquor store located just west of Harrison on Patterson Street (between 30th and 31st). There's a movie theater at the New Gate Mall, which is easily found by driving west on 36th street, from Harrison Blvd., until it dead-ends into the New Gate Mall. An excellent rock gym (Propulsion Climbing Gym) and a climbing store (Canyon Sports) are located next to each other on Riverdale Road (technically in the town of Riverdale, not Ogden) at 697 W Riverdale Rd, and 705 W Riverdale Rd, respectively. Finally, downtown Ogden, on 25th Street, has good restaurants and numerous bars that often feature live bands.

WolverinePublishing   www.wolverinepublishing.com

The best of OGDEN

V0
- [ ] Arrowhead Down Climb ★★★ *page 207*
- [ ] Jail ★★★ *page 213*
- [ ] Clink ★★ *page 213*

V1
- [ ] Transmission ★★ *page 204*
- [ ] Shore Leave ★★ *page 204*
- [ ] East Face Fish Flop ★★ *page 210*
- [ ] #9 Upper Boulders ★★★ *page 212*
- [ ] Jury ★★ *page 213*
- [ ] Lowe ★★ *page 215*

V2
- [ ] Hidden Rock Traverse ★★ *page 204*
- [ ] Disorder ★★★ *page 204*
- [ ] Dead Sun ★★★ *page 204*
- [ ] #16 The Tooth ★★ *page 204*
- [ ] Lobster Arete ★★★ *page 205*
- [ ] Negative ★★ *page 206*
- [ ] Natural Selection ★★★ *page 207*
- [ ] Lock Tight ★★★ *page 207*
- [ ] Toyota Arete ★★ *page 208*
- [ ] Fish Flop ★★★ *page 210*
- [ ] Golden ★★ *page 210*
- [ ] Patriot Crack ★★ *page 211*
- [ ] Hot Joint ★★ *page 213*
- [ ] Dressed in Black ★★ *page 213*

V3
- [ ] Numb ★★ *page 202*
- [ ] Lobster Traverse ★★ *page 205*
- [ ] Arrowhead Arete ★★ *page 207*
- [ ] Suicide Crack ★★ *page 211*
- [ ] LCC ★★★ *page 211*
- [ ] #16 Patriot Crack Area ★★ *page 211*
- [ ] Power ★★ *page 212*
- [ ] Around the World Traverse ★★ *page 212*
- [ ] BW ★★ *page 212*
- [ ] Jack Brown ★★ *page 213*
- [ ] Lowe 1 ★★★ *page 215*

V4
- [ ] Lowe 2 ★★★ *page 215*
- [ ] Worms ★★ *page 215*
- [ ] Mule ★★★ *page 215*
- [ ] Gygi Traverse ★★ *page 202*
- [ ] Mecham ★★ *page 204*
- [ ] Six Foot and Curly ★★ *page 205*
- [ ] Randall ★★ *page 206*
- [ ] Checker ★★★ *page 207*
- [ ] The Boot ★★ *page 212*
- [ ] KG ★★ *page 214*
- [ ] Lowe 3 ★★★ *page 215*
- [ ] Joe Bean ★★ *page 215*

V5
- [ ] Tooth Traverse ★★ *page 204*
- [ ] Pony ★★ *page 205*
- [ ] WD-40 ★★ *page 207*
- [ ] Taddy ★★ *page 207*
- [ ] Mini Cave ★★ *page 208*
- [ ] Leaning Rock ★★★ *page 213*

V6
- [ ] Paulaner ★★ *page 207*
- [ ] ESB ★★ *page 207*
- [ ] Buda ★★★★ *page 210*
- [ ] The Gorn ★★★ *page 212*
- [ ] The Cave ★★★ *page 214*
- [ ] Don't Want To Grow Up ★★★ *page 215*

V7
- [ ] JFC ★★★★ *page 208*
- [ ] Jed's Traverse ★★★ *page 208*
- [ ] Kill Your Enemies ★★ *page 214*
- [ ] Black Rider ★★★ *page 214*

V8
- [ ] Slick 50 ★★★ *page 207*

V9
- [ ] Slick 50 Direct ★★★★ *page 207*

Lower Boulders

The Lower Boulder field is spread out along the lower part of the hillside, spanning nearly half a mile from north to south. Most of the boulders are close to the lower trail that runs under the power lines west (downhill) of the Bonneville Shoreline trail; others are to the east (uphill) of the Bonneville Shoreline Trail. Since most of the boulders here are isolated, they are fairly easy to locate.

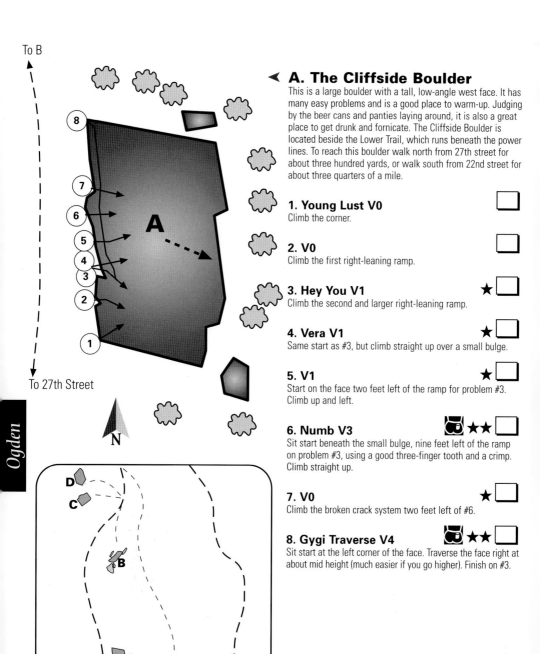

◄ A. The Cliffside Boulder

This is a large boulder with a tall, low-angle west face. It has many easy problems and is a good place to warm-up. Judging by the beer cans and panties laying around, it is also a great place to get drunk and fornicate. The Cliffside Boulder is located beside the Lower Trail, which runs beneath the power lines. To reach this boulder walk north from 27th street for about three hundred yards, or walk south from 22nd street for about three quarters of a mile.

1. Young Lust V0
Climb the corner.

2. V0
Climb the first right-leaning ramp.

3. Hey You V1 ★
Climb the second and larger right-leaning ramp.

4. Vera V1 ★
Same start as #3, but climb straight up over a small bulge.

5. V1 ★
Start on the face two feet left of the ramp for problem #3. Climb up and left.

6. Numb V3 ★★
Sit start beneath the small bulge, nine feet left of the ramp on problem #3, using a good three-finger tooth and a crimp. Climb straight up.

7. V0 ★
Climb the broken crack system two feet left of #6.

8. Gygi Traverse V4 ★★
Sit start at the left corner of the face. Traverse the face right at about mid height (much easier if you go higher). Finish on #3.

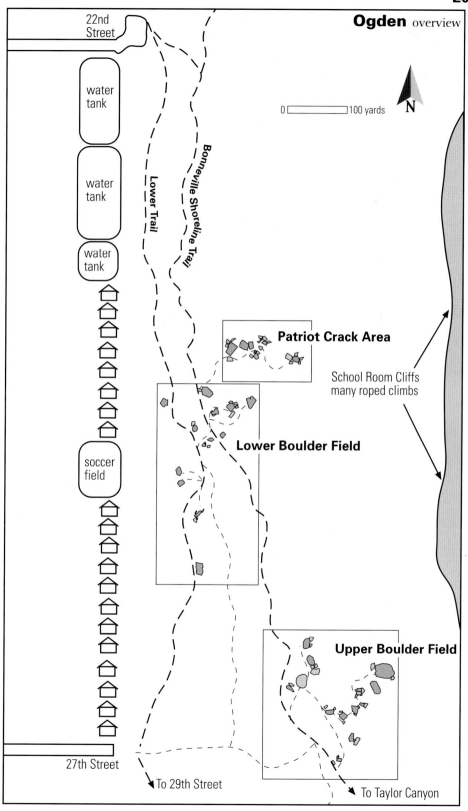

Lower Boulders

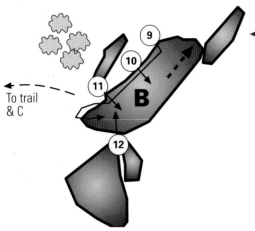

B. Hidden Rock
Hidden Rock is about one hundred yards north of the Cliffside Boulder. It is surrounded by a thick groove of oak trees, and is a difficult to see from the trail. To find this boulder, walk north from the Cliffside Boulder, past the thick grove of trees, then locate a trail heading back south into the trees.

9. Hidden Rock Traverse V2
Start at the left end of the northwest face. Traverse right staying under the small roof and top out on the corner at the right end of the face.

10. Disorder V2
Sit start on a good right-facing sidepull three feet off the ground. Climb straight up, pulling the small roof. Bad landing.

11. Transmission V1
Start on good horizontal edges five and half feet up. Climb the broken crack system.

12. V0
Climb the blocky south face.

C. The Tooth
Located about 50 yards north of the Hidden Boulder, the Tooth is a superb chunk of stone with a high concentration of excellent climbing. The top of this boulder rises above the trees and resembles a tooth, making it easy to locate.

13. Passover V1
Climb the arête on the right side of the southeast face.

14. Dead Sun V2
Climb the center of the thin technical face without using either arête.

15. Shore Leave V1
Climb the small right-facing corner just left of #14. Finish on the arête.

16. V2
Sit start beneath the bulge on the south corner of the boulder. Pull the bulge and finish straight up the arête.

17. Tooth Traverse V5
Start the same as #16, but at the slopey ledge traverse left turning the corner onto the northwest face. Top out the same as #21.

18. Liar V6
Sit start between #16 and #19 with your left hand in a big undercling and right hand using a small, sharp tooth, both three feet up. Slap the slopey ledge and mantel.

19. Singapore V3
Sit start using left-facing sidepulls. Climb the crack system up the center of the face.

20. Mecham V4
Sit start with your left hand on the corner and your right hand on a slopey ledge. Climb the corner.

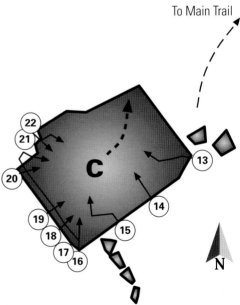

21. November V1
Climb the right-leaning ramp on the northwest face.

22. Lichen V2
Start the same as #21, but move onto the licheny face. Climb the face up and left using hard to find holds.

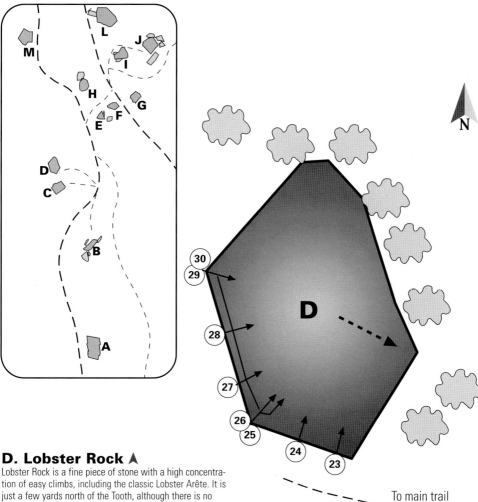

D. Lobster Rock ▲

Lobster Rock is a fine piece of stone with a high concentration of easy climbs, including the classic Lobster Arête. It is just a few yards north of the Tooth, although there is no direct trail because of the trees. To reach this boulder from the Tooth, walk back out to the main trail, then locate another trail heading west to Lobster Rock.

23. V1
Start on a right-facing jug five feet up. Climb the short bulge.

24. Six Foot and Curly V4 ★★
Start on two crimps in the middle of the face, six and a half feet up. Make a big move right to slopers. Using the good holds to the left makes this V2.

25. Sixteen Shells V1 ★
Sit start on flat blocky holds four and a half feet up. Make a couple moves up the arête, and then follow the seam to the right.

26. Lobster Arête V2 ★★★
Sit start the same as #25, but continue straight up the excellent prow.

27. Pony V5 ★★
Start with hands five and a half feet up using underclings in the crack. Climb crimps up the face.

28. Blue V1 ★
Start in the horizontal crack three feet left of #27. Climb straight up the face.

29. Breed V1
Climb the blunt corner.

30. Lobster Traverse V3 ★★
Sit start the same as #29. Traverse the face right and finish on #26, Lobster Arête.

Lower Boulders

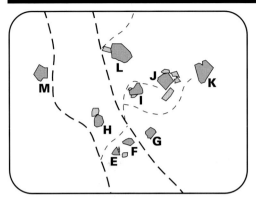

F. The C.R. Boulder
NO TOPO

This small boulder is situated among the oaks, just a few yards northeast (uphill) of the G-2 boulder.

36. Randall V4
Sit start under the overhang with your left hand on a crimpy sidepull and your right hand on some slopers. Surmount the overhang by slapping both sides of the arête.

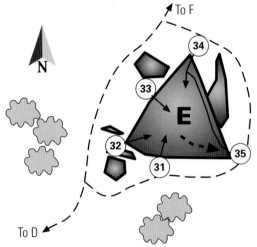

G. The B.M. Boulder
NO TOPO

This boulder is situated just east (uphill) of the Bonneville Shoreline trail, and due east of the C.R. boulder. One decent problem climbs the overhang on its southwest face. Watch out for poison ivy in the area.

37. Poison Ivy V2
Sit start. Climb the overhang on the southwest face of the boulder.

H. The Diamond Boulder ▼
The diamond boulder is 30 yards north of the G-2 boulder. It is surrounded by oaks and a little difficult to approach.

38. Negative V2
Sit start on the left side of the north face. Climb the arête.

39. Creep V1
Sit start on the right side of the north face. Climb the arête.

E. The G-2 Boulder ▲
If you stand at the Tooth Boulder and look uphill at the Arrowhead Boulder, the small G-2 Boulder is in your line of sight. This boulder is 70 yards north of The Tooth, and has G-2 painted in small yellow letters on its northwest face.

31. South Face V2
Sit start. Climb the south face.

32. V0
Start on a small right-facing rail. Climb the arête.

33. G-2 V0
Climb the northwest face, where G-2 is painted on the rock.

34. P.P. V2
Sit start matched on the slopey shelf. Climb the lip of the overhang up and left.

35 P.P. Traverse V2
Start at the left side of the overhang. Traverse the lip right.

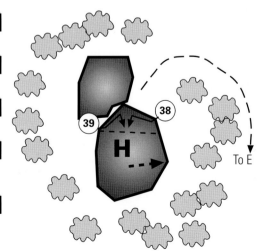

I. The Arrowhead ▶

The superb Arrowhead Boulder has some of best and hardest climbing at Ogden. One of the easiest boulders to identify, it is tall and sits by itself above the Bonneville Shoreline Trail.

40. Slick 50 Direct V9  ★★★★ ☐
This problem would be a classic at any bouldering area. Start in two underclings under the roof and four feet up. Make a hard move left to the slopey lip and follow it to the apex of the overhang. Bad landing.

41. Slick 50 V8 ★★★ ☐
This easier and safer version is the original, the direct was added later. Start the same as #40, but climb left, turning the lip onto the slabby north face. Make the bold finishing moves of Natural Selection, or just step off.

42. Natural Selection V2 ★★★ ☐
Start in the middle of the north face. Climb up to where the thin cracks form an X, then move right and turn the lip. Continue moving right on the slab, making scary committing moves to avoid the moss patch.

43. Checker V4  ★★★ ☐
Sit start using good holds in the dark red rock four feet left of Natural Selection, #42. Climb up the corner, and then move left to a rail on the face. Continue moving left to good holds on the east face. Top out on the arête.

43a. Variation V3 ★★ ☐
Start up start to Checker, hugging both arêtes.

44. Lock Tight V2 ★★★ ☐
Start standing. Climb the center of the east face using hard-to-find edges, move a little right to top out. Easier than it looks.

45. WD-40 V5  ★★ ☐
Sit start three feet right of #46 using an undercling and slopey edge. Climb crimps up the dark red rock, and then move left to the arête. Top out the same as #46.

46. Arrowhead Arête V3 ★★ ☐
Start standing. Climb the arête.

47. Down Climb V0 ★★★ ☐
The beautiful south face makes an excellent highball V0. Keep in mind that this is the easiest way down.

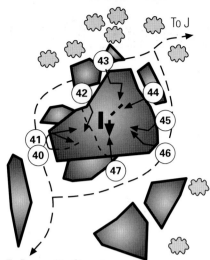

To Bonneville Shoreline trail

J. E.N.M. Boulder ▼

This boulder is thirty yards east (uphill) of the Arrowhead Boulder. It has four good climbs, which are a little harder than most in the boulder field.

48. Taddy V5 ★★ ☐
Sit start in underclings in the cracks. Climb into the shallow corner.

49. Paulaner V6 ★★ ☐
Same start as #48, but climb onto the right side of the arête.

50. Stout V2 ☐
Start standing. Climb the center of the face.

51. ESB V6 ★★ ☐
Start at the right side of the face. Traverse left staying on the face (not the lip) and finish on #49.

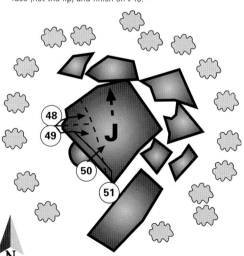

Ogden

Lower Boulders

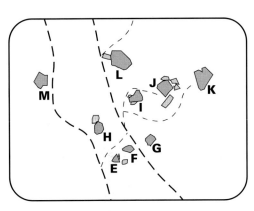

K. The Black Face Boulder
NO TOPO

Although this boulder offers only one climb, it is the best V7 in the boulder field, and well worth the short hike. This boulder lies uphill from the Arrowhead Boulder and has a black west face.

52. J.F.C. V7
Sit start on crimps that are four feet up and just above the lip of the small cave. Climb the gently overhanging west face, moving a little right at the top. Photo opposite.

◄ L. Mini Cave Boulder
This large, squat boulder is about 35 yards north of the Arrowhead Boulder, and about ten yards east (uphill) of the Bonneville Shoreline Trail. It has two great climbs on its southwest face. One is a one-move wonder, the other a stout, pumpy traverse that is perhaps the longest boulder problem here.

53. Jed's Traverse V7
Start with both hands on the lip where the small boulder at the base touches the Mini Cave boulder. Traverse the lip right and turn the corner onto the slabby southeast face.

54. Mini Cave V5
Sit start matched on the only good hold under the roof. Make a big move to the lip, hold the swing, and mantel.

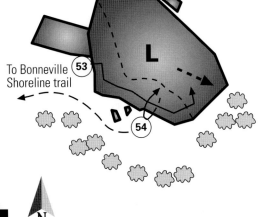

M. Toyota Boulder ►
This boulder is 100 yards northwest of the G-2 Boulder, on the west side of the Lower Trail. It surrounded by large trees, and covered in lots of graffiti, including the word "Toyota".

55. Toyota Traverse V1
Start at the left side of the west face. Traverse the lip right, turn the corner and top out on the south face.

56. Toyota Arête V2
Sit start. Climb the arête.

57. V0
Climb the south face.

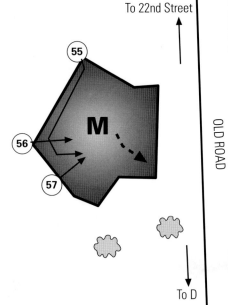

Brent Hadley on *J.F.C* (V7), opposite page.
Photo: Chris Grijalva

Patriot Crack

The Patriot Crack Boulders sit high on the hillside, north (uphill) of the Bonneville Shoreline Trail. To locate these boulders, follow a faint trail northeast (uphill and towards 22nd street) from boulder L, the Mini Cave Boulder, in the Lower Boulder Field towards a dark-gray boulder. This is the Orangutan Boulder. The remaining boulders are due east of the Orangutan boulder. The Patriot Crack boulder is also easy to identify with two cracks splitting its steeply overhanging north face.

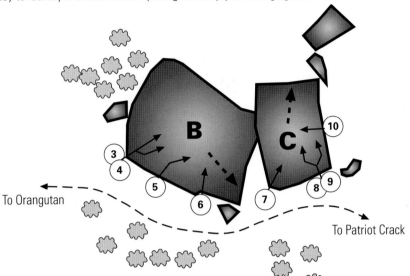

A. Orangutan Boulder
NO TOPO

This square, dark-gray block is the closest boulder to the Bonneville Shoreline Trail at the Patriot Crack area. Two problems climb its steep west face.

1. Anthropoid V2
Sit start using good edges four and a half feet up and between the arête and the rock at the base of the west face. Climb straight up and mantel.

2. Bob V3
Sit start in jugs on the right side of the arête. Climb the arête and mantel.

B. The Deck ▲
This boulder is called The Deck because its top is flat, and level with the bottom of the Fish Flop boulder, providing a great place to unload gear and hang out. The Deck is 15 yards east (uphill) of the Orangutan Boulder.

3. Skoal V1
Start on crimps five feet up. Climb the bulge through an orange rock scar.

4. Drum V2
Same start as #3, but move right and climb the face right of the orange rock scar.

5. Crimper V4
Sit start with both hands in black underclings. Move your right hand to crimpers, then folow the crimpy shallow seam.

6. V1
Start in jugs five feet up. Climb the right-facing corner.

C. Fish Flop Boulder ▲
One of the best boulders at Ogden, the Fish Flop Boulder is just east (uphill) of the Deck and has an excellent bulging prow on its south face.

7. Buda V6
Sit start with your feet between the Deck and the Fish Flop boulders, and left hand on a good incut crimp three feet up. Climb straight up the prow. The standing start to this problem is V5.

8. Fish Flop V2
Start on good holds five and a half feet up. Climb left to good incuts, then go straight up the face.

9. Golden V2
Same start as #8, but move right to the arête.

10. East Face V1
Climb the east face.

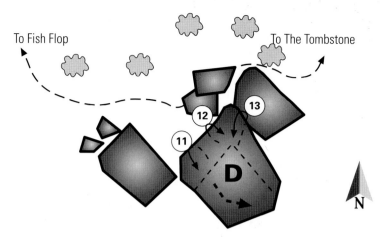

D. Patriot Crack Boulder

Located ten yards southeast (uphill and towards 27th street) of the Fish Flop Boulder, the Patriot Crack boulder has two cracks splitting its steep north face.

11. Suicide Crack V3
Climb the crack on the right side of the steep northwest face.

12. Patriot Crack V2
Climb the crack on the left side of the steep northwest face.

13. Spine V3
Sit start with hands on the left-facing ramp. Climb the bulge staying left of the arête.

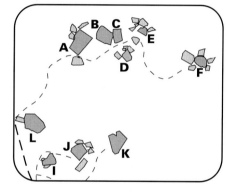

◄ E. The Tombstone

The Tombstone is located amongst the oaks 15 yards northeast (uphill and towards 22nd street) of the Patriot Crack Boulder. It has two good climbs on its southwest face.

14. LCC V3
Climb the arête on the left side of the southwest face.

15. Pain Train V3
Start in the middle on the face. Climb up to the right-trending seam.

F. Boulder
NO TOPO

This tall boulder is located in the talus about 75 yards east (uphill) of the Patriot Crack Boulder. It has one problem on its impressive southwest face above a very bad landing.

16. Brent's Highball V3
Start on incut crimps seven feet up. Climb the face moving a little right. The cave and face to the left has yet to been done.

Ogden

Upper Boulders

The popular Upper Boulder Field has high-quality problems and varied climbing, from horizontal roofs to 20-foot tall V0 slabs. Sitting high on the hillside at the mouth of Taylor Canyon, it offers unobstructed views of Mount Ogden and the valley below. The best approach is to park at the end of 27th street and walk east towards Taylor Canyon, until you meet the Bonneville Shoreline Trail. Walk north on the Bonneville Shoreline Trail until another trail diagonals uphill towards a large rock formation. This is Castle Rock. There is no bouldering on Castle Rock, but it does have one short 10d sport route on its west face. The Upper Boulder field lies around Castle Rock. It contains hundreds boulders; only the best are described here.

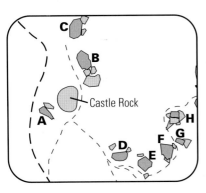
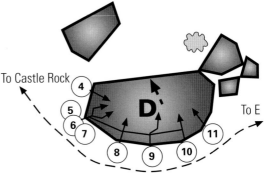

A. 26th Boulder
NO TOPO
This boulder is located in the trees ten yards west (downhill) of Castle Rock.

1. Second Rate V2
Sit start under the roof on the southeast side of the boulder. Climb out the roof.

B. C.V. Boulder
NO TOPO
The C.V. Boulder is about 30 yards north of Castle Rock. It has one good problem on its south face as well a several lines above super bad landings on its west face that await ascents.

2. The Boot V4
Sit start under the roof at the south corner of the boulder. Climb out the roof.

C. The Gorn
NO TOPO
The Gorn is 25 yards north of the C.V. Boulder. There is not much of a trail leading to this boulder, so getting to it is a bit of a thrash.

3. The Gorn V6
Start in the undercling crack under the roof on the west face. Climb out the roof and onto the west face, moving a little left to topout.

D. Around the World Boulder
With several quality moderate climbs, this boulder is a good place to warm up. As it is loaded with features, there's lots of potential for variations, link-ups, and eliminates. To locate Around the World walk a trail from Castle Rock that diagonals uphill to the southeast. Around the World is an obvious boulder that sits by itself at the edge of the trees.

4. V0
Sit start on the left side of the west face. Climb the face and arête.

5. Power V3
Sit start using a big fractured knob three and a half feet up. Climb up and left. Top out on the west face left of the arête.

6. V1
Same start as #5, but move right and top out on the arête.

7. Traverse V3
Same start as #5 and #6, but traverse the face right. Top out on #10.

8. Sunny Days V1
Sit start using the fractured left-facing flake. Climb the face.

9. V1
Sit start four feet right of #8. Climb the face.

10. BW V3 ★★
Start matched in a good hold five feet up. Move your left hand to the mailbox slot, then go straight up the face.

11. Chopper V0
Sit start using the big detached flake. Pull the small bulge.

Wolverine Publishing   www.wolverinepublishing.com

E. 5.7 Boulder ▶

This tall boulder is 20 yards southeast (towards Taylor Canyon) of the Around the World Boulder. It has three easy, but excellent, highballs on its southwest face.

12. Jury V1 ★★
Climb the face left of the center crack.

13. Jail V0 ★★★
Climb the center crack.

14. Clink V0 ★★
Climb the face right of the center crack.

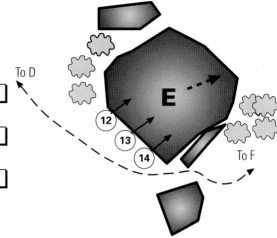

◀ F. Dyno Rock

Located about 25 yards northeast (uphill) from the 5.7 Boulder, Dyno Rock has good climbing on excellent rock.

15. Mini V1
Start in jugs four feet left of the small juniper tree. Dyno to the lip.

16. Jack Brown V3 ★★
Same start as #15, but traverse the seam right, and top out on the right side of the face.

17. Hot Joint V2 ★★
Sit start using the crack in the middle of the face. Climb the left-leaning crack.

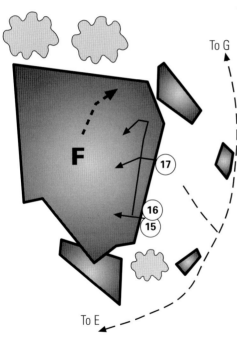

G. Leaning Rock ▶

This excellent boulder is about 15 yards northeast (uphill) of the Dyno Rock. As the name suggests, it leans against the surrounding boulders at a severe angle, making it is easy to identify.

18. Dressed in Black V2 ★★
Sit start using a good incut flake. Climb the face.

19. Leaning Rock V5 ★★★
Same start as #18, but climb right staying on the lip of the overhang then up the face.

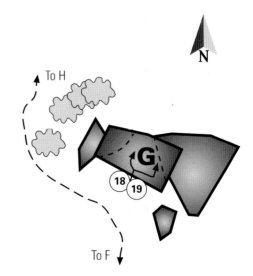

Upper Boulders

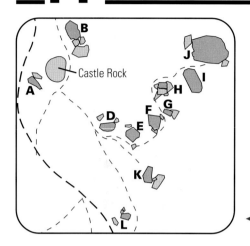

H. Cave Rock
NO TOPO

Situated about 20 yards due north of Leaning Rock, this small, squat boulder doesn't look like much. However, the cave beneath it offers twelve feet of horizontal climbing to a cruxy lip encounter. Just north of Cave Rock is a large rust colored boulder that is not described, but has some highball V1s and V0s.

20. The Cave V6 ★★★
Sit start in the very back of the cave using an undercling crack. Climb the entire roof and top out onto the north face.

◄ I. The Egg
This large boulder is situated at the edge of the talus and has a fairly tall west face. To locate this boulder walk east (uphill) from Cave Rock, and look for a large boulder with an orange-streaked west face.

21. 99 Years V1 ★
Start on the right side of the west face. Climb the face up a dark orange streak.

22. Bid V0 ★
Climb the broken crack system left of #21.

23. Heart Broke V2 ★
Climb the face just left of #22.

24. K.G. V4 ★★
Start in a left-facing jug two feet off the ground. Climb the face to a short right-leaning crack. Follow the crack, and face to the left.

25. 15 Years V0
Climb the dirty crack on the left side of the face.

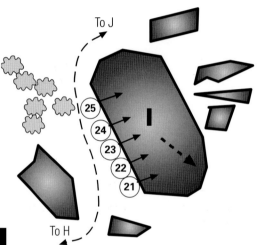

J. The Ute Boulder ►
This huge boulder is situated in the talus, and has a large overhanging south face. To reach this boulder, walk northeast from The Egg, up the talus, for 25 yards.

26. Kill Your Enemies V7 ★★
This short power problem start on crimps under the roof, five and a half feet up. Make one desperate move to the lip and mantel.

27. Grave V1
Start on a jug just below the lip. Make one move to the lip and mantel.

28. Black Rider V7 ★★★
Sit start using two opposing gastons. Climb out the roof.

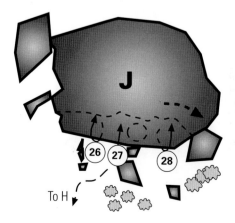

Wolverine Publishing   www.wolverinepublishing.com

K. The Platform ▶

This excellent boulder has some of the finest climbing in the Upper Boulder Field. To reach it, walk from the Around the World Boulder southeast (downhill and towards Taylor Canyon) for 60 yards.

29. Lowe V1 ★★
Climb jugs up the left side of the south face.

30. Lowe 1 V3 ★★★
Start matched on good holds five feet up. Climb the center of the face, move left to top out.

30a. Lowe 2 V3 ★★★
Same start as #30, but move your right hand to a small pocket in the seam, then move your left hand to the good hold in the middle of the face. Finish on #30.

31. Lowe 3 V4 ★★★
Begin the same as #30. Climb to the good hold in the middle of the face, then move right and finish on #32.

32. Lowe 4 V1 ★
Climb the arête on the right side of the south face.

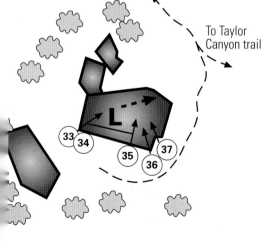

◀ L. The Slab Boulder

This boulder is not a slab and has excellent climbing on its slightly overhanging south face. To locate the Slab Boulder, follow a faint trail 100 yards southeast (directly into Taylor Canyon) from the Around the World Boulder. The Slab Boulder is surrounded by trees, and lies just above the Taylor Canyon trail.

33. Worms V3 ★★
Sit start with both hands on the arête. Climb the arête.

34. Don't Want V6 ★★★
To Grow Up
Sit start the same as #33, but climb right across the face, and finish on #35.

35. Mule V3 ★★★
Climb the big right-facing features in the middle of the face, to a challenging, slopey top out.

36. Joe Bean V4 ★★
Start standing using good holds six and a half feet up. Climb the arête just left of the groove.

37. B-day V3 ★
Start standing with hands matched in the bottom of the V groove. Grovel up the groove. Funky.

OTHER AREAS

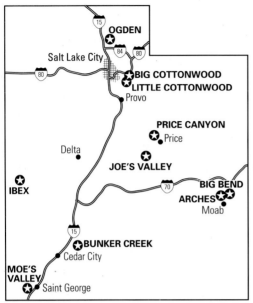

Arches Boulders
A good alternative to Big Bend, the Arches boulders have about 50 problems including several classics. The rock is sandstone, similar to Big Bend but not quite as good. The area is close to Highway 191, just west of the entrance to Arches National Park, about four miles north of Moab. The main cluster of boulders is on the north side of the highway next to a large parking area. A frontage road, which departs from this parking area and parallels Highway 191, leads to more boulders.

Big Cottonwood Canyon
Like nearby Little Cottonwood canyon, Big Cottonwood canyon is loaded with rock, and although better know for its many roped climbs, it offers a wide variety of bouldering possibilities. The rock is well-featured quartzite, like that of Ibex and Ogden, and caters well to eliminates and traverses. Big Cottonwood Canyon is at the eastern edge of Salt Lake City, a few miles north of Little Cottonwood Canyon, at the intersection of Wasatch Blvd (Highway 210) and Fort Union Blvd (7200 S).

Bunker Creek
The welded tuff boulders of Bunker Creek lie at an elevation of 9000 feet and can be a good place to escape the summer heat. The area is located east of Cedar City. Directions were sketchy as we went to press. Our best guess: From Cedar City, follow Highway 14 east to Highway 148. Follow 148 north to the intersection with Highway 143. Follow Highway 143 east to Panguitch Lake. Bunker Creek is just south of Panguitch Lake.

Moe's Valley
This sandstone area is about five miles southwest of Saint George. Like the nearby Virgin River Gorge, it is a good place to climb in winter. The area is on public land but there are access concerns as some of the approach routes cross private land. You can get more information about the bouldering at Moe's Valley from Outdoor Outlet, 1062 East Tabernacle, Saint George; 800-726-8106.

Price Canyon Recreation Area
This recently discovered sandstone area hosts numerous high quality boulder problems and is a good alternative to Joe's Valley. Situated on a northeast-facing hillside the boulders get lots of shade, and can be good in hot weather. Price Canyon Recreation Area is about 10 miles north of Price on Highway 6. The road to the area is marked by a sign on the southeast side of the Highway. The boulders are located in a small canyon at a sharp bend in recreation area road.